Challenges of the Agrarian Transition in Southeast Asia (ChATSEA)

Fields of Desire

Challenges of the Agrarian Transition in Southeast Asia (ChATSEA)

The shift from rural societies dependent upon agricultural livelihoods to predominantly urbanized, industrialized and market-based societies is one of the most significant processes of social change in the modern world. The Challenges of the Agrarian Transition in Southeast Asia (ChATSEA) project examines how the transformation is affecting the societies and economies of Southeast Asia. Headed by Professor Rodolphe De Koninck, holder of the Canada Chair in Asian Research at the University of Montreal, and sponsored by the Social Sciences and Humanities Research Council of Canada, the ChATSEA project includes publications by senior academics as well as junior scholars.

Fields of Desire

Poverty and Policy in Laos

Holly High

NUS PRESS
SINGAPORE

Published by:
NUS Press
National University of Singapore
AS3-01-02, 3 Arts Link
Singapore 117569

Fax: (65) 6774-0652
E-mail: nusbooks@nus.edu.sg
Website: http://nuspress.nus.edu.sg

ISBN 978-9971-69-770-9 (Paper)

First edition 2014
Reprint 2019

National Library Board, Singapore Cataloguing-in-Publication Data

High, Holly, author.
    Fields of desire: poverty and policy in Laos / Holly High. – Singapore:
NUS Press, [2014]
    pages cm. – (Challenges of the agrarian transition in Southeast Asia)
    ISBN: 978-9971-69-770-9 (paperback)

    1. Poverty – Laos. 2. Poverty – Political aspects – Laos. 3. Poverty –
Government policy – Laos. I. Title. II. Series: Challenges of the agrarian
transition in Southeast Asia.

HC443
305.56909594 — dc23   OCN861246598

Printed by: Markono Print Media Pte Ltd

For everyone that helped along the way

Contents

List of Maps

List of Illustrations

Acknowledgements

I have dedicated this book to all the people who have contributed to, encouraged and facilitated its research and writing. I am confident that those people know who they are. It would be tedious in some cases, a breach of confidentiality in others, and perhaps impossible anyway to list each and every one and detail their good deeds. Let me just say that even the smallest of kind words and good advice has had the greatest of impacts.

That said, I do not want to forgo writing a more traditional acknowledgements section altogether, in part because I always find acknowledgements so fascinating to read. This is one of the rare instances where authors who might usually be stuffy allow themselves to mention the conviviality of intellectual friendships and the profound sense of enduring gratitude to field informants, where writers who might usually present smooth and authoritative accounts allow themselves to thank chance encounters and unruly networks of colleagues. This is so precious for our record of how knowledge is produced. With this in mind, what I will present below is an account of the non-linear path this manuscript took from its conception to final rendition. I cannot mention everyone here who helped along the way, but I hope that by tracing this path readers will get a sense of just how deep, and how diffuse, this book's intellectual debts are.

The original research for this book was completed as part of my PhD training at The Australian National University, The Research School of Pacific and Asian Studies, Anthropology Programme and was supported by an Australian Postgraduate Award and fieldwork funds from the Anthropology Programme. My main supervisor was Andrew Walker and other members of my supervisory team included Francesca Merlan, Alan Rumsey and Philip Taylor. It was a line-up of very smart, very conscientious anthropologists. The programme was lively and challenging: I could not have asked for more. I also completed my undergraduate studies at ANU: Ian Keen and Chris Gregory particularly deserve my thanks. The first year of PhD studies was completed at The University of Sydney under the supervision of Peter Hinton. He was an incredibly supportive supervisor, and it was only due to his illness that I later moved to ANU.

It was under Peter's guidance that I completed my pre-fieldwork trip to Laos in 2000 and chose what was to be the area of my study: Sii Phan Don. During that year I also commenced learning Thai with Aacaan Nilawan at The University of Sydney, and she facilitated my enrolment in a summer course at Salaya University, Thailand. In 2001 I suspended my enrolment at Sydney pending transfer to the ANU and arrangement of my research permisions from the Government of Laos. I spent the year living in Vientiane. Denley Pike and the team at Vientiane College must be acknowledged here for providing me with gainful employment and a stimulating intellectual environment in Vientiane. I tried numerous strategies to obtain research permission, determined that my research should be "above board" and legal. After many disappointments, it was with great relief that I met Mr Khamphat Phetlasy of the External Affairs Division of The Ministry of Education. He instructed me on how to submit an application. This was reviewed in 2001 and approved in early 2002. While I waited for this application to be processed (12 months), I continued language learning in Vientiane with private teachers, again arranged by the Ministry of Education. I would like to thank the Ministry staff for their professional and friendly assistance in all these matters.

With news that my permissions had been approved, I returned to Australia to transfer my PhD candidature to the ANU, apply for research funds, and present my pre-fieldwork seminar to the Anthropology Programme, and improve my Lao further under the tuition of Adam Chapman. This was a busy three months that passed quickly in a very supportive new environment. By July, I was back in Laos, research permission letters in hand, and making my way through the Lao bureaucracy from Vientiane, to Pakse, to Mounlapamok, to Don Khiaw. At each step of the way, Ministry of Education staff accompanied me and explained my research permission to the local authorities. This eased my entry to the field enormously.

By late July, 2002, I found myself at last installed on the island of Don Khiaw. All the bureaucrats who had delivered me there went back to their distant homes, and I was faced with the peculiar task of "doing" fieldwork. I was fortunate to be surrounded by an incredibly friendly and generous group of neighbours and co-villagers. Just as this was my first fieldwork, I was their first anthropologist, and we were all feeling our way. If I were to summarize what I learned about fieldwork in that first, astonishing, difficult and humbling year is that fieldwork isn't something that you "do" after all: it is what happens while you are making plans for what on earth it is that you are going to do as one event after another takes hold of you and the people around you. For my first fieldwork I stayed for 16 months. By the time I had left I had forged bonds that I now think will last for as long as more than one of us remains living. I go back every year to Laos and often to that island but I no longer count the months. These people and Laos are part of my life now. To say that I am grateful to them for making this research possible would be true, but it would also be only a very, very small part of the story of these relationships.

On completing my thesis I was fortunate to be offered a fellowship in the Agrarian Studies Program at Yale University. Under the leadership and inspiration of James C. Scott, this year provided the ideal forum to rewrite and re-think much of the material that appears in this book. The book went through a hiatus as the demands of teaching took over with faculty positions first at Deakin University and then at The University of Sydney. My intellectual development did not, however, and I would like to thank the students at both institutions, smart and hungry for ideas and knowledge, who encouraged me to clarify where my research stood in relation to the larger discipline of anthropology. Rohan Bastin, Gillian Cowlishaw, Tess Lea and many other excellent colleagues provided intellectual sustenance through what was often an extremely demanding time. The book began moving again in 2009 when I was offered another postdoctoral position, this one in the Department of Social Anthropology, The University of Cambridge. I would like to thank Henrietta Moore and the Department for making this fantastic opportunity possible, and Clare Hall for offering me a Research Fellowship so that I could also take part in college life. It was in the second year of my time at Cambridge (2011) that I finalised this manuscript. Cambridge was such a rich context in which to work on it that it seems a little pointless to attempt to name all the people who contributed in some way, so I'll just mention a few highlights: The Deleuze Reading Group, The Psychoanalysis Reading Group, The Cosmoeconomics Reading Group, the HAU Network for Ethnographic Theory, The Social Anthropology Research Associates seminar, and all the members, students and associates of the Department of Social Anthropology who generated such an engaging departmental intellectual life. For the hallway conversations, the seminars, the shared meals, the discussion groups, the conferences and the boozy catch-ups that happened afterwards with you, I am truly thankful.

Tania Li deserves special mention for bringing this publication to completion. She has been a great supporter, inspiration and critical interlocutor and her work, along with that of Rodolphe De Koninck, as series editor has surely improved this text. Paul Kratoska has demanded the very best from me, and I thank him for this, and for his patience and encouragement. Tigger Wise provided meticulous copyediting. Ian Baird and another, anonymous, reviewer offered a staggering amount of time to read and suggest improvements for this text. I am very grateful for their kind encouragement and suggestions.

Joann Keong of NUS Press provided excellent editorial support. Material in Chapter Three was originally published in Chapter Seven of *On the Borders Of State Power: Frontiers in the Greater Mekong Sub-Region* (2009) edited by Martin Gainsborough, Routledge, London and New York. A section of Chapter Four first appeared as Chapter Three in *Everyday Life in Southeast Asia* (2011) edited by Kathleen M. Adams and Kathleen A. Gillogly, Indiana University Press, Bloomington and Indianapolis.

Although partial, perhaps this has given a sense of just how many debts I have accrued in writing this book. There is no acquitting these and no full accounting, but they have significantly shaped the pages that follow. The proviso still stands, though, that all the remaining failings are my own.

Sydney, December 2012

Note on Transcription

Lao words are transcribed here in keeping with the method used by Kerr (1972) with the following modifications:

> I have omitted diacritics. This was a difficult decision, and in some earlier versions of this text I did follow Kerr's use of diacritics, but in this final version for publication I have decided to omit them because for the majority of readers they are distracting and not informative. For the small number of readers who are Lao speakers, the context is usually such that they can deduce the tone on their own.
>
> For reasons of typesetting with the press, I have represented certain vowels according to the Royal Thai General System of Transcription where the required International Phonetic Alphabet figure was not available. So *ngán* appears as *ngoen*.
>
> Where Kerr uses as "*v*" as an end consonant, I substitute as "*w*", so that the word for "already" will appear as *laew* rather than *lɛɛv* as the sound an English-speaker would pronounce reading "*v*" does not exist in Lao.
>
> Where Kerr indicates a long vowel with a colon, I double the vowel immediately preceding Kerr's colon. So, the word for "village" will appear as *baan* rather than *bà:n*.
>
> For words used in Lao that have a common transcription in English, I have followed this more common transcription. So, the word for the Lao currency appears as *kip* and the Thai currency as *baht*, rather than *kiip* and *baat*. I have also followed common spellings for place names where they exist, including the word *don* rather than *dɔɔn* for "island" in the title of the fieldsite "Don Khiaw".
>
> All transcriptions, but not personal or place names, are written in italics.

For reasons of confidentiality, the name of the fieldsite where I conducted fieldwork has been changed and the exact location obscured. The term "Don Khiaw" is a pseudonym used throughout the book to refer to the island and village where fieldwork was conducted. Pseudonyms are also used for nearby villages. More commonly known place names (such as the names of towns or provinces) follow common usage. When referring to towns or districts which carry the prefix "Muang", I have used this more common spelling of the term, rather than the conventions outlined above.

All personal names have been changed in order to protect confidentiality. The spelling of personal Lao names follows the conventions outlined above. The exception is the personal names of notable persons, such as Kaysone Phomvihane, in which cases the real name and the spelling that has become conventional for their name has been used. Some personal names are preceded by the title of "mother", "aunt" or "father" following popular usage for the address of some older persons or persons with a particularly close relationship with the speaker.

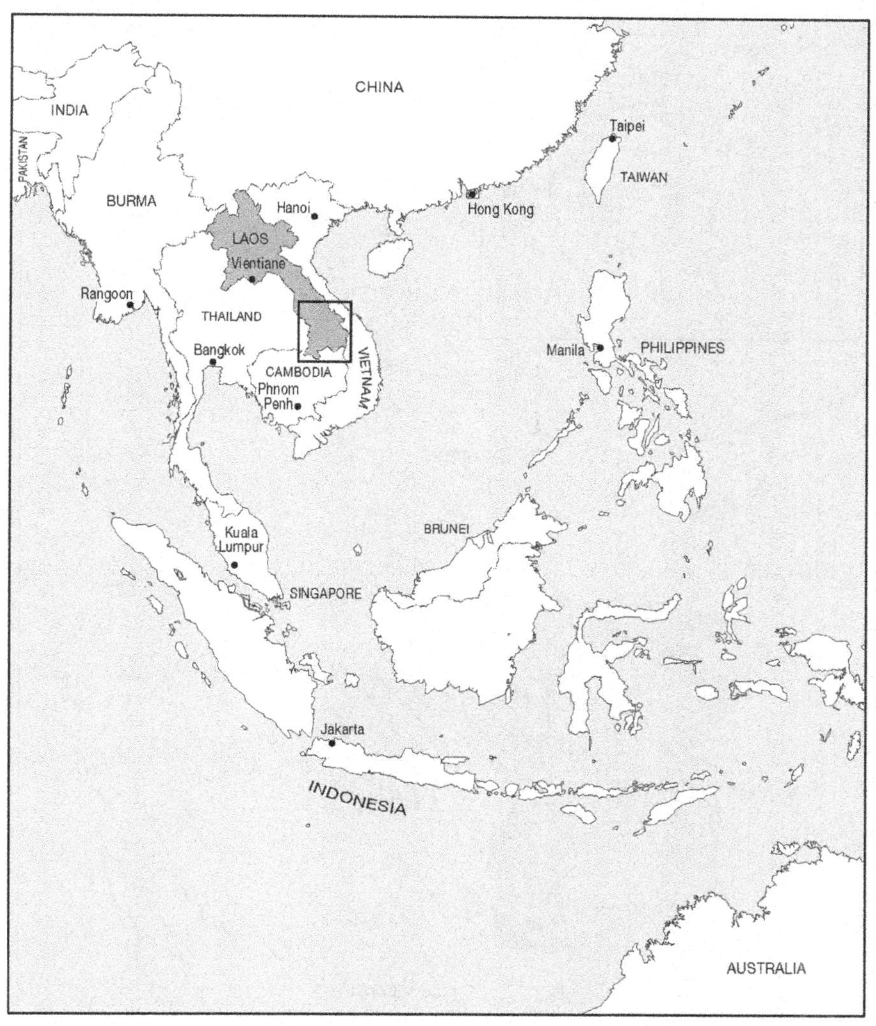

Map 1. Laos in Southeast Asia

Source: CartoGIS, the cartography service of the Australian National University.

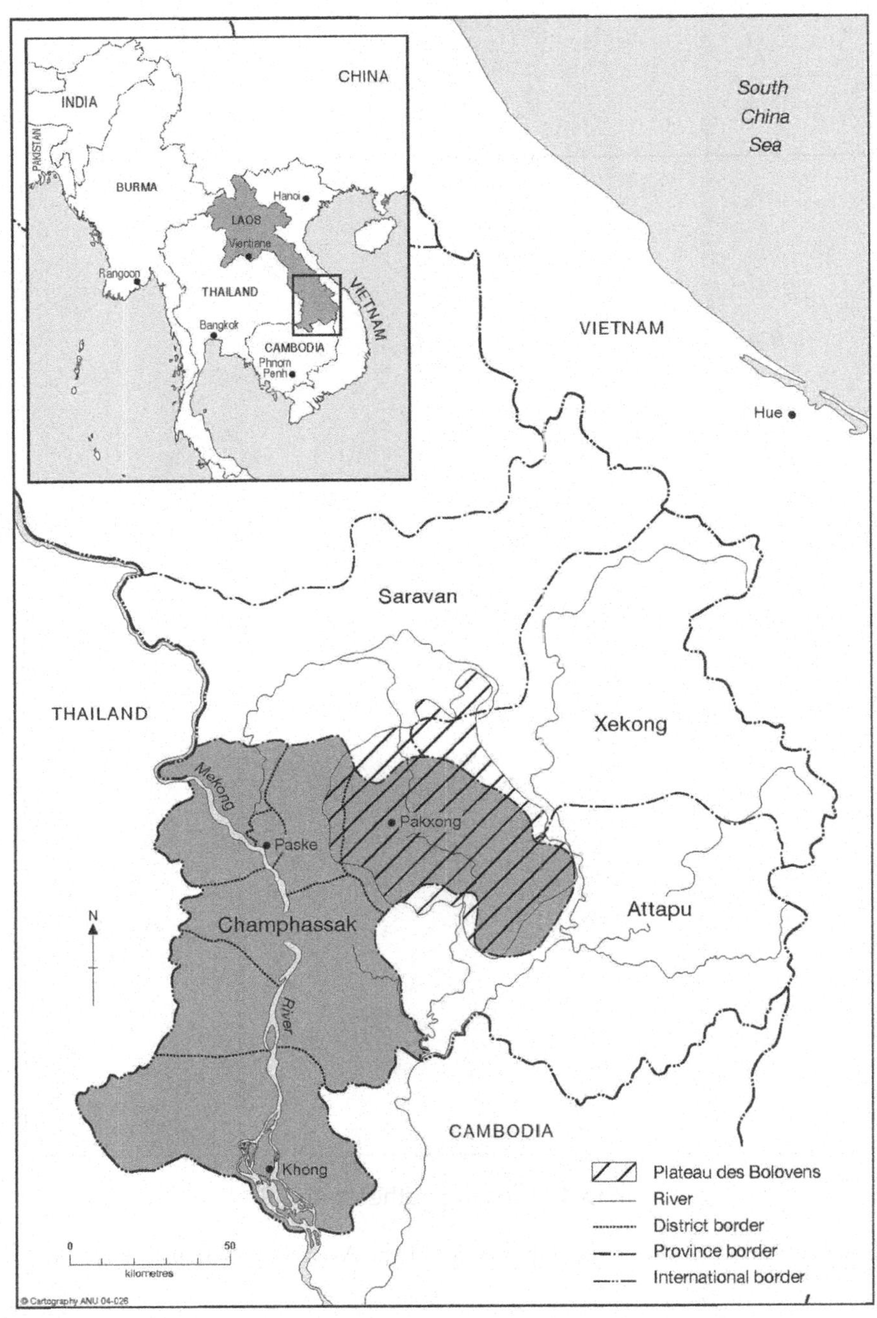

Map 2. Southern Laos

Source: CartoGIS, the cartography service of the Australian National University.

1

Introduction
Towards a Political Ethnography of Desire

This book is an ethnography of the desire that runs through the politics of poverty and development in Laos. I begin with the observation that among the rural Lao residents with whom I conducted fieldwork, disillusionment and suspicion were the dominant frames of reference for interpreting poverty reduction programmes. Yet, despite this, there was a persistent desiring return to these promises, leading people to engage with policy, the state and bureaucracy despite their doubts. Desire in the politics of poverty is the central concept and question of this book.

The setting for this investigation is an island in the south west of Laos, Don Khiaw. Here, the Mekong River spreads wide and slips quietly through hundreds of small islands. I started research here in 2002, initially for 16 months. I continue to return there whenever possible, at least annually, and maintain contacts with residents, but the following chapters are based primarily on that initial fieldwork. This is Mekong valley heartland, ideal for wet rice cultivation. The fields of the islands and plains glow emerald green in the wet season, ripen to gold before harvest and then turn to dust during the wintery dry. From the point of view of rice, a successful colonization of this territory has been achieved via the domestication of human desires: people are settled in an area suited to rice's needs and into a temporal cycle shaped by rice's demands for them to tend to ploughing, transplanting the seedlings, water levels and preservation of seed. In return the rice offers a grain that is heavily symbolized by the people as life itself: it is the archetype of food, and through this, of the productive power of care and nurturance.[1] The domestication of these people to rice is only partial, however, they have desires that lead them further afield. Livelihoods are supplemented by fishing, gathering

1

Figure 1. A mother and three of her sons transplant rice seedlings.

Figure 2. The Sii Phan Don area of the Mekong River is peppered with many islands.

and alternative crops, and many leave the area in the dry to take up seasonal labour in the coffee fields, or more permanently to work in urban centres (construction, garment factories) and Thailand (domestic service, commercial fisheries, factories). All of these migrations, I will argue, are fuelled by significant and sometimes surprising desires.

Historically, the Mekong River has been a centre for trade, settlement and cultural exchange. Through the course of the 20th century, however, the river and its plains became an international border between Thailand and Laos. Today, linguistic, political, economic and kinship ties continue to link the Lao parts of the Mekong valley to those parts that now fall in Thailand. Many of the residents of Don Khiaw that I met were themselves returned refugees who had originally fled to Thailand after the Lao People's Revolutionary Party (LPRP) came to power in late 1975. Many others had wanted to flee, or were relatives of those who had and were now settled in Thailand, the USA, Australia, France and Canada. This area was both the target of and recruiting area for a long-running counter-revolutionary movement that aimed to overthrow the LPRP, a movement that weakened in the 1980s and sputtered to an end in the 1990s. By the time I arrived most locals eyed the current LPRP-backed state and its programmes with suspicion, but they were no longer openly rebellious.

When it came to poverty alleviation and development, this made for a particularly doubtful set of recipients. The people I came to know in my fieldwork rarely took a development or poverty reduction programme at its word, but rather read it in terms of possible exploitation, corruption or futility. This world-weary view of the development industry and its efforts is echoed among academics, development industry workers and bureaucrats in Laos. In the literature—both academic and bureaucratic—it is now not uncommon to see the phrase "development-induced poverty": development programmes themselves are described as harmful and destructive (see Rigg 2006 for an overview). Anthropologists are now used to reading exposés of development: its "anti-politics" (Ferguson 1994), the "rendering technical" of what are essentially political problems (Li 2007), the persistent "logic" of bureaucracies where good policy may be in fact unimplementable (Mosse 2005) with the effect being primarily to maintain, perpetuate and grow bureaucracies themselves (Lea 2008) and so on. In this book I take this critical view of development as an ethnographic fact persistent among not only Lao rice farmers, but also among development workers, bureaucrats and academics: that is, the people directly involved in or commenting on development. I respond to this ethnographic observation by posing the question that flows from it: given this open secret, why is there not more open opposition? Why is it that, among those taking part in some way, almost no one believes anymore, yet the practice nevertheless persists beyond belief, beyond ideology, perhaps beyond reason? By what mechanism does the whole thing continue, anthropologically speaking?

In the context of Laos, a consideration of poverty and development leads directly back to engagements with the state. In Don Khiaw, for instance, the failure of development and poverty reduction programmes was widely discussed as rendering the current state illegitimate: failure was often put down to state corruption. Yet, despite this, the state and its programmes were still able to capture desire: people also spoke to me of their desire for more state largesse, often in the form of development programmes, and when they moved to pursue their own ambitions, it was almost always to areas better connected to markets and state services. Indeed, the strength and depth of their disillusionment with the state cannot be understood without an understanding also of this persistent desire for what the state is thought to be able to offer. My answer, then, to the question of the persistence of development poverty reduction interventions and other state programmes in the face of exposé, begins with desire.

Desire, like any good social science concept, is a concept that is already at work in the world as an explanation for why it is people do what they do. Some of its common deployments already hint at the theoretical directions that have been taken. For instance, it is common to acknowledge that we are motivated by what we want, but we also readily acknowledge that what we want may not be in our best interest, and once we get it, we often find that it isn't what we wanted after all. While we are often tempted to think of desires as personal, even private (such as our heart's desires) it is also easy to show that our own desires are often what we imagine other people have enjoyed or desired. Whose desires are these, really? In this introduction I want to build on the work that desire does in such everyday social analysis in order to produce a more polished social science concept of desire. I will contend that because desires are both unconscious and social, they can produce what I call a "shared delirium": a shared irrationality that produces its own rationalities. These rationalities can be seen in social processes. They are the basis for mutual engagements and critiques, consensus and recriminations, the building blocks of social action and evaluation. I take as my example poverty, and the promise the state offers to alleviate it, because desires and debates related to this were some of the most impassioned that I encountered in the south of Laos.

Before polishing the concept of desire, I will first examine the existing literature on the state, resistance and poverty in Southeast Asia. I will show that desire is emerging as a central concept there, but to date it has raised as many questions as it has answered. I then relate this to a more thorough consideration of the variety of theoretical approaches to desire available, explaining my own use of the concept. I then provide a description of the field-site and the chapters that follow.

From nonrevolt to desire

Above, I noted that while most locals in Don Khiaw viewed the current LPRP-backed state and its programmes with suspicion, they were no longer openly rebellious. In this respect, they can be thought of as post-rebellious. They are occupying a moment of nonrevolt after a period of more open resistance. Within Southeast Asian studies, it was James C. Scott who took up peasant rebellions, resistance and then nonrevolt most tenaciously and influentially. In *The Moral Economy of the Peasant* (1976), Scott paid attention to the sensational rebellions that had flared up in the colonial era. He asked the next question, "why don't peasants rebel?" explicitly in the final chapter of that study, noting that in reality the vast majority of peasants in exploitative conditions lived their entire lives without engaging in anything so remarkable as open revolt (Scott 1986). Building on his argument that it was threats to normatively sanctioned subsistence levels that had provoked outright rebellion, he speculated that "safety valves" could ease pressure on subsistence and may stave off open revolt, without radically challenging exploitative arrangements. These might include off-farm work opportunities, state welfare, or other forms of patronage. These may also have the effect of undermining peasant autonomy, producing what he (somewhat reluctantly) called "post-peasants". Fear could play a major role in repressing revolt, too, even where other factors were in place, especially among those who have experienced harsh defeat in the past. Yet throughout this consideration of "nonrevolt" he was at pains to argue that any apparent quiescence need not be interpreted simply as false consciousness or successful hegemonic incorporation. Even among defeated "post-peasants" he suggested that researchers could usefully look for a "symbolic gap" (1976: 234) between elite and rural culture, or indeed "symbolic reversal" (1976: 236) where elite culture is stood on its head in vernacular expressions. Even in apparently hegemonic situations, where to all appearances peasants simply reproduced elite narratives, this need not be taken at face value. Folktales or plays, off-stage complaints and gossip, or behaviours, such as foot-dragging or absenteeism might allow an attentive researcher to read against the grain. In the final lines he argued that:

> This symbolic refuge is not simply a source of solace in a precarious life, not simply an escape. It represents an alternative moral universe in embryo—a dissident subculture, an existentially true and just one, which helps unite its members as a human community and as a community of values. In this sense, it is as much a beginning as an end (1976: 240).

This was the launching pad for the everyday forms of resistance literature that were to follow through the 1980s, and which remain today perhaps Scott's greatest legacy to political anthropology.[2] Scott's answer to the question "why don't peasants rebel?" was, in effect, to reply that they *are* rebelling, at least sometimes (in peasant wars, as Wolf had demonstrated) but also at other times less easily recognized. Even when confronted with apparent peasant quietude or compliance, the researcher who is aware of the nuance and subtlety of cultural expression and off-stage performance would be able to locate less obvious forms of resistance: in effect, they are rebelling: you just need to know where to look. This is a surprising answer, because while it opens the door for a consideration of apparent quietude and cultural expression as possible forms of (or covers for) resistance, the question of nonrevolt itself recedes one step further away from analysis.

Ortner, in a well-known argument, suggested that the resistance literature (such as that which has followed Scott and his contemporaries, often picking up the idea while losing some of the complexity of its original formulation) often appears "thin" to an anthropological eye because it is ethnographically thin (1995: 190). Ortner noted there seemed to be almost a kind of embarrassment, as if acknowledging the complex interweaving of domination, complicity, ambivalence, and contradiction that ethnographers actually encounter in the field would concede too much, and perhaps even provide a weapon to justify injustices and violence. Ornter has called this "The impulse to sanitize the internal politics of the dominated" (1995: 179). I can only agree with Ortner when she argued that self-censorship is not a solution to the question of how we can provide ethnographically thick descriptions of what we encounter in the field while maintaining a firm footing in a politically engaged academia.

For Ortner, ethnographic thinness in resistance studies is a kind of refusal of the challenges and implications posed by the ethnographic method. Ethnographic thickness, on the other hand, in her view could indicate many things, including exhaustiveness, holism, or—influential at the time she wrote—contextualization. I would add another form of ethnographic thickness: desire. Often the characters we meet in the field and the dilemmas in which they find themselves are not clear cut: people find themselves faced with competing desires, conflicts between their desires and their self-interest, and desires which remain opaque and puzzling even to themselves, and when they pursue what they think they want, they often end up with something quite different. An ethnographically thick description must have the ambition to take into account not only ever more detailed wholes, but also such holes, contradictions and gaps. A nuanced concept of desire can help us craft ethnographic accounts that are thickened in this way.

In my interest in desire, I join a number of other scholars of the region who, unsatisfied with the thinness of resistance studies, have responded with ethnographic attention to what it is that marginal people desire in and from these situations. Tongue-in-cheek, I refer to this as the "resistance to resistance studies". For instance, Tania Li (2014) writes of how a shift to cash cropping in upland Sulawesi resulted in landlessness, a dramatic rise in inequality, and very real livelihood problems for the new class of rural residents who now rely solely on waged work, work which is scarce and getting scarcer. Yet this all-too-familiar process of differentiation was not the result of a bungled development programme or state initiative. Rather, she suggests that in this case, it arose internally, from a configuration of desires. This process, she suggests, is best thought of not in terms of coercion, but seduction. In an explicit rejection of Scott's concepts of a highland preference for anarchy (Scott 2009), she outlines the strong desire for order in the form of submission to authority and the appeal of the promise of development. In an explicit rejection of Geertz' concept of shared poverty (Geertz 1963) and Scott's concept of a moral economy with a subsistence ethic (Scott 1976), she argues that the ethic, rather, was that of an eagerness for modernity, sometimes at tragic cost. In a rejection of a Polanyian "double movement" (Polanyi 1957), she shows how the uplanders of Sulawesi actively dismantled their own commons, voluntarily. All of this fueled, she tells us, by desires: for modernity, for food, and for security.

In a similar take, but from the perspective of Vietnam, Oscar Salemink (2011, 2012) presents a counter-narrative to that reading of the uplands as spaces of state evasion and escape that has become associated with James C. Scott's *The Art of not being Governed* (2009). Salemink writes, "I have hardly ever encountered any highlander who did not wish to partake in the promise of modernity, especially as exemplified by consumer goods ... the desire for goods and prestige link highlanders firmly to state- and market driven development programs" (2012: 5). He describes the lowland states of Southeast Asia as capable of enchantment and attraction, both historically and today. The highlanders he encountered were originally convinced by and committed to the "profoundly modern desire" shaped by the new Socialist state: their disaffection came often from those promises and benefits failing to materialize.

Sarinda Singh, in her recent monograph (2012) uses the example of forestry, wildlife and conservation in Laos. She argues that studies of conservation in the developing world are often framed in terms of "domination and coercion" (Singh 2012: 58). Contrary to this tendency, her aim is to show how "forests can symbolize social identities and desires for development" (Singh 2012: 58). She emphasizes in her introduction that Laos is "authoritarian" and that dissent is stifled, yet she argues that even in such a context, the state is seen as a field of natural potency and potential source of social improvement in much the same way that forests are. This culturally informed desire may go some way to explaining why Lao citizens keep returning to, and thus socially reproducing, the state despite their criticisms and distrust of it. Likewise, Andrew Walker (2012), writing of Thai politics, argues that, far from resisting the state, Thai peasants desire an attachment to it: it is "The desirable state", as one of his subheadings has it (2012: 27). He writes: "Rural Thailand's new "political society is energized by a fundamental desire to be productively connected to sources of power" (Walker 2012: 6). Walker is careful to develop a local, cultural concept of what power means in this context, based on Mulder's (1979) discussion of power as potential and potency in Theravada Buddhism. Yet, like so many other contributors to the "resistance to resistance" literature, he does not provide a similarly-grounded analysis of what desire means in this milieu or in his analysis.

This is by no means an exhaustive survey of the "resistance to resistance studies" literature, but it does give some idea of the direction in which the debate is heading. My sympathies, too, lie in this direction, but there is a danger here that I would like to point to and address. The danger with using desire in this manner, as a kind of resistance to resistance, is that desire is treated as somehow self-evident. It is what people desire, the objects of desire, which have been the focus of regional explication. We have ethnographic accounts of local concepts of power, potency, prosperity, security, modernity and so forth in the region: these are the objects of desire. But the theorization of desire itself seems to have remained somehow "thin".

Theories of desire

This is peculiar, because it is not as if we are short of theories of desire. Some readers, by the end of this introduction, may indeed think we have far too many. Below, I set out five ways of thinking about desire, and there are of course many more that I do not cover. I will try to relate each of these to the main questions that have been raised so far: "what is desire?" and "does it have anything to do with the current post-revolutionary, post-rebellious politics of Laos?" Perhaps, by bringing various existing theories of desire into mutual critique and by opening them to the objections, modifications and developments demanded by one another and by my fieldsite, a thicker sense of what we mean when we speak of desire can be crafted.

1) **Desire is just another word for "wants": these are universal, insatiable, and the driving force of the economy.** I have stated the position a little bluntly, here, but this is the approach taught in any standard introduction to

economics textbook. Take, for instance, this statement, made as "an introduction to the economic way of thinking":

> Our world is a finite place where people, both individually and collectively, face the problem of scarcity. Scarcity is the condition in which human wants are forever greater than the available supply of time, goods, and resources. Because of scarcity, it is impossible to satisfy every desire. Pause for a moment to list some of your unsatisfied wants. Perhaps you would like a big home, gourmet meals, designer clothes, clean air, better health care, shelter for the homeless, more leisure time, and so on. Unfortunately, nature does not offer the Garden of Eden, where every desire is fulfilled. Instead, there are always limits on the economy's ability to satisfy unlimited wants. Alas, scarcity is pervasive, so "You can't have it all." … all individuals, whether rich or poor, are dissatisfied with their material wellbeing and would like more…. Because of the economic problem of scarcity, no society has enough resources to produce all the goods and services necessary to satisfy all human wants (Tucker 2011: 3).

This author explains that the discipline of economics can be summed up as "the study of scarcity and choice". While the tone is down-home common sense, the substance is quite remarkable. This is a theory of desire as infinity: unlimited and insatiable. This inexhaustible energy collides with the equally immutable fact of resource scarcity. The result is the inevitability of "choice". We are all imagined as endlessly desiring subjects unendingly evaluating choices in a frustratingly finite world.

Anthropology has been in a tussle with this kind of thinking since the discipline's earliest days. In his preface to *Argonauts*, James G. Fraser denounced what he called "this horrible phantom … actuated by no other motive than that of filthy lucre, which he pursues relentlessly … along the line of least resistance" (1966). Malinowski (1966) pointed instead to excess, the constant give and take, the adventure, magic and aesthetics of Kula exchange to argue that, whatever desires are evident in economic action, these could not be understood purely as rational wants, or as unlimited. Rather, they were specific and importantly informed by cultural values. The subsequent amassing of ethnographic data has only confirmed this, as do the chapters that follow.[3]

The appeal of "desire," I suspect, for ethnographers of contemporary economic and political change in Southeast Asia is precisely the way that it somewhat vaguely and poetically gestures towards this finding: that we cannot continue to assume that "wants" are as simple as introductory economics would imply. The term "desire" seems to offer a tantalizing glimpse of an awareness of these complexities: it is suggestive of sex, psychoanalysis, continental theory and cultural considerations, which leads us to a second stream of thinking.

2) **Desire lies at the heart of the human psyche, and thus, perhaps of symbolic communication itself.** Psychoanalytic theories are diverse, many are mutually antagonistic and many also repulse anthropologists because of a sometimes gob-smacking glibness about the role of cultural difference. Henrietta Moore (2007) has made an important contribution here, though, subjecting Lacanian and object-relations theories to an anthropological critique as a way of discerning what a psychoanalytically inspired reading of desire might yield to ethnographers. She suggests a reading whereby desire emerges from an original infantile blissful state which is then lost: the gap left by this lost object is desire. The infant is then forced to learn a system of culturally specific symbols through which its dissatisfactions with this loss can be expressed in the form of demands. However, the range of possible ways of communicating this is never fully adequate: articulations always say too much or too little. Desire is the remainder that exceeds symbolization: it is inarticulate yet seeks expression, and thus drives renewed articulations. Since it is impossible to adequately express or indeed to satisfy, desire is thus a constant source of culture-work.

This takes us back to the reassuring ground of a culturalist explanation. This Lacanian-inspired model allows for (indeed insists upon) a specific "symbolic" learnt from one's environment though which desire is expressed as particular kinds of demands. However, this reintroduces the cultural at the cost, perhaps ironically, of its own (cultural?) prior commitments. The way desire is taken as a core of human experience here at first glance is very similar to the idea of desire found in the pages of any economics textbook: infinite, insatiable and everywhere. Yet Lacan himself expressed doubts about the infinity of desire: in his later work, he suggested that "Desire, more than any other point in the range of human possibility, meets its limit somewhere" (Lacan 1977: 31). It is more accurate to understand Lacanian desire not as a general explanation of everything in the universe, but a specific explanation of a particular element of the human experience (Moore 2011). Furthermore, while mainstream economics has tended to emphasize the rationality, obviousness and presence of desire, psychoanalytic approaches have viewed it in terms of the unconscious, of what is lost and inarticulate. This leads to important differences in interpretation, and in the chapters that follow it is this revised Lacanian model of desire that I will often use to thicken ethnographic accounts through attention to holes, gaps and ambiguities in meanings that are nonetheless compelling and formative. This distinction between the two approaches to desire (as a presence and as an absence) is important and returns in my next example, which is an even more extreme formulation of the first approach that sets no limits to desire at all.

3) **Desire is "life itself".** Deleuze and Guattari (1983) were great critics of psychoanalysis, arguing that the Freudian approach seemed so closed, narrowing desire down to set answers that locate it in sex and the domestic circle. They wanted to throw open a window to the wider political economy. Deleuze and Guattari also critiqued Lacan's concept of desire as generated from an original lack and argued instead that desire is a positive force immanent in a larger political economy. They argued that desire is generated in "assemblages"—such as capitalist, agrarian or fascist ones—and also generates such assemblages, while also being a revolutionary force that overthrows them. Drawing on both Marx and Freud they argued that economy is always at once both political and libidinal. They wrote of "desiring-machines" as a way of thinking about desire as both produced by and productive of wider social, political and economic context, in much the way that machines produce parts and components that go on to make up other machines. Desire is thus gigantic, operating on the scale of an entire socius. But there is also a "dwarfism" to desire, in that it resides in the smallest details, in the most routine daily acts. Deleuze, drawing on Spinoza and Nietzsche, also developed an understanding of desire as immanent—a force that arises within, but is also basic to, life itself. For example, beings not only persevere in life, they desire to do so. As life itself is nothing more than this desire, then life is "to desire one's own desire" (Agamben 1999: 236).

There is an irresolvable nub of difference, here, between psychoanalytically inspired views that locate desire in specific stages of human development, resulting in a particular structure of lack, and these philosophical concepts of desire which view it, somewhat mystically, as an immanent positive force. Moore has described this latter version as a "reworked vitalism": while starting with the specific embodied human experience, via a process of analytic reduction, it ends with an idea of disembodied affect running through all things, not only people (2011: 176).

While Deleuze and Guattari presented themselves as critics of classical economics and psychoanalysis, there is also an uncanny resemblance here: Deleuze and Guattarri have not so much overthrown Lacanian psychoanalysis and neoclassical economics as stretched them to a breaking point. They have taken the core concepts of these traditions—most especially desire—and attempted to make them subversive. Desire, the darling of ascendant capitalist models, was framed by them as "revolutionary" and "libratory", as that which not only ran through capitalism but could overthrow it. In the process, desire was amplified even further: now it was the property not just of (rational or irrational; consciously or unconsciously) desiring subjects, but of life itself thought of broadly, as inhering in all things.

4) **Desire is a western fantasy.** Thus, for all their apparent quarrels, there is a common thread here. The consensus seems to be that the human condition (and perhaps the condition of "life itself") is one of being a desiring subject. But for Foucault, this was a way of thinking characteristic of what he called "the West". He suggested that, "the West has managed ... to bring us almost entirely—our bodies, our minds, our individuality, our history—under the sway of a logic of concupiscence and desire. Whenever it is a question of knowing who we are, it is this logic that henceforth serves as our master key ... the matrix not only of the living, but of *life itself*" (my emphasis 1976: 78).[4] He set out to draw a genealogy of desire where individuals were "led" to interpret "themselves as subjects of desire" (1984: 5). This ambitious plan of work was not completed upon his death, but he completed enough to sow seeds of doubt about what we mean when we talk about desire. Foucault was able to show that the particular constellation of ideas about truth, the body, sex and confession that he outlined in the first volume were not constants in the history of "the West". They took time to emerge, and did so only in fits and starts, with other constellations also possible and in formation. Desire, then, is not universal or eternal, nor is it "life itself". Rather, it was a way of seeing life, of investigating and debating about it, one that grew out of a very particular context.

Is it possible that one reason why so many ethnographers of Southeast Asia have lately turned to desire in their discussion of politics and economy is because it is, as Foucault suggests, already a key concept in our ideas about what constitutes "the truth of their being"? This might also explain that uncanny convergence between mainstream economics, Deleuzian philosophy, and psychoanalysis on this concept. If the idea that desire can illuminate "the truth of their being" is so thoroughly embedded in "the West", how useful is it for cross-cultural ethnography?

This is a question worth asking and I think the answer is to be found in yet another question: Is desire an indigenous concept in our fieldsites, or only in this amorphous thing Foucault called "The West"? If it is found at work in the world, how can everyday concepts of desire be utilized to hone and improve social science uses of the concept? In the chapters that follow, I will show that desire works on multiple registers in Laos: as a part of lives as lived but also as a meta-representation (among others) of how Lao people themselves understand and interpret those lives. If we read Foucault's use of the concept of "the West" as the polar opposite of all things eastern, and therefore that desire is something we have, conceptually or experientially, and they do not, then the example of Southeast Asia is an excellent counter-argument. This brings me to point number five below.

5) **Desire is an indigenous, live concept.** In Laos, the liveliness of desire can be seen in the unresolved debates that circulate around it. Take Buddhism, for

instance. In the Theravada tradition practised in Don Khiaw, desire is a key concept via doctrinal renunciation. Reynolds concludes that the Buddhism characteristic of the region teaches a "simplicity of desires" (2005: 224). *Nir + vana* means "freedom from desire." However, Buddhist societies are also some of the most openly avaricious and acquisitive. This has been the focus of some debate in regional literature: why this materialistic acquisitiveness when Buddhism teaches simplicity and renunciation? Why are even the most holy Buddhist practices—doctrinally aimed at freedom from desire—in practice associated with obtaining one's heart's desires? Why are the key holy days of the Buddhist calendar in practice celebrated in ways geared towards material or karmic gain?[5] A clue might be found in Devereux's suggestion that, "culture itself produces all the value systems in terms of which culture as a whole is criticized and sometimes arbitrarily condemned" (1980: 308). Each culture, indeed each individual, he maintained, has some capacity for the full range of the human experience. So where one finds an intense negative association, as with desire in doctrinal Buddhism, it is almost inevitable that one will also find an alternative and equally intense elaboration in the opposite, positive direction. Certainly in Don Khiaw, local concepts such as *"yaak day"* (desire, greed) and *"ao"* (want, take) are not only condemned. They are also taken as basic explanations for human behaviours, sentiments and motivations. Following this way of thinking, we might see desire as a major indigenous field of worry and work in Theravada Buddhist Laos precisely because it is the subject of elaborate condemnation and incitement simultaneously. This is a view of desire that takes it as a symbolic elaboration that can vary culturally in terms of intensity.

In recent years, Marshall Sahlins has been pursuing the concept of desire as one particular cosmological commitment among many other possible alternatives, especially in terms of the way it underpins economic rationalities. He notes that the "Judeo-Christian" tradition fostered a view of humanity as full of unsated desires, and that this fed early anthropological concerns, for instance with functionalism. But, Sahlins writes, "the critical discovery of anthropology" has been that this view of humans, as simply "desiring" ultimately reveals nothing: objects of desire are only constituted through symbolic schemes. It is the meaning of things which determine their value and these meanings are determined culturally. Far from meaning and symbol being extraneous to economic calculation, "exogenous" or even "irrational", as the economists would have it, Sahlins argues that: "We live in a world enchanted by symbolically constituted, culturally relative 'utilities' such as gold, oil, diamonds, Pinot Noir grapes, Mercedes cars, heirloom tomatoes, silk clothing, hamburgers from McDonald's, and purses from Gucci" (2010: 383). Our economies are cultural constellations born of our cosmological commitments.

Scholars of Southeast Asia who have been writing against the ethnographic thinness of domination and resistance approaches have touched on something important in their uptake of the concept of desire. The ethnographic observation that people in the region do not only resist the state and markets, but appear to also demand them, has become impossible to ignore. Ethnographers are grappling with how to account for Southeast Asian change in terms that can explain not only nonrevolt, but also everyday nonresistance including daily aspirations, in ways that allow for both reason and fantasy, repetition and creativity, and for both the respect implied by cultural relativism, and a clear-eyed understanding that the cultural may not be so exotic after all. Desire hints at a way of dealing with this range. My sense is that, when scholars of the region speak of these "desires" for economic and political engagement in Southeast Asia, they are employing the term in this alternative sense offered by Sahlins: one that critically recognizes the influence of the classical economic notion of human behaviour as "functional" and "rational," but nonetheless insists that the functions and rationalities of desires are rooted in the specificity of particular symbolic cosmologies, thereby allowing us to make desire a question, rather than a prior commitment, in cross-cultural analysis.

Desire and delirium

It is this last model, where desire is understood as a locally charged concept and as a way of thinking about the cosmological and symbolic commitments behind particular arrangements of economics and politics, that I will employ in the chapters to follow. But by what mechanism does desire acquire this "charge"? One way of thinking about it is in the terms Devereux used in the example above, as the charge generated between two poles of an ambivalent structure. Another is offered by Lacan (via Moore) where desire is understood as charged by the circulation around an original and permanent lack. The charge is generated by the gaps, missing parts and contradictions that seek resolution yet can't be adequately resolved. If there is an order to desire, it is not an order of clear, conscious rationality but rather an order of this kind of circulation or ambivalence. Deleuze used the term "delirium" to describe how a particular rationality or cultural frame "works" in the sense that it produces its own persistent orderings and arrangements even when it does not "work" in a coherent, holistic manner. "Delirium" refers to the way a certain kind of sense can be compelling even when not making sense rationally. It is this delirious "sense" of politics and poverty I set out to grasp and communicate ethnographically in the following chapters.

The example Deleuze gave was of the stock market. On one level, everything about it makes perfect sense: it has rules and regulations, practices and regularities; it is even possible to gain qualifications geared towards mastering the stock market, and some claim to be able to predict it. But on the other hand, Deleuze commented, "it's nuts." It only makes sense if one takes as given certain fundamental premises about property, value and exchange that are themselves in fact exotic and historically specific cosmological commitments. Nevertheless, these hang together in such a way that they produce a rationality of their own: "it is demented and it works."[6] Attention to delirium in this sense equips ethnographers to make thicker descriptions not only of symbolic wholes (via contextualization in the cultural fields of meaning from which desires emerge) but also of the holes: the missing or hidden parts where meaning fails, is contradictory or incomplete, but nonetheless compelling.

Desire can produce resistance to the dominant assemblage, but it can also inspire normativity and aspirations for conformity. Speaking of the question that interests us here, that of non-rebellion, Deleuze and Guattari, in characteristically shocking tones, wrote:

> ... the astonishing thing is not that some people steal or that others occasionally go out on strike, but rather that all those who are starving do not steal as a regular practice, and all those who are exploited are not continually out on strike: after centuries of exploitation, why do people still tolerate being humiliated and enslaved, to such a point, indeed, that they actually want humiliation and slavery not only for others but for themselves? (1983: 29, see also Deleuze 1993a: 231).

This is not some kind of rationalistic desire, as assumed in classical economics, where desires match one's self-interest. But, like Scott and Sahlins, Deleuze did not wish to reduce the observation of nonrevolt to "ignorance or illusion," hegemony or false consciousness. All these thinkers pointed instead to more subterranean levels: for Scott this meant the rich culture of resistance below surface conformity, for Sahlins, the cosmologies that underlie economies. By "delirium" Deleuze was indicating much what Sahlins was suggesting through the use of "cultural-symbolic schemes": a shared irrationality which provides the basis for the particular rationalities of that assemblage. The appeal for me of Deleuze's term "delirium" rather than Sahlin's "culture-symbolic schemes" is that delirium points much more clearly and directly to the holes, gaps and contradictions, rather than the coherent and credulous wholes with which the culture concept has historically been linked. And it is by attending to the holes, to the moments where "it's nuts" but also produces rationalities, moments where what is missing is just as important as what is present, that we can produce thicker descriptions of the politics of poverty and development, the persistence of a programme when no one any longer believes, but almost all nonetheless continue to take part.

The lie of the (is)land

The island of "Don Khiaw" has been inhabited mainly by ethnic Lao for as long as anyone there can remember. The Buddhist temple on the island has an inscription claiming it was built in 1859. Early accounts of this region describe it as densely populated, especially along the riverbank and islands. Pavie, for example, wrote:

> ...the banks of the Mekong appear more populated. The villages succeed each other without interruption ... the small Province of Si Phan Don (4.000 Ssles) [sic], the name of which simply means that it is composed of a great number of isles and is a rich district, very densely inhabited, whose population lives from their rice fields and which also owes its wealth to the commercial traffic on which the barrage of the rice imposes inland water transport (Pavie 1999: 427).

He recorded that Vientiane (now the capital of Laos) at that time had a population of only 2,000, while Bassac (the centre of the *mandala*[7] where Don Khiaw was located) had 10,000, and Mounlapamouk and Khong (two other local centres) numbered 2,300 and 1,500 respectively. Similar observations were made by Garnier in 1866, who noted on his river journey that, "Everywhere, the densely populated and cultivated banks present convenient and well-stocked places to stop over" (1996: 76). He described the islands as "very highly populated and densely cultivated" with a "continuous line of palm trees, houses and gardens beside the banks (that) is most pleasant" (1996: 73) a description that could well have been written today. With an eye for the economic standing of the region, Garnier wrote that, "The location ... makes it quite an important commercial center" with Chinese traders and a "rather busy" route heading east to the "wild tribes" of the Bolaven Plateau (1996: 74). In addition, Siam was attempting to draw the region more closely into its administrative framework. Garnier wrote:

> At this time, the whole of Lower Lao was swarming with envoys from Bangkok charged with cranking up the zeal of the government and, in the name of the king, organizing some sort of forced commerce in addition to the taxes levied on the population. It was in this way that His Siamese Majesty fixed for himself the quantities of wax, ivory and other local products that had to be turned over in exchange for the cotton cloth and other European export products that could not be sold in Bangkok (1996: 117).

Figure 3. The main hall of the Don Khiaw Buddhist temple also served as the venue for most village meetings.

Figure 4. A boat moored by the shore of Don Khiaw. Boats were the main form of transport during my fieldwork.

The demand for taxes had sparked gold panning, gem prospecting and slave raids in the Plateau to the east, trades which passed through this Mekong region for exchange and transport. The position of Don Khiaw on an island in the Mekong placed it in the thoroughfare of these flows of trade, transport and politics.

Siam and France were in contest over the rich and well-connected area in which Don Khiaw was located. This dispute continued up to and throughout WWII (a more complete account is offered in Chapter Three). As a result, Don Khiaw island was consolidated into Laos only in 1946. Older residents of Don Khiaw have memories of both corvée labour on French road building projects on the mainland and Thai schooling in the temple grounds. Soon after WWII Laos was drawn into the Second Indochinese War. Conflict did not take place on Don Khiaw, but the island was affected by the large population movements triggered by the protracted civil war that emerged over the ensuing decades between rightist, leftist and neutralist factions in Laos, combined with the wider effects of the US bombardment.[8] Many moved to urban centres that were not only relatively spared from the bombardment but were also experiencing a boom due to an injection of American aid and bureaucratic presence. In 1975, the communist Pathet Lao came to power, introducing a suite of major changes to the Mekong Valley economy, which had not previously been "liberated". In Don Khiaw, this was perhaps most keenly felt in terms of direct state intervention in the rice economy, such as bans on the private trade in rice and the collectivization of agriculture. These years were marked by significant food shortages which in turn drove many urban residents to relocate again, this time to rural areas. In the late 1970s and early 1980s, Don Khiaw saw a significant proportion of its population flee to Thailand. While the harshest controls on the rural rice economy were reversed relatively quickly, people continued to flee Laos in large numbers into the 1990s. Many became refugees and some sought resettlement further abroad, while others were involved in counterrevolutionary incursions back into Laos, but these fell off in the late 1980s.

Official statistics estimate that during my research about 80 percent of the population of Laos are engaged in agriculture, although rural residents also engage in migrant labouring, receive remittances from relatives abroad, and undertake multiple livelihood strategies which tend to be overlooked in such statistical representations. Likewise, even those who live and work in cities commonly remain existentially linked to agriculture, making Laos an importantly rural nation despite growing urbanization. Laos now receives one of the highest rates of international development assistance in the Asian region. One of the latest phases of development policy has been the push for "decentralization", which has involved, among other things, the relocation of some significant aspects of bureaucratic work (such as tax collection, recording citizenship status, and school building) to the village level. This corresponds with international trends in development practice, but it is taking place in a context that was weakly centralized in the first place. The effect has not been to strengthen local autonomy, but to require rural residents to integrate more intimately with the nation state through a particular, and very "near", form of bureaucratic practice.[9]

From the perspective of Don Khiaw, within the space of a single generation, national borders have been solidified to an unprecedented degree, a new tax regime has emerged, entailing new modes of land ownership and the closing of a formerly rather open land frontier, education has moved out of the temple and into the remit of the Ministry of Education, and citizenship has been documented and regulated. The modern state has arrived in rural Laos, but the dust swirled up from its arrival still hangs in the air. In this context, development projects play a very particular role as a rationalization for new forms of rule. In rural Laos, this rationalization takes the form of promises of development and poverty reduction. The Party is committed to "graduating" Laos from Least Developed Country status by 2020. Catchy phrases such as "addressing poverty is everyone's work" and "National poverty reduction and growth strategy" adorn t-shirts and key government documents, seemingly aware on some level of the need for constant repetition of this key rationalization for rule. Echoes of this idiom and the interventions carried out in its name are found in even the most remote and supposedly inaccessible parts of Laos.

Laos is currently undergoing a period of significant economic change: economic growth stood at 8.4 percent in 2010, with rates projected to climb in 2011. Yet in this period of growth and apparent commitment to development, Don Khiaw has moved, while staying in the same place, from being described by Garnier and Pavie as in the heartland of a "rich" and well-connected area to being described by the Lao regime and its international backers as poor and remote and in need of intervention. In terms of official definitions, Don Khiaw was considered "poor" largely because incomes were low and the island lacked many government services.[10]

There was also a loud self-definition from many people who lived there that they were poor (even though I have certainly seen poorer places in Laos, particularly in the remote east). There was a pervasive feeling in Don Khiaw of being poor and marginal, and as a local perception this is worth taking seriously. Two important elements of national development have contributed to this sense of growing marginalization: roads and electrification. While the river was once the mainstay of transport in this region, making islands the most central location possible, today it is roads and motor vehicles that are the symbols of everyday mobility. So, where Garnier and Pavie observed houses clustered along the river, palm trees reaching out over the water, now throughout Laos it is possible to see houses clustering by roads, electrical wiring and satellite dishes radiating around them. This has raised concerns about the often unplanned-for rush of resettlement towards roads as they are constructed. By contrast, there are no roads on Don Khiaw, other than the dirt footpaths that are called "roads" (*thaang*) because they were the site of previous food-for-work "road" construction programmes. More importantly, there are no bridges to the mainland to connect any would-be drivers to the growing national road network. There was also no link to the national electricity grid at the time of writing. When my fieldwork began in the early 2000s, there was a kind of equality in this lack of roads and power: not only Don Khiaw, but all of the surrounding villages lacked these. Now, however, there is a vehicle-worthy dirt road on the mainland adjacent to Don Khiaw, and along it have come power lines. When I started my fieldwork, there were 66 households on Don Khiaw. By 2011, there were 50: "If the electricity won't come to find the people, the people will go to find the electricity" people joked. Don Khiaw is being made marginal by the transformations of rural Laos. It is now considered a poor place by bureaucrats and local residents alike.

The book

The state and its poverty reduction policies are subjects of constant criticism in Don Khiaw: this is no adoring peasantry. They—like so many others in or observing Laos—"see through" poverty reduction policies and speculate about the political motivations behind them. False consciousness and hegemony, as both Scott and Deleuze predicted, cannot explain this mode of political engagement. What is required is a more nuanced study of the political field in terms of the desire that produces the delirious rationalities for sometimes diametrically opposed evaluations, agreements, condemnations and actions. Chapter Two begins an outline of this delirium with an analysis of the phrase "eat with you". This is a particularly evocative phrase in the Lao rice economy, because it can refer to both forms of building and confirming solidarity and to forms of corruption and exploitation. This dualistic interpretation of eating can be observed in folktales, religious observances, common courtesies and sayings regarding rice, but also in everyday encounters with the state. I suggest that this example of "eat with you" hints at a broader ambivalence in the Lao political field between power as nurture and power as destruction.

Chapter Three narrates the history of the region in four registers—a Lao propaganda document denouncing insurgency, a family history of one household in Don Khiaw, retrospective narratives from returned refugees now living in Don Khiaw, and conventional written history. These show how the region has been, over time, enmeshed in a specific set of territorial and administrative constraints which now entangle Don Khiaw residents in a particular regime of citizenship. Entrenched poverty, marginalization, and increasing regulation are now part of the context that rural residents confront when pursuing their desires. With their migrations, their past defeats, and their compromises with expanding capital and state projects, the people of Don Khiaw closely resemble the "post-peasants" that Scott described, and in many ways their situation seems difficult, if not hopeless.

Scott suggests that, when confronted with a situation of post-peasant defeat and apparent hopelessness, analytical advance can be made "by asking directly whether the values embodied in peasant culture do in fact accord with the dominant myths of the social order" (1976: 240). He predicted that such an investigation will reveal difference, the "embryonic form" of a dissident culture. Cuing from Deleuze, I develop this idea to suggest that there are multiple embryos—some of them revolutionary, some of them with aspirations for conformity, some of them mutations and others replications. Chapter Four presents character sketches of particular Don Khiaw women in their fluttering attempts to break free of poverty. I frame these in terms of desire to indicate the way these pursuits were often pursued passionately (sometimes beyond reason), but did not always match self-interest, and produced results that were not as intended.

In Chapter Five, I introduce the "stories of state" that are told in Laos. Using the example of the collectivization of agriculture, I investigate that persistent gap between the official story told about the Lao political structure in the public realm and the officially unknown exposés that are made of corruption, secrecy and violence. Such stories of state are often only told in private moments. I understand these off-stage stories as more than simply memories. They communicate a particular knowledge about the state and how to effectively engage with it today. These stories draw a picture of the state as an external entity, above and beyond society, oppressive, extractive, dangerous and dishonest. Even though this portrait of the state is not supposed to be spoken openly, these tales are essential to ongoing engagements with development and poverty reduction projects as these are understood as state projects. Despite the apparent divergence of the on-stage and off-stage depictions of what the state is and what the intentions of poverty reduction programmes are, there is also a shared delirium that underlies and links both of these.

I trace this out in terms of the linked dualism of nurture and devouring, echoing the ambivalence of the rice economy outlined in Chapter Two.

Strikingly, the state is viewed as an external entity, yet this is an intimate externality. Despite the condemnation of it as corrupt and untrustworthy, the state continues to be understood as essential to the politics of poverty, which is often a politics of sheer bodily survival. While the exposés of state violence and corruption revealed in intimate moments often teach that the state is oppressive, extractive and immoral, the state nonetheless continues to be approached as a potential dispenser of relief, development and assistance to the poor. In Chapter Six, I examine how an irrigation project was resurrected after it had fallen into disuse. The project had originally been abandoned and at that time the farmers involved had spoken to me of the project as flawed and essentially extractive, landing many poor people in debt. Using subtle, on-stage manouvering they had been able to negotiate away from the project, leaving the island dotted with abandoned irrigation pumps and the District Agricultural Promotion Bank account books smeared with unpaid debts. The very next year, however, a drought struck and rice shortages loomed. The Don Khiaw village meeting voted to request yet more irrigation pumps from the local authorities because they feared starvation otherwise. A village leader explained that *more* irrigation investment was now the "will and desire" of the people. Here, a renewed engagement with a previously rejected state intervention was initiated by villagers on the basis of another kind of intimacy, the intimacy of a politics of survival and the state's promise to intervene there, at the very least. There is thus an ambivalent, even physical, intimacy with this reified and reviled entity, a process similar to what Lacan referred to as extimacy (*extimité*).

Lest this sound altogether too determinist, Chapter Seven provides a narrative to show how the delirium of desires operates as an open-ended process. I describe a particular series of events surrounding The World Bank Poverty Reduction Fund. In this narrative, I show how my own interpretations changed over time and were indeed part of the events as they unfolded. My purpose is to show how the political field is negotiated, with varying interpretations held by different actors altering and clashing over time. The concepts of fear and nurture, intimacy and reification that I traced out in the previous chapters are useful throughout the narrative for understanding why people reacted or interpreted the way they did, but these appear in this narrative not as cultural determinations but as the building blocks from which people constructed and reconstructed their responses and interpretations. This narrative shows how these shifted over time, were tentative and uncertain, and often formed within a context of incomplete knowledge, disagreement and struggle.

Chapter Eight consolidates what has been learnt through the previous chapters by taking a look at one thread that has run through the descriptions of collectivization, mechanized irrigation and the Poverty Reduction Fund. This is the notion of "mutual aid". It seems that there has been for decades a continual policy push for Lao rural residents to pursue development and poverty reduction through "mutual aid", although the language and methods have varied with the times, from high socialism to contemporary "participatory development". Chapter Eight examines mutual aid as a delirium in its distribution throughout the wider social field, from mortuary ceremonies in rural Laos to critical evaluations of the contemporary regime. I argue that "mutual aid" is a particularly powerful image for constructing images of political virtue and disgrace.

2

Eat with you
Power as Nurturing and Devouring

In the beginning, there was only one woman. She lived with a dog in a cave, and they lived as husband and wife. The woman gave birth to children, human children, but the dog would eat them, each and every one. One day, when the dog was out hunting, the woman gave birth to a boy. She hid him in a secret cave where the dog could not find him. The next time, she gave birth to a girl. She hid this child in a different cave. Eventually, when the boy and girl grew up, they found each other. They had children and their children had children too.

This tale was told to me in Don Khiaw by a man who claimed it was the story of "where people come from". He often delighted in telling me what he called "*nithaan*" (folktales) although his stories rarely coincided with any well-known canon of Lao folktales: he had an eye for the obscure, amusing and irreverent. This particular story is not found in other anthropological accounts of the ethnic Lao or Tai of this region, nor is it the kind of "official myth" that features in preserved manuscripts, Lao nationalist mythology, Buddhist religious performances or schoolbooks. It does, however, have some resonances with minority folktales in the region.[1] When I tried to follow the tale back to its source, I asked as many locals as I could about it, and in the process I participated in spreading the tale to many who had not heard it previously: some enjoyed it, others were baffled, some disapproved and thought I should stick to Buddhist morality tales. Others had heard it before, and speculated on its origin: all agreed it was likely local.

The story of the dog and his human wife is worth considering, I suggest, because it is evocative of something key about how power and people are understood in the south of Laos. The tale pivots on eating. The dog-father is a hunter but he also eats his own children. The mother, meanwhile, is a nurturing figure. The drama of the story is about how these two characters either eat or do not eat the people in their care. I suggest this hints at an ambivalent but compelling understanding of the power that feeding and eating entails. Van Esterik (1996) has suggested that the Thai (and Lao) term for feeding, *liaang*, can be translated as "nurture" and that it is also "the most widely understood arena for negotiating and displaying power and hierarchy" (1996: 23). *Liaang*, she suggests, is most widely elaborated in connection with "feasting, partying and banqueting" (1996: 33) where it refers to how a host or patron feeds his guests. And unlike the English idea of nurture, *liaang* does not entail the idea of gendered duty. Rather, it entails a sense of the potency inherent in feeding, a potency that both men and women can engage with, although women do have a particularly close association with it through idealized images of motherly care.

Cuing from this notion of feeding as a form of potency, I interpret the story of the dog and his human wife as a story about the very different potentialities of power. Power can be wild and dangerous, and mean being fed upon and thus destroyed. But domesticated, power can also be nurturing, a source of protection from rapacious forces, of sustenance and perhaps even of the creation of life. In this chapter I will trace out this ambivalent understanding of power in contemporary state relations. I use this to begin my investigation into why people from the south of Laos at once fear and seek nurturance from the state. To put it bluntly, the state is perceived as a powerful entity, and therefore ambivalently: it is seen as a possible source of both sustenance and destruction, nurturing and devouring.

Some time ago, Scott noted that, "food and the imagery of food is at the center of peasant notions of equality. Equality and redistribution are also, of course, an integral part of the ideological vision propagated by revolutionary elites" (Scott 1979). Food is central to the rationalization of rule in Laos. The promise that the people will, at least, *mii khao kin* (have rice to eat) has been a consistently important part of the political project of the Pathet Lao, and later, the Lao People's Revolutionary Party (LPRP). Lao agriculture was referred to in early announcements as isolated and backward and the Pathet Lao announced they would deliver food security through modernization. Irrigation, collectivization and controls on the trade in rice were aimed at achieving national self-sufficiency in food. During the war, producing food to support the war effort was imperative for the Pathet Lao. After the 1975 revolution the LPRP denounced the ousted RLG (Royal Lao Government) as decadent and dependent on foreign powers. Chomsky (1970) reported that in 1963, the Kingdom of Laos imported 40 times the value of its exports. This was linked by commentators at the time to corruption, social decay and loss of national autonomy. Part of the populist platform of the incoming LPRP regime was a promise to overcome this malaise through self-provisioning of essentials, most essentially rice. When self-sufficiency in food was declared achieved in 1999, the rationalization of delivering prosperity remained. The 1991 Constitution replaced the previous slogan ("Peace, Independence, Unity and Socialism") with a new one: "Peace, Independence, Unity and Prosperity" (see Ivarsson et al., 1995, p. 38). While goals of a socialized economy have been deferred, the goal of provisioning prosperity was intensified.

However, this is a rationalization that leaks out on all sides: it is not fully contained by LPRP promises, and is indeed used in strong condemnations of the current regime. In this chapter, I will argue that this rationalization—that the LPRP are the ones who will ensure that Lao people *"mii khao kin"* (at least have rice to eat), and perhaps have more than enough—saturates power dynamics but often in an ambivalent way. Rice itself is an ambivalent symbol. The force of feeling attached to rice is not limited to the political realm, and indeed draws much of its political force from the way it circulates through economic and familial relationships more generally. In the way that it leaks between such contexts and is charged with ambivalent dynamics, the rationalization of rice operates more as a shared delirium that reaches well beyond the apparently practical purposes of having rice to eat.

Rice, eating and solidarity

The word "eat" in Lao is, as in so many other Asian languages, literally "to eat rice" (*kin khao*). In the south of Laos, rice is the staple food of every meal. It is grown in dry fields (*hay*) and wet fields (*naa*). These are cultivated areas of intense human effort, and this makes them distinct from the wild places of *paa* (forest). There was no mechanization of rice production in Don Khiaw during my fieldwork: buffalo, wooden ploughs and harrows, and pedal-powered threshers were the main additions to human labour. It was often said, "to eat rice, one must work, and to work one must eat rice". These fields produce heavy, glutinous rice that is said to be the most appropriate food for those who labour in them: glutinous rice is considered sustaining and invigorating for the sturdy, hardworking people of the rice fields. The phrase *"saaw naa"* literally means "people of the rice fields", though it is often translated as "farmers". By contrast, I was warned that if I ate this rice it would make me feel tired and heavy: Mother Phong, my adopted mother, would often insist on cooking a special pot of lighter, non-glutinous rice for me, as a sign of her attentive care to my perceived needs as non-Lao and a non-farmer. Rice has a special, reciprocal relationship with the "people of the rice fields": it is a material consolidation of their labour, skill and effort spent in the fields. The vulnerable seedlings are cared for, fretted over and nurtured into golden sheaths of grain, and these grains in turn nurture these people, or so common wisdom has it. In what follows, I will trace out such common wisdoms. Although these often sound rather idealized when parsed into English, my purpose is to first examine seriously the way eating is linked to nurture, before turning to its more destructive associations.

Common wisdom has it that you cannot grow rice alone. Of course, people can and do grow rice alone, but they speak of this as a disadvantage, a problem, and those growing rice alone often plant fewer fields than they would wish. Wet rice has been shown to be responsive to labour intensity: increased labour results in increased yields (Bray 1986, Geertz 1963). Rice, then, is a thoroughly social crop. It often involves a group effort. However, in southern Laos there is no set arrangement for how these groups will be arranged: the style of production is called *phay heet phay man* (each to his or her own). People own land and means of production privately and are

Figure 5. Harvesting rice.

Figure 6. I have translated *haa kin (find and eat)* as "a hand-to-mouth existence." It often includes gathering wild foods, such as this assortment collected from the forest.

Figure 7. A woman prepares a meal using herbs grown in a homestead garden.

responsible for their own subsistence needs. Most commonly it is households that form the core groups of rice production and consumption. Before the rains come each year there is speculation about how labour, land and equipment will be assembled that year, each household pulling together a different assemblage, each year producing rice in a changing mosaic of people and resources often not finalized until the last moment. One couple might have land but no buffalo to plough it, so they plan to rent buffalo with a promise to send some of the harvest to its owner in return. Another woman has land and buffalo but no one to plough while she transplants, so rather than farm rice alone she elects to rent out her fields and animals, while working herself as a hired labourer elsewhere. A third family might be owners of land and buffalo, with more fields than they can plant on their own, so they seek out labourers to come for peak periods—the harrowing and ploughing, the transplant, and the harvest. Others have no land, and these landless farmers are perhaps the most fluid of all in their strategies, experimenting each year: establishing new fields to the west one season, the next renting out other's land in Don Khiaw, the next eschewing rice production altogether in favour of migrant labouring.[2] Workers may receive a standard wage (10,000 *kip* or 1 USD a day during the main period of this fieldwork) but more often they operated under an idiom of help (*sooy*). Assistance can be rendered under this idiom sometimes for weeks, sometimes just for a day. Helpers share meals provided by the host household, and may be offered gifts: perhaps a share of the harvest if their contribution was sustained and substantial, or perhaps an overflowing bag of fruit for a day's work. Rice production is expressive of, and dependent on, such varied forms of exchange or mutuality between specific, often unequally placed, people.

Perhaps this helps explain why the eating of rice is ritualized at each meal in small ways that express both mutuality yet also, often at the same time, inequality. Meals are taken two or three times a day. Rice is served in large bamboo containers, usually one shared between each cluster of two or three people, with the group as a whole sharing a common central tray of soups, hot sauces, vegetables and perhaps some fish or meat. The most senior diner will eat first, taking a small ball of rice in hand and eating it, plain. Common wisdom has it that rice (and eating more generally) is not delicious if a person dines alone (*kin khao phuu diaaw bo saeep*). Any visitor to rural Laos will have noted the remarkable habit there of calling anyone in earshot, including passers-by, to join the meal: "*kin khao*" (eat rice!) they call. Even if one is a guest, and eating a meal prepared by hosts, it is still usual to call out this invitation to any and all before starting. Even when a passer-by has no idea that the people inside a house might be eating, it is still common to hear a voice call out through the split bamboo walls, inviting any and all to "come and eat." When making small talk in general, the most common question after the ubiquitous "where are you going?" is "have you eaten rice yet?" And if one answers in the affirmative, the next question is "what did you eat with the rice?" This often sparks the patter of daily conversation about bounty and scarcity that is the common fodder for small talk in southern Laos. These are the daily micro-rituals that express the social nature of rice: socially produced, it is socially consumed.

Eating rice together also marks major moments of social solidarity. It is perhaps not surprising that events such as weddings, *phuuk khaeen* (calling of the souls) and New Year parties are marked by a meal shared *en masse*. What strikes the visitor to Laos, however, is how often eating is also intermingled with work. A house-raising event will be marked by at least one major meal. Visiting government officials, even those who have come to collect bank debts, expect to be offered a meal when in the village. In Don Khiaw the Village Chief and the Women's Union Leaders bore the burden of preparing these meals. Male village leaders, meanwhile, entertained official visitors with rice whiskey. It is often claimed that it is impossible to decline a shot of rice whisky offered in such a situation, even if it is still early morning. "*Kin, kin,*" the reluctant drinker will be urged, as the word for "drink" and "eat" are the same: *kin*. Rice whisky is usually offered from a single, shared glass: this is explicitly explained to anyone who might hesitate or balk at the often fiery-tasting liquid that drinking it is a sign of solidarity (*saamakhii*), as are the joint meals that follow. Eating with each other, particularly eating rice, is conspicuously and loudly declared on such occasions as a sign of social solidarity.

Lao understandings of relatedness also draw heavily on the idiom of eating rice together. Theirs is a cognatic, matrifocal patterning where the emphasis is placed on female-centred households and families. While each individual is understood to have many relatives (indeed it is often said, half in jest, that "everyone" is related), family, true family, are only ever a small selection of the larger group. One of the characteristics of family is that they are the people you eat with, or have done so in a sustained way in the past. The word for family, *khoop khua*, is made from the words for "to cover" and "to cook" respectively. Family are those who are covered by the same hearth, the same meals.[3] Biological relatedness is only one factor in forming such groups: it is not uncommon for children to be raised by parents who are not their biological progenitors, for adults to adopt new parents, and for good friends or even colleagues to refer to each other as siblings, and so on. There is a great variety in how these "love" (*hak*) based familial ties are enacted: some are virtually in name only, but for much of the time these are profoundly important relationships based on sharing the windfalls and hardships of everyday life, especially food. Hearth groups are often also core units for producing rice.

Thus, when Jane Hanks asked so perspicuously why it was that, when rice itself is considered "drearily tasteless…. What makes these people gorge themselves on this admittedly vapid food?" her answer pointed to the relationships that sustain and are sustained by rice production. As she puts it: "As each person partakes of rice, he demonstrates that he (or at least someone) has reciprocated his obligations in the past, and by eating it contracts new obligations to reciprocate. Rice nourishes his soul, which is eternally dependent on feminine mercy" (1960: 151–3).

At the heart of each hearth group is often a mother. Women are often responsible for preparing meals for household members. In addition, mothers are heavily symbolized as archetypes of the kind of nurturance that creates family bonds. It is a mother's provisioning of shelter, material needs, food and support for her child that is said to generate the sense of endless "debt" that some Lao speak of: *tit nii bun khun maee* (indebted by the virtue of the mother). In contrast to Euro-American notions of kinship (Schneider 1972) which foreground metaphors of shared biological substances (Carsten 1995), Lao kinship focuses on intimate exchanges of nurture and care as the substance of relatedness. A mother's daily preparation of rice for her children (biological or otherwise) is a key symbol of this kind of nurturing love and resulting obligation that is the foundation stone of Lao notions of relatedness. I have argued elsewhere (2011a) that these familial gifts in daily life and the reciprocal relationships that they incur are thought of in terms not so much of acquittal over time but as ideally deepening, so that one gift engenders yet another, each one cementing the bond between the pair.

The local economy is centred on rice, as are idioms for describing economic fortunes. Comparing their lives to those of urban people or market gardeners, it was observed that at least here, on Don Khiaw, there is rice to eat (*mii khao kin*). In the city, by contrast, you have to find money first to buy rice. To *mii khao kin* (have rice to eat) is an idiom expressing relative comfort, indicating that even if things are not great, they are not as bad as they could be. It carries with it an implicit comparison, as most people have experienced at one point or another periods of time when there was not enough rice to eat. The opposite phrase, *bo mii khao kin* (no rice to eat) is an idiom used to refer to poverty.

Rice is grown in Don Khiaw primarily for subsistence needs, but people will also sell it, use it to pay debts, or to produce noodles, alcohol or sweets for sale. Rice production is the core economic activity over which other activities are overlain. Petty trade, picking coffee in the Bolaven Plateau, and migrant labouring in Vientiane or Thailand are significant alternative sources of income, and often timed to slot in with the demands of the rice season. Nonetheless, most people do not grow enough rice to sell or trade in significant amounts: most do not even grow enough rice to cover their own needs. This is a below-subsistence rice economy. The classificatory scheme used locally in the village to determine relative wealth between households, such as when determining how much each household will contribute to the village festival, divides households into those with "extra" (that is, more than enough for their needs, often because they run successful businesses), "enough" (meaning that their harvested rice from the previous year ran out roughly as they harvested the new rice) and "not enough" (meaning the rice from the previous year ran out often months before the new rice was harvested). In Don Khiaw, of 66 households, three households had "extra", a dozen had "enough", and the rest had "not enough". The three with "extra" did not farm rice for a living, though they lived and owned fields on the island: one was a spirit healer, one a moneylender and rice dealer and the third owned a cargo boat.

Amongst those who have "not enough", their poverty is measured in terms of which month the rice ran out. How do people survive without rice? The answer, most typically, is _haa kin_ (find and eat). This is an umbrella term that indicates the multiplicity of strategies used to get by until the next harvest: foraging in the forest, digging up wild root vegetables, looking for work with neighbours or in the city, begging, pressing relatives abroad for remittances, anything and everything. Perhaps the best translation is "a hand to mouth existence". Such people often eat the new rice as they harvest it. Soft and bright white, the new rice is valued for its flavour and appearance, and for the return, for a brief time at least, of steady sustenance.

Rice and eating are also key symbols in supernatural relationships. As any visitor to Laos will have observed, the most common daily act for lay Buddhists is not praying or meditating, but feeding the monks. In Don Khiaw, the bell strikes at 6am announcing that the novices will set out with their begging bowls for the south of the island, following the single path that weaves from house to house between the river and the rice fields. People at each of the houses (mostly women) place cooked sticky rice in their begging bowls. At _phaen_ (11am) the bell rings again, and a group of women from the north of the island take the second and last meal of the day to the temple. These two strikes of the bell—early morning and late morning—are key references for marking daily time. Likewise, the lunar months and annual calendar are punctuated with Buddhist holy days and larger festivals. Again, the act of feeding the monks takes centrestage. Offerings of food generate merit, which in turn is thought to bring rewards to the donor in this life and the next, rewards that may be transferred to others, such as distant or deceased loved ones. At death, monks are invited to the family home to eat an elaborate meal, importantly rice based, to generate merit which is then transferred to the deceased. This is called the *caeek khao* (the distribution of rice). Without a *caeek*, or in the period between death and a *caeek*, the dead are hungry. They remain with the living hearth group, seeking to eat rice with them at meal times, haunting them in their unsatisfied need. The feeding of the monks at a *caeek* satisfies this hunger, fulfilling the duty to care for and feed loved ones even after death. The monks thus importantly act as catalysts transforming this-worldly rice into other-worldly merit and familial nurture.

This element of rice and feeding is also evident in those parts of religious life that are not strictly Buddhist. At the end of the harvest, the spirit of the rice is called into the granary and offered small gifts: candles, perfumed water, an egg, flowers, a cigarette, betel nut, string, rice, bananas. Attracted by these gifts, the spirit of the rice enters the granary with the harvest and dwells there, offering in return bounty and beauty to the next rice harvest. This closely mirrors the gifts made twice a year to the *puutaa* (territory guardian), in a ritual that is called *"liaang puutaa"* (nurturing or feasting the *puutaa*). The *puutaa* is offered alcohol, candles, rice, a chicken or egg, flowers and rice, and is then asked to care for the health of the livestock (buffalo particularly, but also chickens, ducks and pigs) and to care for people of the island, and in particular to avert epidemics, illnesses and accidents (High 2006a, 2009).

When out in the forest—perhaps to collect tubers, mushrooms, firewood, or coffee beans—it is a wise precaution to place small balls of glutinous rice on the branches of surrounding trees at meal times to feed whatever unknown spirits that may reside there. Generally, nothing is asked in return, but the rice may placate whatever ill ease, surprise or jealousy unseen spirits may harbour on seeing people eat. During the *suu khwan* (calling of the souls),[4] the 32 souls of the body are called to return and are tied onto the body with string, either to alleviate illness or to ensure good outcomes for the future. At the core moment of this ritual, rice is scattered over the bent head of the patient or supplicant as the cry *"maa doee, maa doee"* is raised (please come, please come). The souls are attracted by the rice and re-enter the body through the head where the rice falls. In private houses there is often a small shrine to *khuubaa*—ancestors, revered monks or other powerful entities. There may also be a spirit house built outside the main household, where local spirits (*phii*) or further *khuubaa* can be appeased through food. There is an anarchic element to these: people follow their own preferences and habits in household propitiation of *khuubaa* and *phii*. However, the common feature is again that these entities are approached and pleased via food, particularly rice. Throughout these disparate spiritual practices, feeding is used to attract, placate, satisfy and nurture.

Feedings are often hierarchical. Rice is offered by less powerful beings (ordinary humans) to more powerful beings (spirits, souls, monks, *khuubaa* and territory guardians). Feeding powerful beings is a means of ensuring right relationships with them, and of thereby attracting benefits to oneself, perhaps through their support or protection, or perhaps merely through their withholding harm, or indeed perhaps merely from the merit inherent in the act of generously offering food. This echoes the feeding of visiting officials: there the insistence is again on offering rice, other food, alcohol and cigarettes with a similar logic that solidarity and positive relationships can be formed via such feedings. Feeding among humans often goes the other way along the social hierarchy: the more affluent may be pressed to give rice to the poor, not as a duty or requirement but as a sign of their elective virtue. Likewise, mothers feed children as the ultimate picture of virtue. The witnessing of helplessness, poverty or need in the supplicant is thought to produce pity and generousity in the heart of a superior and virtuous person. They can display this virtue through the gift of foods, and these gifts are explicitly thought to produce a sense of indebtedness in the recipient. Again, this is a question of individual virtue on the part of the donor, not one of expected roles or duties. Children are indebted to the virtue (*bun khun*) of the mother, and even the very poor who are forced to beg are often endeavoured to make some small token of return—a woven basket, some gathered mushrooms—for the rice that they are given. Gifts of rice then provoke a form of reciprocity in unequal, dyadic and ideally ongoing relationships. Indeed, small exchanges in unequal relationships of this nature are the very stuff of the most basic relationships in the south of Laos, such as familial, patron-client and neighbourly ones. Small gifts of food are part of the daily pattern of life in the south of Laos. Feeding, then, is the symbol itself of nurturing solidarity among unequal entities.

Yet, to be fed upon by powerful beings involuntarily is a nightmare. Some malevolent beings (*phii poob*) are capable of feeding on the livers of sleeping bodies. Forest spirits (*phii paa*) are thought to be dangerous partly because of their rapacious appetites. Likewise, when it is said that a fellow human "eats with you", this can be an indication that they are exploiting you, sucking your resources, taking advantage of you, living freely from your labour without proper reciprocation. "Eat with you" (*kin nam cao*) is also a euphemism for corruption.

It is striking, given the central role of rice and eating as a symbol of building and expressing social solidarity, that we find this subtext of eating as a sign of danger, exploitation, illegitimacy and deceit. Attention to one narrative, where the image of eating was used repeatedly will cast some light on this apparent paradox. Father Khong was an elderly man when he related to me this set of reflections on the changes he had seen in his lifetime. He said,

"I am so poor. But I've never worked for anyone else. Never in my life. I've never put my work in so that someone else can eat from me. They offered me a lot of money to be a soldier, but I didn't do it. I found food for myself. But I am poor now. I can't find food—I don't know how. I am already old.

They didn't used to *kin nam pasaason* (eat with the people). *Bo ao* (they did not take/they did not want to). Now, they *maa kin nam hao* (come and eat with us). Before, we did not have to pay for land or animals. Now, we have to pay. They count from your bicycles through the rest of your possessions. If we had the same system as before, Laos would be really developed now.

In truth, we do not eat with them. They eat with us. That's all. If a civil servant comes here, he or she can expect to eat with the people everywhere he or she goes. All the American houses (in the cities) belong to the government officials now. You don't find houses like that belonging to ordinary individuals. The Soviets are finished already, they don't help us. We don't have a king to help us, like in Thailand. We don't have a government to help us, like in Australia. They come and eat with you."

The soldiering that Father Khong mentions here refers to those ample opportunities for Lao men to become soldiers during the civil war and international conflicts that plagued Laos from the Second World War until the socialist revolution in 1975, and indeed after it. Father Khong did not join the army, but his life was sharply shaped by the conflicts nonetheless. In the 1960s he and his wife moved from Don Khiaw to the Bolaven Plateau where they raised cattle and vegetable crops for *falang* (the French/the foreigners). He often recounted this as a time of hard work but plenty: their crops were reliable and fetched a good price, the cattle quickly grew to a large herd, they had a cosmopolitan and supportive circle of friends, and health care was not difficult to access. The couple were able to save money. However, in 1970 they were forced out of this area due to heavy fighting and US bombardment. The couple, by then with a young son and daughter, became refugees, travelling on foot to Pakse where they used their savings to construct a house. Father Khong's wife, Mother Phong, began a trading business, but with the consolidation of LPRP power in 1975, this too was disrupted. In 1977, the small family moved back to Don Khiaw to look after Mother Phong's mother and take up rice farming once again. This was a story that I heard many times after I came to know this family well. Father Khong refers briefly to it here in order to draw a comparison between his prosperity in the past and his current state of poverty.

In Father Khong's narrative, eating is used as a means of emphasizing this contrast. In the first paragraph, Father Khong claims with pride that "I found food for myself" and that he avoided working for others, because that would only mean that they could "eat from him". To find food for one's self is depicted here as a valued sign of independence, while employment means another can "eat" from your labour and is a sign of exploitation. In the second paragraph, the contrast Father Khong draws is between the previous regime (prior to 1975) and the present one: the previous regime did not "eat with" the populace, he claims, but the current one does. Eating here again stands for extraction and exploitation. I take this contrast as a rhetorical and metaphorical one: it is not accurate that the previous regime made no extractions from the populace and in other conversations with Father Khong it was clear that he was perfectly well aware of this.[5] His point here, rather, is to express his discontent with the onerous extractions he associates with the state today. He mentions the counting of possessions: this is a reference to the incredibly detailed taxation system that levies annual taxes not only on land and buildings, but also household possessions including boats, white goods, televisions and, as he notes, bicycles. In the third paragraph, he moves from the extractions of taxation to allude to perhaps more overtly corrupt state practices: he sketches a picture of rapacious civil servants expecting to be fed wherever they go, and occupying the most prestigious homes. His story concludes with the observation that not all states are of this ilk—he imagines that the Australian or Thai situation may be more benign but the state under which he lives he characterizes vividly as parasitic. Father Khong's allegation is that the current regime in Laos is corrupt, both in its everyday extraction (such as taxation) and in the degree of personal gain appropriated by government officials: this is the meaning of his closing statement "they come and eat with you".

In the Lao language more generally, images of eating are found in other evocative phrases indicating official misdealings, such as the very common euphemism for small cash payments made to officials to ease any kind of dealings with them: *ngoen kin nam kin nay* (lit. money/silver eat water eat something, perhaps best translated as "money for something to drink or whatever"). There is also *kin muang* (eat the District, corruption) and *kin sin bon* (take a bribe). *Kin* is used as a prefix for a number of idioms that indicate misdealing, deceit or exploitation more generally, such as *kin cay* (suspect), *kin dook* (charge interest), and *kin kan* (deceive each other). Mother Phong, in attempting to explain the phenomenon of *kin num pasaason* (eat with the people) used the example of toll ways, where she said officials would intercept goods being taken for trade because officials *kin paa khoop cay, kin paa free* (eat fish and give nothing but a thank you, eat fish for free). Her account in that instance made no distinction between legitimate road toll collection and illegitimate abuse. The motif of eating straddles both of these realms. I heard the phrase *kin nam pasaason* (eat with the people) regularly used to cast a pall of suspicion over what appeared to me oftentimes to be perfectly normal state activities, such as contributions to the local school, special levies for District festivals and taxation.[6] Perhaps not coincidentally, the word for receiving a salary in city work, as opposed to "finding to eat" (*haa kin*) as most rural people do, is *kin ngoen duean* (eat monthly money/silver). *Kin* (to eat) also has the meaning of using up, depleting or wasting, such as when it is said that an activity "eats time" or "eats money", or that a philandering person has "eaten" wives or husbands. To portray the state and its employees as "eating" rather than "finding", then, is to portray it as extracting from the work of others, often illegitimately, always onerously.

Requests and demands for contributions to state activities from village residents form a slow drip in everyday politics in the south of Laos. Village meetings often focus on the latest demands received from the District, Provincial and National levels. These demands are regularly not met and they become standing items on the agenda returned to at each meeting, meaning that a central feature of village politics is the discussion of incoming, overdue, and contested requests for payments to various state bodies. For instance, in Don Khiaw, some of the requests for payment that were channelled through village meetings were:

- District Boat Racing Festival in the District capital:[7] Don Khiaw village is asked to contribute 100,000 kip (roughly 10 USD).
- Boat racing festival in a neighbouring village: request 200,000 *kip* and 50 kilos of rice at the rate of one ladle of rice and 7,000 *kip* per household.
- The villager currently serving as the policeman requires 100,000 *kip* to fund a study trip to the District capital.
- A beauty contest in Wat Phu. Don Khiaw is asked to contribute 150,000 *kip*.
- A neighbouring village requests 100,000 *kip* towards the construction of their school.
- The Don Khiaw school needs a new fence: one fence post per household is to be donated.
- New signs for each house, assigning them a number: cost 7,000 *kip* each.
- A new system for approving travel: leaving the village for up to seven days costs 2,000 *kip*, up to a month is 8,000 *kip*.
- New citizenship regulations require that each resident be entered in a "household registration book". Books cost 15,000 *kip* each and each household is required to have one.

Other small but constant contributions were announced and discussed at village meetings, too. These were often not fully paid. 16 months after the introduction of the "household registration book" in Don Khiaw, the Village Chief was still attempting to "name and shame" residents into paying the 15,000 *kip* fee (1.50 USD). While this strategy made some subdued in the village meeting, others vocally protested this and other fees, claiming loudly that they would not pay. Such examples were used to illustrate to me how the state "*kep kep kep nam pasaason*" (takes, takes, takes from the people), and this was a major and continuing bone of contention throughout my fieldwork.

These levies and charges were in addition to the dauntingly complex lands and goods taxation system (which, in contrast to the ad hoc fees listed above, is paid into the National Budget). Like the ad hoc levies, the taxes were often openly complained about in the village meetings, and underpayment was endemic. The District office furnished me with the following summary of tax collection in the District.

	98/99	99/00	00/01	01/02	02/03
Plan	1,376,000,000	1,600,000,000	1,824,000,000	2,240,000,000	3,251,000,000
Actual	874,430,000	732,039,848	1,432,000,000	1,735,093,413	1,701,902,807

When I asked tax officers why there was such a consistently large gap between the planned and the actual, they replied that if there was a flood or a drought the collection would be lower. My sense is that this explanation cannot adequately account for the consistency of underpayment nor why, given this consistency, the plan was not revised accordingly over time. There is a political dynamic that consistently produces a gap between the planned and the actual in policy: expectations were consistently put forward but rarely fulfilled. The political terrain was thus one of continual recrimination against these unfulfilled plans, both on the part of the state (in their judgements of popular action, such as in paying their tax) and on the part of regular people (in their judgements of the state, such as in evaluations of state service provision).[8]

In addition to the complaint that the state *kep kep kep* (takes takes takes) from the people, there was also the complaint that the state was not forthcoming enough in giving back to the community, especially in the form of government service provision, social welfare, and general maintenance of the economy. For instance, when attempting to explain corruption to me, one woman pointed out that even though taxes were collected, the salaries of the local school teachers were often not paid: "where does the money go?" she asked, pointing to this gap as proof of corruption.

I witnessed a meeting where a District education officer exhorted village school teachers to struggle harder in their teaching, even though their salaries had not been paid for months. Assembled in one of the local primary schools, the teachers sat in rows facing the front, exactly as students are arranged during class time: a reminder that going to a meeting and studying can be indicated by the same word, *hian*, and of the often starkly hierarchical format of these meetings as one-way transmissions of information from District to village level. At the front sat the District education official, Phao. My field-notes of the meeting record that he spoke for three hours without a break, and only took questions at the end. The main thrust of his presentation was to address the various gaps and lacks that were shot through the local schooling system. Pupils graduating from the schools in this District could not add or spell, he claimed, and sometimes teachers did not come to work, doing other work instead to find food for their families. He extolled the teachers to carry out their duties, and especially to not skip workdays.

In the background of this lack (the absent schoolteachers) was another lack: their salaries which were so often late, the inadequate teaching equipment, and the dilapidated school buildings. He explained that the teacher salaries come from tax collection by the District offices. The District needed to find 76,000,000 *kip* for one month just for the teachers' salaries alone, but revenues were shaky and the District had difficulty finding this money with any regularity. In view of this quandary, the District was calling on voluntary sacrifice from the teachers. He referred to instances of District solidarity, such as the fun times of the District Boat Racing Festival when the District Chief himself had danced with the villagers: "Do it for your country, for the people, for us." He announced that the new District policy was to have no tolerance for teachers skipping school. He noted that school employment came with benefits, such as a pension scheme and health coverage. He went on to remind the teachers, however, not to rely on the District for support in building and maintaining schools: that would have to be done at the village level.

What was notable in Phao's plea to the schoolteachers was the rationalization he employed. He did not mention the possibility of taking disciplinary action against teachers who skip school. Rather, his position was part desperate plea, part rousing narrative about the importance of their work and the virtue of their sacrifice for the good of the nation, the District and the children. He portrayed the nation and the District as poor and thus needing to call on virtuous donations from the teachers. Contrary to images of an authoritarian regime governed at gunpoint, this is a context where the modes of negotiation between policy and practice (also) drew on appeals to a shared (ir)rationality.

Phao's impassioned plea was only partly successful. Some village-level primary teachers in the District did indeed struggle valiantly against the difficulties of unpredictable salaries, a lack of teaching equipment, dirt-floored classrooms, and roofs that leaked like sieves in the rain, to teach students that often came from homes where Lao was not the first language spoken, where parents might be illiterate themselves, and which might also be food insecure.[9] Many teachers phrased their work to me in the terms Phao had used: as a sacrifice, a duty, and a service to the region and the nation. But I also observed that teachers continued to skip school, often closing it altogether if other duties (such as work in the rice fields, weddings or meetings) arose. The local teachers explained that they had no choice: they were *thuk lay* (so poor). They made a plea to their own personal poverty to justify their continued disobedience of Phao's direct and strongly worded order not to skip school, just as Phao had made a plea to District level poverty to explain why the salaries had not been delayed. Both sides in this tug-of-war employed poverty to seek a recognized legitimation for their failure to fulfil the terms of their agreement. Poverty, then, entered the political realm here as part of the positioning of parties within a common rationalization that could be employed for diametrically opposed ends.

I have already mentioned that ideal images of food include its exchange in unequal relationships of enduring reciprocity. I have also mentioned that such giving and eating is cast in frameworks of either virtue and courtesy, or exploitation and deceit. My argument is that relationships between state and society, or individuals and state organizations, are also cast in these terms. By virtue of salaries that are not released for the "eating", unmaintained school buildings, and missing equipment for teaching, the state was described to me by teachers and ordinary citizens as a non-provider. The problem of the absence of education support was only one example given to me of a more general pattern of the non-provision of state services. In local eyes, this was an example of extraction without virtuous return, and thus of the immorality of the state. "In truth," Father Khong said, "we do not eat with them. They eat with us. That's all."

In the wider moral reading of eating, a sense of exchange is often explicit. People speak openly and normatively of the forms of reciprocity and entanglement that arise from eating with another. These kinds of reciprocal arrangements are apparent in spiritual uses of food too. After offering the spirit of the rice various forms of food, one woman recited the common wisdom that: "The rice *hak saa* (loves, cares for) people and people *hak saa* rice." She then turned immediately (and to my mind unexpectedly) to a critique of the state, saying, "Their policy was 'when I have enough I will let the people have some.'

They lie.'" Her point, I now believe, was to contrast the virtue of the sustaining and deepening exchanges of nurture that take place between people and the spirit of the rice, and the exploiting, draining, one-way extractions that she associates with the state. In the complaints levelled against the state in Don Khiaw, the state is depicted in parasitic terms: as that which eats, but does not return.

Conclusion

This sense of transgression of reciprocal norms conforms closely to the kind Scott, in his *Moral Economy* (1976), identified as influential in sparking peasant rebellion. So why, in this case, was not there more open rebellion? In Don Khiaw I was told directly that people were afraid of the government and that it was impossible to directly dissent from state policies. In many ways, this was a post-rebellious moment for the people of Don Khiaw. I will turn to histories of defeat and the way these are communicated in Chapters Three and Five. But fear alone cannot explain how people also go forward to actively engage with state policies in the rural south of Laos, despite their sense of disillusionment. I observed them attend the interminable meetings that are called, put their minds towards producing the proposals and plans that are required to be in the running for state financing of village projects, and sign the contracts and take the loans for state-sponsored irrigated rice (Chapter Six). As I will show in that chapter, when crisis strikes, such as with a drought, it is often to the state that these people turn.

My argument is that despite the common depiction of the state as a parasite that I have attended to in this chapter, the state is seen not only as preying (like the dog-father) on the populace. It is also seen as a potential source of largesse (the mother-nurturer). The state can be and is approached as a potential destroyer, vampiristically sucking the resources and vitality of the populace. It can also be and is approached as a potential nurturer, offering care and protection. It is to this second aspect of the state that Lao people appeal when, in response to the latest extraction, they claim poverty. Claims of poverty would surely find no traction with a state that was only extractive and rapacious. Lao rural residents make claims on the pity and virtue of state officers, just as is common in other hierarchical relationships. Through feeding official guests, agreeing to and entering into development projects they attempt to activate these kinds of relations, to gain some benefit from the endless cycle of policy that confronts them. To eat with you can be interpreted as a sign of courtesy, solidarity and mutually beneficial relationships *and* as a sign of exploitation and misdealing. Engagements with the state, likewise, can potentially be either. In their dealings with the state, the residents of Don Khiaw work towards the former while maintaining a wary eye on the latter.

In the origin tale of the father-dog-eater and the mother-nurturer-protector, the original scenario is one of stasis: the mother reproduces, the father consumes, children are born, but none survive. The mother subverts this balance when she protects two of the offspring. In this myth, mother-cover literally creates human society by allowing reproduction to flourish into a human population. The children in this tale—the ancestors of each and every one of us by implication—were thus born into a dynamic dominated by two forms of power. The father: feared, half wild, destructive and devouring; and the mother: domestic, life-giving, protecting and nurturing. White ventures to suggest that, wherever the dog appears in such origin-mythology, it takes a liminal position. Dogs are threshold creatures: among the first (if not the first) wild animals domesticated by humans, they represent the threshold between the wild and the domestic. In homes, they are often gatekeepers, marking and guarding territory. In a wide-ranging survey, he found that dog-men in myths are often paired with human wives, but remain guilty of "animal immorality" in their relationships with humans (1991: 69).

The dog and his wife can be interpreted as two possible valences that can be attached to power. They stand for two possibilities for how one may benefit from (or be harmed by) powerful entities, two outcomes: eat or be eaten. These are two forms of understanding the self, too. The dog-man myth of Don Khiaw reminds listeners that, after all our claims to humanity, there is still a bit of dog in us. No matter how loud the proclamations of care and *samakhii* (solidarity), of virtuous pity and pious reciprocity, there is always a subtext of possible exploitation, destruction and harm in these relationships. In everyday life, one valence of power must be repressed if the other is to take centre stage.

There is thus a kind of vigilance at portraying everyday instances of eating rice as a sign of solidarity, nurture and care. This is a necessary vigilance, because if these interpretations fail, the alternative reading—of eating as exploitation—quickly fills the interpretive space. This is one way of understanding those ubiquitous calls to "come and eat" made to one and all before every meal: these are loud proclamations of solidarity in an effort to shout down the interpretation of everyday eating as exploitation. Indeed it is in those potentially awkward meals shared between villagers and visiting government officials that one finds the loudest and most repetitious statements of "solidarity" and the most forceful insistence on sharing rice and rice whiskey. These direct claims about solidarity are comparatively absent from intimate meals with family and friends, where solidarity and sharing are more assumed.

As Phao explained to the teachers how salaries would *not* be forthcoming, how school-building would *not* be funded by the District, he phrased this in terms of a three-hour exhortation on the topics of love of the nation, solidarity and sacrifice, in denial of the interpretation of these events as exploitation and illegitimacy. These efforts at the assertion of one interpretation over another are efforts to repress the ever-present alternative—but those repressed elements do not go away. They remain if not conscious then unconscious, charging the political domain because unknowing them needs constant work. For this reason, rationalizations offered in the political sphere of Laos have a repetitious, compulsive and passionate nature. These rationalities often have irrational outcomes, contain contradictions and encounter failures, but they nonetheless make sense in the shared delirium from which they emerge.

3

The Mobility of the Marginal

In this chapter I describe some of the historical context in which the residents of Don Khiaw found themselves. I take as my example the historical formation of the current "regime of citizenship" (Kipnis 2004) that marks these people as Lao citizens, and limits and shapes their movements accordingly. This regime of citizenship is, in Deleuzian terms, a form of "capture". But as I will also show, this capture is not complete, and the desires and lives of Lao rural residents continue to flow beyond it, although the channels they take remain profoundly shaped by it.

While once Don Khiaw's position in the Mekong's busy flows meant that it was well enmeshed in the Kingdom of Champassak and the Tai world, Don Khiaw is now a place far from roads, offices and markets, the hallmarks of modern integration. Nonetheless, the people of Don Khiaw continue to live in a social world of connectivity and mobility. They cultivate social, economic and political networks that extend regionally and globally, and their travel to and fro across borders is an important part of these. Common-sense understandings of globalization, the impacts of transport and communications technology, and the splintering of the bamboo curtain might suppose that borders are less salient now than they used to be, and in some senses this is true. Yet, for the people of Don Khiaw, this is not necessarily so. Many of the recent modifications in border controls have eased the mobility of the rich more than for the rural poor. Some of the modifications that have affected Don Khiaw residents the most appear to have been aimed more at controlling than facilitating their migrations. Other forms of migration particularly common among the poor have been outlawed altogether—undocumented labouring, human trafficking, asylum seeking, insurgency and smuggling among them. Thus, although this region has historically been integrated and mobile, and although the people of Don Khiaw continue to constitute themselves importantly through travel and geographically broad networks, this cross-border mobility sometimes brings them into conflict with contemporary regulations of citizenship. The current regime of citizenship, as well as the political conflicts that have been a marked part of its establishment, are two of the most important contributing factors towards the poverty that is now characteristic of this place. Yet, despite the apparent firmness of this regime of citizenship it continues to be subverted by the cross-border activities of the rural south, sometimes in oddly casual ways. This contrast—between the bold assertion of the power of the state and its oddly casual subversion—forms one theme of this chapter, as it is a feature not only of border regulations but state relations in Laos more generally.

This chapter approaches the history of the Thai-Lao border from four directions: first, a recent Lao propaganda document provides an "official history" of the local border, one that insists on the unity and continuity of the Lao nation. Second, a family history: this lived experience reveals just how very recent and arbitrary this nation seems in the context of local lives, and how it "leaks on every side". Third, I draw on conventional historiography to investigate the precolonial past of Champassak, the years of colonialism and war, the new regime and recent attempts at regional cooperation, all with an eye to the formation of the Thai/Lao border over time. The fourth is retrospective narratives of the southern Lao insurgency. Through this interweaving of historiography and narrative, I aim to show that residents of Don Khiaw live in a social world of mobility, that this mobility has changed over time, and that restrictions on mobility are an important contributing factor to the poverty that Don Khiaw residents now experience, even if these restrictions are—like so many of the spectacular manifestations of state power in Laos— often ignored or undermined.

The lecture

It was 21 September 2002, the day of Bun Khao Salak when the people of Don Khiaw wear their best clothes, gather at the temple and donate gifts, money trees and food to the monks at the temple in order to generate merit for deceased relatives, all amid excitement and bustle. Afterwards, when we were listening to the sutras in the temple hall, a bell rang. It was a signal that we were to go to another meeting. No one had thought it worthwhile to tell me prior to this that there was a government meeting planned that day. I joined about half the congregation in moving to a second, smaller hall further north in the temple grounds. We spread out woven mats over the floorboards and sat in our festival best, waiting. I was told that some officials were going to report to us on current events. Half an hour later some visiting District officials came and sat at the front of the meeting along with the three Village Chiefs. With little fanfare, the officials proceeded to read out a document entitled: "The annihilation of those who plundered the Vang Tao/Chong Mek border crossing on 3/7/2000: Lecture paper for all civil servants and the people."

They did not pause to discuss or interpret the document, but simply read it verbatim, passing it from one to another when their voices became tired. It began to rain, the drumming on the tin roof only a couple of metres above our heads made it difficult to hear. People were chatting among themselves by then anyway, laughing occasionally at little jokes of their own and trading news. Coughs, sneezes and burps went unstifled. As the minutes turned into hours and the officials' voices grew more hoarse, people became more restless. We sat in various poses of discomfort, stretched sore legs, some pounding them to fight the pins and needles. The shuffling, rain and chatter sealed the impossibility of hearing the speakers. I gave up attempting to understand, and made a note that the next time I was in the District capital I would try to get a copy of the lecture to read. Fortunately, one particular official whom I knew there undertook to make me a copy himself—with no photocopier in the town he had to hand copy it, which he agreed to do over a few weeks. He delivered it to me in person, at home, at some inconvenience to himself, giving it to me when we were alone together. Later, when I had read the contents of the paper, I wondered at his unexpected act of generosity and bureaucratic openness.

The written document was even more sensational than the words I had been able to catch in that rainy, raucous day in the village temple. It was a condemnation of Laos' perceived enemies and a statement of renewed resolve to tightly control the countryside framed as a historical narrative culminating in the violent clash on the Vang Tao/Chong Mek border crossing in 2000. It described first the international setting, then the region, the nation, and the province before turning to the border incident. Each section was progressively more detailed until the conclusion, which was outlined in broad brush strokes the future implications for the local area. What is striking about each of these is the sensational, alarmist nature of the language and the contents.

The first section, describing the international setting, began with the observation that, although world politics had shifted to a multi-polar arrangement, nonetheless there continued an observable tendency towards attempts at domination through war, aggression and conflict. Within Southeast Asia, stability, economic growth, and peace had been achieved. However, there were still "nations, large economic blocs, imperial groups and current powers that are our enemies and have the American Empire as their head" attempting to cause division through trickery and sabotage. The paper noted that, "concerns about human rights, democracy, religion, minorities are tools and pretexts for interference, threat and containment. Economic and military interventions are employed against those countries which do not surrender their opposition and change sides."

Turning to the situation in Laos, the lecture paper observed:

> Since its establishment until the present, The People's Democratic Republic of Laos has faced powerful imperial enemies. These have taken a new strategy: peace. They implement a two-faced policy. On the one front, they hope that what they cannot take by force, they can attract slowly, so that we will change our ideology to that of the west. On the other front, they allow individuals a place to hide, individuals who then infiltrate and sabotage us. They use ideology, hateful propaganda, and military attacks while seeking for themselves popularity, affection and respect. This is false and distorted.

The lecture paper worried about insurgency as a current problem that threatened national security. This theme was continued in the next section, examining specifically Thai/Lao relationships. It traced a history of conflict and oppression between the two nations beginning with the fall of the Kingdom of Lan Xang and the subsequent sacking of the kingdom by Siam. The Lan Xang territories then became vassals of Siam (1777). "Lao people fell to be slaves of Siam," the lecture paper explained, and many died building the canals of Bangkok. In 1829, the rebellious Chao Anuvong was executed in public in Bangkok as a traitor to Siam. After that, in the 19th and 20th centuries, the French and then the Americans "took Laos to be robbed and looted, governed by tyranny, extorted by noblemen and empires. Our lands and waters, of incalculable value, have been taken by Thailand." The paper drew a picture of an enduring enmity between Laos (imagined as Lan Xang) and Thailand (imagined as Siam).

The lecture went on to argue that despite this enmity, the Lao people have heroically survived because: "Lao people are by nature patriotic, beautiful, courageous and will not submit." The paper described how, after the revolution in December 1975, Thailand and Laos signed a series of agreements formalizing the border and agreeing to peace. However, the lecture continued, there were some Thai for whom this cooperation was about as comfortable as "a fishbone stuck in the throat". Even though the public declarations were of closeness, in reality the border was marked by infiltration, military attacks and provocations. Border skirmishes were much reduced in the current day, but there were still "bad people who have not changed in Thailand". These people continued to cause trouble, the lecture warned, by selling narcotics, falsely accusing Lao people of producing narcotics, arresting and imprisoning innocent Lao people, smuggling Lao people into Thailand to work illegally, trespassing on Lao territory with ground forces, airplanes and spies and, finally, by allowing insurgents to hide in Thailand so that they could infiltrate and disrupt Laos.

Turning specifically to Champassak province, the lecture noted that it had a particularly strategic role because of its land border with both Thailand and Cambodia. "It (Champassak) is a Province of strategic importance. It is the fortress at the face of the nation…it is at the centre of the economic, political and social fronts, it is the southern entry and exit…" The Vang Tao/Chong Mek border-crossing became an international check point on 2 March 1999. The lecture enumerated the incidents, presumably gathered from Lao police reports, of unauthorized Thai incursions across the border into Laos, including 153 cases of Thai people crossing into Laos to cut timber and 28 cases of cross-border cattle theft. There were a number of other provocations leading up to the events of 3 July 2000, including leaflets left in a village school, arson, and some suspicious movements of people. On 3 June 2000, over 30 people bearing a range of firearms including AK-47s and M16s entered Vang Tao in Laos from Thai territory. They moved in three groups; the first attacked the bank and taxation office, the second attacked a government boarding house, and the third attacked some other private buildings and took 17 hostages. Lao forces responded immediately and retaliated, recovering the hostages and forcing the insurgents into retreat across the Thai border where Thai forces arrested them. Ten insurgents were killed and 28 arrested. The Thai media had reported the incident as a domestic rebellion in Laos against the Lao government. The lecture was adamant that this was not fact: the point of the lecture was to put forward the interpretation that this was an attack on Laos by outside forces. Laos was depicted as coherent, continuous, and virtuous, with its territories synonymous with its peoples. The touchstone here was the ancient kingdom of Lan Xang. Outside Laos, on the other hand, lay "bad people", encroaching empires, attackers and enemies of Laos. When Lao people moved outside Laos in this historiography, this was always presented in negative terms—as slavery and domination.

In the concluding sections of the lecture paper, the subject matter shifted to the ways forward from this situation. It noted that, in the history of Laos, national independence had been most threatened when disunity had spread. A lack of solidarity, the paper argued, will lead to national decline, possibly renewed war, and the inability to attain development. The solution must start, then, with solidarity (*saamakhii*), unity, love of the nation, and love of the "new system" (a euphemism for the LPDR regime). The focus must be on the nation's own strength and self-confidence, and following the directives of the Party: this would make the nation wealthy, strong, and prosperous, with contented people and a just and civilized society. In particular, in order to rectify the mistakes of the past it would be necessary to work on village level politics. The Party and the mass organizations would need to cooperate and redouble their efforts to govern the people. The local militia and police services would need to expand and improve. Villages in the region would need to become "fighting villages", ready at all times if the nation should need to summon them. Party members, especially those working at the lower levels, would need support and encouragement through Party cohesion. Another strategy mentioned was to encourage rice production and small production with the aim of improving living standards. Finally, it was resolved that a way forward was to follow the resolutions of the 7th Assembly of the Party, the 4th Assembly of the Provincial Party organization and the District, and to rouse a sense of political coherence with reference to the history of the nation, the Party and the army. This would ensure peace, order, social and economic development: the Province could then act as an example for the entire nation.

The lecture was sensational: it had it all—spies, guns, allegations of international conspiracies, heroic histories of struggle, the triumph of the underdog and rousing cries to rally around the existing regime. I was faced with a puzzle then: on the one hand, the lecture was an instance of the sensational aspect of state power, a bold declaration of the continuity and coherence of Laos inside its borders, its distinction from those outside its borders, and a call to protect and identify with this entity as the one and only truth permissible. On the other hand, we have the oddly casual or at least dispassionate delivery of the lecture, and the seeming irreverence with which village residents received it. The officials who read the document aloud seemed bored, and the people gathered to form an audience averted their eyes, chattered idly, and did whatever was necessary to be comfortable. The disjuncture was that of brute power and its casual disruption.

I will return to this disjuncture in the following sections of this chapter and the next, where I look at how Lao people negotiate their position today, particularly in terms of how their current day travels disrupt the narrative of a stable Lao population, and in Chapter Five, where I look at the divergence between the "known knowns" and the "known unknowns" of the Lao state. But first, in the next section, I want to focus on the formation of this particular set of state relations through attention to the border and the current regime of citizenship over time. To pursue this, I next present a vignette which describes a very different meeting and which contains a very different understanding of the history and meaning of the Vang Tao/Chong Mek border.

Lai's dreams

The last moments of sunlight in Don Khiaw were typically busy: times to wash, pack away and prepare before the darkness closed in around us. I was surprised, then, when Lai, a teenage girl, appeared at my home one day at this hour. She seemed restless. After some small talk, she said, "It is not fun here, is it? It is silent. I sit at home all alone. Every day! Muey comes to visit. She visits often. Twice in one day." After some time Lai looked at me intently and said: "Holly, I came to tell you something. Remember this afternoon I said I had business with you?" I did remember—she had said she wanted to talk to me in private, but we had not been able to find a moment alone together. She knew that I would likely be alone now in the twilight, though. Lai said: "I'm running away. Tomorrow I will leave." She had come to say goodbye.

Lai had been particularly friendly towards me during my time on Don Khiaw, perhaps because I was one of the few young single women resident in the area. She was the youngest daughter of an aging couple who were too weak now to do heavy agricultural work. Lai's ten older brothers and sisters had all moved to other places, including the Bolaven Plateau, Pakse, Vientiane, and Thailand. It remained to Lai, then just 16, to cultivate her parent's land and assist them in day-to-day living. Not only had her siblings left, but so too had her neighbourhood friends and age-mates. Muey, Laeng, and Ten had each been resident when I arrived, but they moved during the course of my fieldwork to the Bolaven Plateau, a Vientiane factory, and a Bangkok factory respectively. I had met other friends and age-mates during the *pii may* (New Year) celebrations, when migrants flock back to their rural homes. For most of the time, Don Khiaw was not a place that young people flocked to. It was a place they left. For many young people, dreams and aspirations were focused resolutely beyond the village bounds, and Lai was no exception.

"Where will you go?" I asked.

"Thailand," she said, her excitement was now evident. "My friend En from across the river came to ask me today. She is a *khon song*.[1] She said that the next bus will leave tomorrow morning." En charged 4,000 to 5,000 *baht* to arrange a bus to Vientiane, a seven-day tourist visa, and delivery to Thailand. Migrants were then responsible for finding their own work. Domestic and factory labour for women, and fishing, factory or construction work for men, were the most usual. Lai and I spoke of all the things she hoped for and desired from migration. She wanted to see other places, experience other lifestyles, and wear fashionable clothes. She speculated that she would earn around 4,000 to 5,000 *baht* a month and planned to save it to buy gold "because you can sell gold when you need money". At my prompting, Lai estimated that she would be gone for ten years. I expressed surprise since we had only recently talked about her plans to marry in a couple of years. Lai shrugged playfully: she was absorbed in this dream of a life beyond the border, or perhaps it was bravado. Even as we spoke, I suspected that this conversation was more about aspiration than realization. Nevertheless, I agreed to go to her home the next morning to bid her a last farewell.

When I arrived just after dawn, I was not completely surprised to find that Lai was in fact not going. Her mother explained, "It is too dangerous. She is a woman—I won't let her go." She also said *"bo mii khon yuu huean,"*[2] meaning that she needed Lai to stay behind to work in the fields and at home. She and her husband had decided that Lai's brother, Win, would be sent to Thailand instead (he was at that time in the Bolaven Plateau working on the coffee harvest). Lai's father was sympathetic to Lai's aspirations. "The *khon song* came yesterday looking for people to go" he told me, "and all day, Lai was saying 'I will go, I will go.' But in the end, her mother would not let her." Her parents, however, did not seem at all surprised by their daughter's desire. Lai lived in a social world of mobility. The friends, family, siblings, age-mates and older generations that formed her personal network regularly migrated to find work and earn money. Even for those who stayed behind, such as herself and her mother, migration remained an essential ingredient of their experiences and expectations. Migration is firmly entrenched in what Lao labouring youth perceive to be possible, desirable, and probable.

Lai's family includes several members in Thailand. Lai could trace her family line on Don Khiaw back to the 1800s when her father's mother's mother was born on what is now the family plot. Her father's mother, too, was born there. It was in Don Khiaw that this grandmother of Lai's eventually met a Thai solider. He was stationed across the river as part of Thailand's administration of the area between 1941 and 1946. They married. Their first child, Amnuay, was still an infant when the French reclaimed the area that included Don Khiaw. Abruptly, Amnuay's father was required to leave Champassak. He asked his new wife to accompany him to Thailand, but the infant was left with his mother's mother on Don Khiaw. Amnuay's Thai soldier father is now dead, but his mother still resides in Ubon Ratchathani, the large urban centre on the Thai side of the border that now divides Champassak from Thailand. Amnuay has four brothers and sisters, all in Thailand. One of his own children left Don Khiaw to live in Ubon Ratchathani with this branch of the family. Family members still visit each other and exchange gifts across the border when they can although, due to age and lack of funds, these exchanges are not frequent.

Lai's family are far from unusual. It is estimated that approximately ten percent of the population of Laos fled the country in the years following the 1975 revolution, some relocating to third countries including Australia, Canada, France, New Zealand and the USA, while many remained in Thailand, only a few hours travel away. The rates of post-75 emigration appear to be much higher than ten percent in the Champassak region: this region shares a long land border with Thailand, and has historically been westward-leaning in political orientation.[3] These distant household members are often important in household economic strategies. The New York Times has estimated that total global remittances are over 200 billion USD a year (three times official aid budgets).[4] The International Fund for Agricultural Development estimates that remittances to Laos alone were 1,175 million in 2006, or 34.52 percent of total GDP.[5]

The lecture paper described in the previous section depicted human mobility in purely negative terms: border crossings were associated with the invasion of foreign, often harmful forces or loss to extractive exploitation and slavery. In contrast, Lai's playful imaginings and her familial networks associated cross-border mobility with aspiration and pursuit of desires. While the lecture paper drew Thai and Lao history as being at odds, Lai's family history criss-crossed this shifting border. Below, I take a third look at how this border has changed over time: this time one distilled from conventional history texts.

Lao historiography

The comment is often made that in pre-colonial Tai polities, the index of power was not simply territory, but people (Scott 2009, Wolters 1982, Gesick 1976, Thongchai 1994, Condominas 1990). Correspondingly, it was not only land but human bodies that were fought over and marked by leaders. The populace could signal their displeasure with a leader, onerous demands, or instability by emigrating (Condominas 1990: 63, Grabowsky 1995: 114). Viewed from the leaders' perspectives, this constant possibility of population movement was a problem to be avoided: rewards were offered to local leaders who could "entice" people to settle and establish rice fields (Gesick 1976: 15). Viewed from the perspective of ordinary people, however, this arrangement indicates a life premised on the constant possibility, if not actuality, of mobility and relocation. It was common for victors in war to seize the defeated populace and forcibly resettle them closer to the victor's centre of power (Gesick 1976: 47). The Burmese invasions and the fall of Ayutthaya were a turbulent time for the Tai world. Wyatt (1997) estimates that during this period, *most* people were living in a place distant from where they were born.

Cholera epidemics (Ayonmier 2000: 10, Harmand 1997: 60) and wars characterized the pre-colonial borderlands and added a further impetus to movement. When Siam overran Vientiane in 1778 and again in 1827, hundreds of thousands of people were forcibly relocated across the Mekong River, leaving the left bank virtually depopulated. Rebellions and uprisings, such as the Ay Sa rebellion of Southern Laos, also led significant numbers of people to relocate (Baird 2007).

The region where Don Khiaw is located was known as the Kingdom of Champassak from 1713 to 1945. The kingdom was established when over 3,000 refugees fled the breakup of Lan Xang (Grabowsky 1995: 112). The capital of Champassak, located a few tens of kilometres upstream from Don Khiaw, was at that time ruled by an aging queen who allegedly offered the incoming refugees the chance to rule several years later (Achaimbault 1961, Grabowsky 1995: 112, Simms and Simms 1999: 163). Taksin brought Champassak into the Siamese orbit in 1777 (Gesick 1976: 104). Attapeu and the Bolaven Plateau to the east, Stung Treng to the south, Roi Et in the northwest, Salavan to the north,[6] and Ubon Ratchathani in the west paid tribute to Champassak (Grabowsky 1995: 113, Simms and Simms 1999: 164). From the 18th to the 19th century, the population grew substantially, partly from the continued flows of refugees following the Mekong River downstream (Grabowsky 1995: 114). From 1809, Rama II (1809–1824) and his Ministers devoted every effort to creating a "Tai land" made up of all the Tai people, of which Champassak was a small but important part (Simms and Simms 1999: 168). This included rationalized administration, standardized education, monastic arrangements, military presence, and eventually a telegraph line from Champassak to Bangkok (Grabowsky 1995: 148, Simms and Simms 1999: 178). Siam was emulating the colonial administrations observed in Java, India, and Singapore (Thongchai 1994: 103), turning away from the indeterminacy of the *mandala* system and attempting to consolidate their borderlands in the image of a modern state (Thongchai 1994: 105).

In October 1893, France forced Siam to cede all territories on the left bank of the Mekong, slicing the Kingdom of Champassak in two. For almost ten years, the capital of Champassak was Thai territory while a great deal of its former possessions now lay in French Indochina. The old tribute relations that had sustained Champassak were upset, causing significant "suffering" for the King of Champassak (Baird 2013: 10). In 1904, France added to their possessions some territories on the right bank, including the capital of Champassak. However, the French recognized only the King of Luang Prabang: Champassak's Chao Nyuy, who had been recognized by the Siamese as of a high-rank but had not been formally declared King by Bangkok, and had only been appointed by the French merely as governor (Stuart-Fox 1997: 29 and 212).

The earlier forced resettlement of Lao-speaking people, along with the voluntary movements into Thailand that many elites and regular people made, meant that now many more Lao people lived on the Siamese side of the border than in the French territories of Laos. By some accounts Lao people made up almost half the population of Siam (Toye 1968: 48). Both the French and the Siamese attempted to attract and keep people in their territories through lowered taxes, handouts, and force (Thongchai 1994: 165). Until 1907, the French left an open invitation for these resettled Lao to return to the French side of the new border, and many did.

Strong affinities remained between the French and Siamese Lao populations in terms of language, religion, annual events, trade and kinship. Even after the French consolidated their claim to Indochina, and perhaps even facilitated by the relative peace that ensued, "Lao people mingled freely across their great river" (Toye 1968: 48). Toye perhaps overstates the peace of this period: from 1901 to 1935, there was a series of rebellions led by *phuu mii bun* ("people with merit" or spiritual leaders) in the Champassak area. These were religious and charismatic leaders who challenged the administration on both the Siamese and French sides of the new border (Simms and Simms 1999: 180, Ishii 1986: 182). Grabowsky reports that the aim of the movements was to establish a Lao state independent of both the French and Siamese (Grabowsky 1995: 150), although interpretations of the political motivations of the movements differ (see Pholsena 2006 and Gay 2002). Baird suggests that the movements must be understood in terms of the way the authority of the Kingdom of Champassak had been successively undermined by the French. There is evidence that the rebellions were supported, and perhaps in some cases instigated, by Champassak elites disaffected by the decline of their own influence. In addition, there is evidence that this decline was resisted by former vassals as well. The famed uplands rebel Kommadam reportedly articulated his demands at one point in terms of a request to be able to pay tribute once again to Champassak, as his people had previously done (Baird 2013: 23).

Siamese nationalist premier Phibun Songkhram came to power in 1932 and was implacably opposed to French ambitions in South-east Asia. In 1935, Siam was publishing maps showing the area of Don Khiaw as part of the "territories lost to France", and denouncing the "false frontier of colonialism" with leaflets and radio broadcasts aimed at French Indochina (Mayoury and Pheuiphanh 1994: 60–61). This strategy gained particular support in southern Laos "where people had always tended to look across the river to Siam

rather than upstream to Vientiane" (Toye 1968: 56). The need for iden-
tification papers or residence certificates for people crossing into Siam from
French Indochina was suspended (Mayoury and Pheuiphanh 1994: 60–1).
Indeed, commentators at the time record a "cordial" reception of refugees from
Indochina by frontier authorities, with the government waiving "immigration
formalities" and the public offering relief and donations to the newcomers
(Sivaram 1941: 36). In the perception of one writer, "[refugees from Indo-
china] were Thai people and were treated as such" (Sivaram 1941: 37).

With France weakened by German occupation in Europe and Japanese
forces in Southeast Asia, Phibun demanded the return of territories to the
right of the Mekong, including part of what is now Champassak Province
that is on the western side of the Mekong River. There followed a military
build up on both sides of the border, and then active hostilities. In January
1941, Thai[7] forces pushed across the land border east of Ubon Rathchathani,
forcing the French into retreat. In less than a week, they had raised the Thai
flag in Champassak Province, "in a most impressive ceremony attended by the
local people" (Sivaram 1941: 97–8). On 22 January, Champassak town was
occupied by Thai troops, and the Prince of Champassak, Boun Oum, made a
speech on Thai radio speaking "excellent Thai."[8]

The Japanese, who had maintained a military presence in Indochina since
1940 while allowing France to continue to rule for most of the war, brokered
a truce. The deepest channel of the river was taken as the dividing line between French and Thai forces in the Mekong area, and both forces withdrew
ten kilometres on either side. The Japanese occupied the neutral zone. Don
Khiaw lay in this neutral zone on the Thai side. In the peace deal brokered
by the Japanese, the deep channel was confirmed as the border between
Thailand and French Laos. Thus, Champassak, along with Sayaboury, was
confirmed as returning to Thai control. Don Khiaw fell under the sway of
Thailand once again. Health services, relief aid, public lectures, and a Thai
administration were installed (Sivaram 1941: 130). Older residents of Don
Khiaw remember learning to read and write Thai during these years at the
school established in the temple. Thai administrators and soldiers were also
stationed in the area, and a romance blossomed between the man and woman
who were to become Lai's grandparents.

However, by the end of 1946, Thailand had been pressured into returning
Champassak and Sayaboury to the French. Prince of Champassak, Boun
Oum, was pro-French and was instrumental in their return to the region. For
the first time, Laos became a unified entity under a single king, generating
in the process considerable resentment in the south (Toye 1968: 74). Fleeing
the returning French forces, Viet Minh and Lao Issara members were offered

safe haven in Thailand. From there, they were able to organize their resistance, launch raids and disseminate propaganda against the French (Toye 1968: 79) until the end of French colonial rule in 1954.

Meanwhile, on the Lao side of the border, domestic politics soon became polarized between the US-backed right-wing, the neutralists, and a left-wing sympathetic to the Viet Minh. With hostilities escalating, the border between rightist southern Laos and north-east Thailand was traversed not only by supplies for rightist forces, but eventually by bombing raids into Lao territory. Thailand served as the United State's "unsinkable aircraft carrier" (Randolph 1986: 49). In 1964, operation "Barrel Roll" commenced bombing in the east of Laos, and in 1965 operations "Steel Tiger" and "Tiger Hound" were launched targeting the south.[9] The bombings, which halted in 1973, came to an estimated total of some two million tonnes.

In November 1975, the Pathet Lao and Thai forces clashed, leading to a complete closure of the border by Thailand. With the ascension to power of the Pathet Lao the following month, Thailand continued the policy of trade restrictions. Mayoury and Pheuiphanh have suggested that the border became an "ideological boundary" (1994: 71). Thailand imposed "Blockade, embargo, closed frontiers, abusive taxes, unfair transport fares" (1994: 71). Well into the 1980s, Thailand continued to ban the entry of 273 "strategic items" from Thailand into Laos, including consumer goods, spare parts, and fuel. Meanwhile, ties with Vietnam were intensified. Their "special relationship" was formalized by the signing of the 1977 "Treaty of Friendship and Cooperation" (Stuart-Fox 1997: 177) which provided the legal basis for the stationing of Vietnamese troops in Laos.

Tensions with Thailand and the friendship with Vietnam made the Thai-Lao border near Don Khiaw into the "bamboo curtain", an ideological as much as a regulatory boundary. However, the border was, perhaps inevitably, still permeated by some illicit trade. The long-running trade and barter across the Mekong, however, was now designated as "smuggling" and "illicit trade," and accordingly these activities were fraught with danger (Walker 1999: 58). Also, in a move reminiscent of Phibun's earlier policy, refugees were accepted from Laos with no need to offer proof of their refugee status. According to Mayoury and Pheuiphanh, Thailand's aim was to "bleed the Indochinese countries white" (1994: 95). But in a counter-claim to this view, Sarasin in a pro-Thai defence of Thailand's policy towards the Lao border has claimed that Thailand always behaved towards the border as a technical, not a political issue and that, "After 1980, Thailand's policy has been to treat those coming in from Laos as 'illegal entrants' subject to deportation. This policy remains valid today. Furthermore, a number of refugee camps were closed as part of the effort to stem the flow of refugees as well as for security reasons"

(1985: 1273). Either way, even during the era of the strictest control, the border was not made impermeable.[10] In particular, the long border with Thailand was criss-crossed by insurgents opposing the regimes on both sides: the LPRP by some reports tolerated sanctuaries for the Communist Party of Thailand on Lao soil and insurgents opposing the LPRP operated from bases and refugee camps in Thailand. It is to this last insurgency that I turn next.

Local Insurgency

The insurgencies in the south of Laos commenced with the 1975 consolidation of LPRP rule, reached their height in the 1980s, before falling off sharply in the late 1980s, with continued smatterings of unrest into the 1990s and 2000s. In this section, I will describe the local insurgency as my fourth and final example of how the Thai/Lao borderland came into existence, and is experienced, in Don Khiaw.

Most writing about post-revolutionary insurgencies in Laos have focused on those that took place in the north and among the Hmong (Lee 2007, Tan 2007, Time Asia 2003, Baird 2010b). The region where Don Khiaw is located, with its flat plains and Mekong trunk and tributaries, has historically been inhabited by ethnic Lao and Khmer residents and the insurgency movements there have only been sketched in the broadest outlines in the literature.[11] In summary, after the establishment of the LPDR in December 1975, conflict continued in the historically westward-leaning south, particularly Champassak, where right-wing political tendencies were influential, although not universal. Security measures, such as control of the media, were put in place and approximately 50,000 Vietnamese troops were based in Laos, many of them in Champassak. The unpopular collectivization of agriculture was initiated, and applied with unusual zeal in Champassak (see Chapter Five). Economic hardship ensued. Finding these conditions intolerable, large amounts of disaffected rural residents left the country. Most ended up in refugee camps in Thailand and many of these sought resettlement in third countries. Insurgents solicited recruits from villages within Laos and refugee camps in Thailand.

The "Lao People's National Liberation Front" was declared on September 15, 1980 in Champassak Province (Gunn 1983: 328). In addition to disaffected rural residents, Radio Beijing claimed former officials and military officers from both the former regime and the LPDR had joined the movement (cited in Gunn 1983: 329). Gunn speculates that the 1980 announcement was an attempt to capitalize on regional pressure against the Vietnamese in Kampuchea at that time which had brought together an unlikely coalition of anti-Vietnamese forces including China, Thailand and the Khmer Rouge. The right-wing southern Lao argued that, likewise, Laos was subject to Vietnamese hegemony and deserved recognition and support. The group submitted a 12-page submission to the U.N. highlighting what it called the Vietnamese "colonialization of the Lao people" (Gunn 1983: 328). A meeting of Lao, Khmer Rouge and ethnic minority delegates reportedly took place in Preah Vihear Province, Cambodia, on November 3, 1980 to discuss a unified resistance, including the provisioning of weapons originally from China. The key activities of the southern insurgency were "armed propaganda" within Laos, and sabotage, harassment and hit-and-run attacks on Vietnamese and LPR outposts. In the early 1980s, the movement claimed to control parts of Champassak near the Cambodian and Thai borders (Gunn 1983: 331). However, most Lao insurgents operated from sanctuaries established on Thai territory. The Internal Security Operations Command (ISOC) in Thailand offered support to the movements until at least 1988, when the Chatchai Choonhaven government reduced this under the policy of "battlefields to marketplaces," aiming at rapprochement with Vietnam, Laos, and Cambodia (Baird 2013b: 132). Nevertheless, it also appears that local provincial heads, military and even Buddhist temples in the region gave tacit approval and support for longer periods of time (Baird 2013b: 138). The insurgents were reportedly armed by the Khmer Rouge (Gunn 1983: 330) and China, and it was even claimed that they were visited by Chinese military advisors.

From 1988, growing friendship between Thailand and Laos led to the movement coming under pressure. UNHCR repatriation schemes were stepped up, and moves were made to wind down the camps. This undermined the movement, and many insurgents elected to return to Laos on the UNHCR repatriation programme, sought resettlement abroad, or remained in Thailand. All commentators agree that the southern insurgency was never a serious threat to the LPDR. Gunn wrote that, "The highest estimate (5,000) of rebel manpower in the southern area of resistance in Laos suggests that the regime will not be overthrown tomorrow" (1983: 336). Other estimates put the number twice as high (Baird, personal communication). The movement was very fluid, with recruits entering and dispersing constantly, so firm numbers are difficult to determine, though they were certainly in the thousands.

Evans and Rowley refer to the "endemic factionalism of right-wing Lao" (1990: 225) and point out that the movement never obtained the external support it sought. They also suggest that the insurgency lacked a constituency internal to Laos (Evans and Rowley 1990: 223). It is not quite accurate to argue that a local constituency for the insurgents was lacking: using interviews conducted with refugees settled in North America, Baird (2012) records how some local monks went to great lengths to support the movement, such as drying out the rice left over from festival days in the temple, offering this as well as medical care and Buddhist teachings to the movement. In the region of Don Khiaw, support was widespread but not universal. Many local people entered the insurgency knowing that it would put their own lives, and the lives of their loved ones, at risk. The movement in hindsight seems frail, but at the time it was able to attract people to make life-changing decisions and sacrifices. Below, I provide three retrospective narrative accounts from some of those in Don Khiaw who were prepared to speak with me about the insurgency. My aim is to contribute to the slim but growing knowledge of the insurgency and to add a further dimension to my argument about the changing nature of the Thai-Lao border.

According to Don Khiaw residents, open hostilities accompanied the beginning of the LPRP regime and continued into 1977. The most intense fighting locally, however, was located on a neighbouring island, not on Don Khiaw itself. Don Khiaw in fact appears to have served as a secure base for LPRP and Vietnamese cadre. Refugee movements were significant during this period, and people continued to flee up until the rapprochement between Thailand and Laos. Local residents and refugees refer to the resistance movement as the *phatthin* (the expatriates).[12]

Si was born in Don Khiaw (he was not quite sure of the exact year) and went to primary school in the village temple (up to grade five) and in his final year was ordained as a novice. After three years he was ordained as a monk and remained such for a further four years. Don Khiaw was a key centre for Buddhism then, he noted, with people from surrounding villages and further afield attending the temple for study, ordination or worship. He then left the monkhood and married. He had farmed for a few years when the "new system" of the LPRP was established in 1975. He found it intolerable. He was convinced to join the *phatthin* and fled to Thailand with two friends: Lot, who is the husband of one of his sisters (and currently also lives in Don Khiaw) and Nyueang (from a neighbouring island, who was later killed in action). They walked for three days and three nights, living on the kindness of the people they met on the way. They crossed the border illegally at a point south of Vang Tao/Chong Mek and joined a *phatthin* base. Si was responsible for taking supplies to active soldiers. He had a gun, but he claims that he was such a bad shot that he was not much use as a soldier: a farmer and a monk in the past, he had no soldiering experience to build on. At one point they were surrounded, and his friend Nyueang was shot in the stomach. They both managed to escape and the injured man was taken to the hospital in Ubon, but he died before arrival. Soon after this incident, Si decided to leave the insurgency movement and slipped off to an internationally supported refugee centre. Another of his older sisters was there: she had married a Cambodian man who she had met at the camp. Inmates there were not permitted to work. He remained there for about six years.

Meanwhile, his wife was still in Don Khiaw. She had been pregnant once, but his child had died. In 1981, she made the journey by foot to a *phatthin* base in Thailand with a large group of people hoping to find him. From the base she sent word to him at the refugee centre to join her. Si escaped from the camp and became a soldier with that *phatthin* for another year. He remembers the danger, particularly land mines. His unit was composed of about 70 or 80 people, under a local leader from a neighbouring island who was eventually killed in action. The unit disbanded in about 1985, with the leadership fleeing to the US and France.

Si did not stay that long. After just over a year he snuck away from the insurgents again, this time taking his family to join his older sister who had moved to a Thai village. He lived there for about three years, his family growing with the arrival of more children and him earning a living by market gardening. Eventually Si's illegal immigrant status was exposed and he was forced to enter another refugee camp, this one without international funding. He had to find money to support his family through occasional work such as cutting wood. He was then transferred to a third refugee camp which did have international funding. He lived there for about three years. He remembers that, although he had a lot of friends, his children were not able to study because there were no teachers and he was not able to work. Si said that, in truth, this was really a prison.[13]

His sister was accepted to the USA as a refugee. Si decided to return to Laos, explaining that he missed his parents and relatives in Don Khiaw and his sister wanted someone in Laos to care for them. In 1992 the process of return began. The family were provided with seven sacks of rice and 400,000 kip. On the Lao side of the border they were given three days of "education and training". Then, they boarded a large boat, which he says was crammed with returnees, and it made a slow journey down the river, discharging its passengers at villages and islands along the way. Arriving in Don Khiaw, the family stayed with Si's mother, but by then the family had no fields to work on the island. Si now works some fields on the adjacent mainland while maintaining a home on Don Khiaw: he has one hectare of his own, and he rents more. During my fieldwork, Si moved to the mainland to be closer to his fields when his older sister sent money from the USA to build a house there.

Wilay, too, joined the *phatthin* in his youth. He had wanted to simply be a refugee, but he explained to me that it was no easy thing to flee to

Thailand, so he had joined the local resistance because they offered to help him out of Laos. He reports that his division was provisioned by the Khmer Rouge and China. Wilay remembers it as a very difficult time: "In 1975, the regime changed, a new system. They would arrest ex-soldiers, and no one knew where they went or if they would be released. I was afraid, so I joined the *phatthin*." He claims that his main work was entering Laos along the border and talking to people, asking them how things were, and listening to their opinions and views. After a year with the *phatthin* he spent three years in various refugee camps in Thailand. He finally agreed to return to Laos in a UNHCR sponsored programme. He was "trained" for five days near the border, and then released with basic food and supplies. His wife and child had been waiting for him on Don Khiaw. Of the eight men from this village whom he knew had joined the *phatthin* but that I was unable to meet for one reason or another, he reported: one was shot dead; two moved to the USA; another went to France and did not return to visit his wife here, his wife whom I came to know. She lived on the central spine of the village in desperate poverty with her daughter and grandchild. She told me he sent money once in the 30 years since he had been gone. Another, Lum, lived in Thailand. Another, Seng, lived in Pakse. Seng had a colourful past—he had gone to fight for the Khmer Rouge, was shot in the leg and arrested by the Vietnamese. Yet another, Khian was shot dead in Thailand by Vietnamese, or so the story had it. Khun, the older brother of one of my neighbours, moved to the USA but died there soon afterwards. Another man, Heng, came back on a UNHCR programme only to collect his family, then fled again to Thailand and then to the USA. After recollecting these stories of a fractured and scattered generation, Wilay explained:

> These days it doesn't matter—we don't resist them now. We don't evade their policies. If we evade their policies, they'll arrest us for sure. But we go along with them now. It doesn't matter. It is nothing. We cooperate. We do whatever they tell us to do. We will build the school if they tell us to. Whatever they tell us: we cannot *not* do it.

Ruefully, Wilay said, "Who would not want to go to the USA? They didn't tell me I could go! I would have if they had told me, I would go and find money for my wife". He laughed, but there was pain there, too. He said that once, in the refugee centre, he had received an offer to be assessed as a refugee, but when they called his name he was afraid it was a ruse: perhaps they would take him out the back and shoot him? Wilay has no rice fields at all. His wife brought in some rice by offering to help others in their transplant and harvest. Wilay earned some money in his roles as the officiant of the territory cult and as the *luuk khii* (lay worker) at funerals. Some of their children are grown now, and have moved to a newly established "development" village in an attempt to find food and money for the family. Wilay and his wife care for their grandchildren while these young adults work.

One final retrospective narrative will round out this account. It is from Father Hian, who did not join the *phatthin* and thoroughly disapproved of it. He had been a solider for 15 years for the Royal Lao Government, and was the head of a squadron in Naadii for the old regime, so he had reason to fear the new regime. He had retired in 1973. He said, "I did not like the *phatthin*. 'Aren't you tired of fighting?' I asked. 'Why fight with your own people? Why leave our country like that?'" He stayed in Don Khiaw, and contrary to fears that the new regime would arrest all former RLG soldiers, in addition to the currently serving soldiers, he was in fact appointed as Village Chief. He says it was a comparatively peaceful time—no one from Don Khiaw was sent to a re-education camp, but people were taken from neighbouring areas, especially the neighbouring island where prolonged fighting against the new regime had taken place. These cases of "re-education" generated widespread fear. He said that, at that time of open conflict, Don Khiaw had in fact been considered a safe haven for the new regime. Cadre would sleep and eat on Don Khiaw if they were in the region, because it would not have been safe for them on neighbouring islands or on the mainland. Don Khiaw, accordingly, was made the head of the local canton (*tasseng*) and housed the government store selling essentials such as soap, salt, cloth and buckets. Father Hian, as Village Chief, said that he advised people simply to go along with the new regime. He explained: "If people spoke against them or did not go along with them, then of course those people would go to re-education camps. But in our village no one had to go. Everything was normal. There were lots of emigrants, though. Lots of people left around 1977—so many!" He shook his head, "So many. They did not like the new system. So they left. They left for the USA." He started to list off names. "I didn't try to stop them. I didn't know they were going. They would go in secret, agree between themselves and go. It is nothing, I said: if you want to go, go!"

Retrospective narratives are difficult sources to work with: they are prone to the vagaries of memory, the mutations of hindsight and the colour of current concerns, and the great history of the southern Lao insurgency waits to be written. All that I can offer here, based on these minor and incomplete fragments, is a sense of how significant this insurgency was for the lives of these men and their families. In terms of the larger story of this chapter, these retrospective narratives present a very particular image of the border: as a very stark manifestation of the power and importance of the new regime as marginalizing, and yet also something that could be subverted (albeit at great risk). This was a period of hostility and wariness between the governments of Laos and Thailand, when the border was policed and enforced in particularly harsh ways. Like the lecture paper, the border was an expression of the sometimes sensational claims of state power: of Laos as a coherent entity, where people are sharply demarcated between insiders and outsiders, and where crossing the border was viewed in overwhelmingly negative terms. Yet from the point of view of the residents of Don Khiaw, these sensational claims of this power, while formative, were not exactly carried through. The border was not as seamless as it claimed. For those brave or determined enough to risk the violence of the border, the frontier was in some ways permeable. As refugees or rebels, rural residents crossed the border in what might most accurately be termed the mobility of the marginal.

Control through cooperation

By the late 1980s, support for insurgencies such as these was waning. Despite the sensational language of the lecture paper that I described in the opening section, Thailand is no longer the sanctuary for insurgents or the refuge for refugees that it once was. Compared to earlier times, cooperation between Thailand and Laos means the border is becoming less porous for these kinds of border movements, but more porous for other kinds of movements.

Both Thailand and Laos are members of the Association of South East Asian Nations (ASEAN), and both are involved with regional integrative initiatives such as the Greater Mekong Subregion, the Economic Quadrangle (Walker 1999) and joint hydroelectricity schemes. At a recent ASEAN meeting, the commerce ministers of Thailand and Laos announced an arrangement to make their joint border a "model boundary". In a move symbolic of the shift from "battleground" to "marketplace" since 1988, a number of bridges have been constructed across the Mekong from the 1990s onwards. Pakse airport has been upgraded with a low interest loan provided by the Government of Thailand's Neighbouring Countries Economic Development Cooperation Agency, with the explicit purpose of easing air transport to Bangkok. Agreements have been signed between the Lao and Thai governments on a series of border related issues, such as labour migration, cross border trade, and security.[14]

In December 2009, 4,500 Lao Hmong, including 158 people who were already recognized as refugees by the United Nations High Commissioner for Refugees (UNHCR) and had been offered resettlement elsewhere, were forcibly returned to Laos. They had been staying in a camp in Phetchabun, Thailand, where the Thai government had refused the UNHCR access to them, so the vast majority had no opportunity to prove their claims to refugee status. The Lao government has refused the UN and other monitors access to the asylum seekers after their forced relocation to Laos. Journalists were informed by a spokesman for the Lao government that "all of the Hmong decided to live in their homeland forever" (Amnesty Urgent Action 13 January 2010). This was only one of a series of recent incidents where asylum seekers from Laos have been identified as "illegal entrants" and returned to Laos without having access to the UNHCR.[15]

A similar shift can be seen in the treatment of the men who were captured in the 2000 border incursion, described in the opening section. It is still unclear what motivated the attack, although most commentators believe it was supported by royalist émigrés: the men hoisted the pre-1975 flag in Laos before they were driven back (Tan 2007: 49). The men were arrested in Thailand. Laos initially sought their extradition but this was refused on the grounds that the men would be in serious danger if returned to Laos. They sought asylum in Thailand, but the UNHCR was repeatedly denied access to them to assess their claims. The Lao government appealed the extradition refusal successfully, and in July 2004, 16 Lao citizens were extradited from Thailand to Champassak Province charged with looting and destroying the Vang Tao checkpoint. Amnesty International claimed "forcibly returning them to Laos was a breach of the customary law principle of *non-refoulement*, which prohibits the return of a person to a country where he or she would be at grave risk of human rights violations" (Amnesty 2004: 1). The Government of Laos has made assurances that the men were treated correctly and were in good health, but they refused requests to observe the trial or access the men. The men were tried in The People's Court of Champassak in October 2004. All 16 were found guilty and given prison sentences ranging from two to sixteen years.[16] It is unknown if those with shorter sentences were released at the end of their terms (Amnesty International personal communication 5 November 2010). The shift from the time when the aim seemed to be to "bleed Indochina white" by accepting Indochinese refugees and allowing insurgents safe haven on Thai soil could not be clearer. Now the public message is that such asylum seekers are not welcome.

The border is being rearticulated in another important aspect: the joint Lao-Thai effort to control the "undocumented" Lao workers in Thailand. It has been reported that illicit Lao migration into Thailand has reached an "acute" level (Petcharoen 2006) and the media regularly features alarmist articles about "people trafficking." A memorandum of understanding signed between the two governments in October 2003 allowed for some Lao workers to be employed in Thailand. However, the number permitted was significantly less than the number of Lao at that time known to be working illegally in Thailand. Moreover, this legally sanctioned pathway for migrants submits would-be workers to bureaucratic red-tape and fees designed to ensure that workers return to Laos after a maximum of four years, including wages held in trust. Cooperation here is designed less to facilitate than to regulate people's movements.

It is common to read in the literature on "trafficking" the complaint that the "victims" consistently do not realize that they have been trafficked, typically referring to their marginalization in other terms.[17] Molland has recently demonstrated the slipperiness of defining trafficking within anti-trafficking organizations in Laos. He reports that although most definitions include ideas of "coercion", "force" and "exploitation" these terms are rarely problematized and anti-trafficking workers express frustration with the difficulties of interpreting and using these ideas when confronted with real world examples (2011: 246–50). Potentially *any* kind of labour arrangement that the observer finds unacceptably exploitative might be defined as trafficking, but almost all labour involves some kind of exploitation. The everyday tactics used by the marginal to manoeuvre within a regulatory regime that offers them few alternatives might be condemned and criminalized as slavery. It is interesting to note that the activities of En and other *khon song* fitted into the definition used by Interpol at that time of "people smugglers" as those who "smuggle human beings for financial gain" (Interpol, November 24, 2005). This organization concluded that people smuggling is "not only a transnational crime, but also an enormous violation of human rights and a contemporary form of slavery" (ibid). While I think it hardly needs to be stated that I am opposed to slavery, my concern with anti-trafficking is when it appears to campaign against human mobility itself, rather than the conditions which make this mobility dangerous and exploitative in the first place. By a sleight of hand, it comes to seem as if illicit cross-border mobility itself is the crime against the marginal, that migration itself is the dangerous act that creates risk and exploitation. The criminal, in this view, is Lai's friend En whose business it is to ferry would-be labourers across the border. I would like to suggest, in light of the history and ethnography presented here of the Thai-Lao border, that it is not "people smugglers" like En who creates this risk and exploitation but the historical solidification and regulation of the border itself.

It cannot be said today, as in Toye's description of the colonial era, that "Lao people mingled freely across their great river" (1968: 48). It is now not an option to display one's displeasure at a leader by emigrating, as in pre-colonial times, and nor is it possible to claim "refugee" status in Thailand simply by virtue of being Lao, as it was during and directly after the war. Insurgents in the region are no longer considered "freedom fighters", as Reagan described them (Evans and Rowley 1990: 232). They are considered terrorists, and are singled out for control.[18] It is specifically the kinds of mobilities that the people of Don Khiaw have historically engaged in—insurgency, asylum seeking, and irregular border crossings, the mobilities of the marginal—that are being targeted for elimination in the era of regional cooperation. Meanwhile, airports and foreign direct investment are encouraged and paraded as the symbols of so-called regional integration, an integration accessible in reality only by a favoured few.

Conclusion

The recent re-articulation of the border is symbolized aptly by the physical nature of the Chong Mek/Vang Tao border crossing, the site of the 2000 incursion that was the subject of the lecture described at the start of this chapter. The checkpoint is also locally simply known as *tokheet*, "the border". It is the legal avenue into Thailand closest to Don Khiaw, and one I have crossed countless times since 2002. It became an international crossing in March 1999. While best known for the border skirmish mentioned above, for most locals its significance lies in the fact that Lao and Thai people are permitted—for a small fee of 1,000 kip—to cross the border for one day within a one-kilometre radius of the border without passing passport clearance. A Lao immigration officer explained to me that the arrangement was necessary because people in the area were "related and you can't really stop them anyway." Combined with the Japanese-funded Mekong bridge at Pakse and feeder road to the border, completed in 2000, this policy saw a boom in trade at *tokheet*. When I arrived in 2002, *tokheet* was swamped by trade. Lao market vendors would catch small, cramped, open vans to the border and hire a cart at the border to fill with Thai products to sell on in Laos. On the Thai side of the border stalls were jammed one after another selling the full array of household and commercial goods, from live fish fingerlings and fertilizer to Thai fruits and packet noodles. The stalls formed a tangled mass—several rows deep—on either side of a single dirt road that bore a constant traffic of carts, buses, and pick-up trucks.

By contrast, the office where long-term travellers were required to show their papers to Thai officials in order to obtain an entry or exit stamp was a single-story affair tucked away down an unassuming-looking dirt path. The markets were so dense that the untrained eye easily missed this administrative post: the "trade" aspect of the border visually eclipsed its "administrative" aspect. More than one tourist failed to gain the requisite stamp there, because it seemed more obvious to directly board one of the many conveyances on the main road offering transport. At police checkpoints a few kilometres further into Thailand, public buses were stopped and papers are checked. While unwitting tourists were sometimes caught, the police's main targets were Lao labourers attempting to enter or exit Thailand without proper documentation. Some of the men I knew from Don Khiaw reported being caught when catching a bus from Ubon Ratchathani to the border crossing. They had no identification with them, and were carrying their entire savings from the trip: the money was confiscated, and the men deposited on the Lao side of the border. These men felt they had little choice but to immediately return to Thailand to try to recoup their losses. The next time, the men were more careful, they told me, depositing their earnings in a bank to be accessed once they were back in Laos and hiring a private vehicle to whisk them past the checkpoint uninterrupted. Once at the border, the confusion provided a safe haven for returnees.

Tokheet has changed in the ensuing years, however. Beginning in 2003 and more or less completed by 2005, a new, multi-story immigration office now dominates the Thai side of the checkpoint. It is located in the middle of a single, paved road, so that all traffic must move around it, regulated by heavy boom gates. Passengers alight and pass through on foot, corralled in barricaded queues in the manner of a cattle yard. The market stalls have been moved to an orderly pavilion far off to the side of the road, but they lack the vibrancy and variety of the former markets. Today, the chances of a Lao labourer slipping past the border post undocumented are much reduced. The building again seems sensational: it is a loud declaration of the strength and standing of state power. However, this loud claim to regulate the border is also being subverted in new ways. In the next chapter, I will describe some of the ways that undocumented labour is continuing.[19]

As the relationship between the Lao and Thai governments solidify their territorial claims, their borders grow more orderly, distinct and regulated. In the era of being "good neighbours" the two governments have prioritized the enforcement of "good fences." While officially monitored and recorded trade volumes across the border continue to increase, other forms of mobility have been targeted for elimination in sometimes sensational and costly interventions.

I have written this chapter in two registers. The first is a sombre accounting of suffering. If one wants to understand why Don Khiaw is poor, one need look no further than the stories told here. Caught on the wrong side of a revolution by a border that has become more and more fixed over time, some of these people launched rebellions against the new regime, but now these too have come to an end. This is a region that can be considered in terms "of a "post-conflict" situation" (Baird and Le Billon 2012). The current regime of citizenship attempts to capture and corral the flows of rural people. It criminalizes poor people when they seek work elsewhere, and exposes these already vulnerable people to the dangers of other criminal elements, such as police on the take or unscrupulous employers. The border regime creates an order based not on merit or effort but on the papers one carries. This is a global hierarchy of citizenship. It is not simply a matter between Thailand and Laos, but a global regime that is perhaps one of the most powerful forces separating humanity into differentiated classes today (Kipnis 2004). Another register has played alongside this sombre account. Lai's imaginings of her trip to Thailand were rich with speculation, hope, inventiveness and desire. In the next chapter I will show how, despite capture and corralling, Lao rural resident continue to sprout new desires and experiment with new possibilities. Here, I will simply ask: can we, like Lai, dream beyond borders? This historical and social analysis of Don Khiaw has demonstrated that the regime of citizenship is not only linked to contemporary poverty and vulnerability, but also that it is not inevitable. Historically, the enforcement of the border at Champassak is relatively recent. While recent events have made the border a very real and influential factor in local lives, it is important not to be overwhelmed, either perceiving the regime of citizenship as inevitable or so pervasive that it is invisible and "natural". People have not always been ordered according to their citizenship papers, and perhaps it is now time to consider whether they ought to be.

4

Poverty becomes you
Black, White and Gold

In the previous chapters I sketched out the development of some of the contemporary context in which Don Khiaw residents find themselves. When viewed through the lens of family, oral and written histories it is clear that poverty on Don Khiaw is shaped by factors well out of local control. In this chapter, I follow Deleuze's suggestion that, even in contexts such as this, where opportunities and alternatives are shut down and constricted, that there are always lines of escape. These are not necessarily successful: he acknowledges that there are always "sticking points to cut off" or re-routings of these escapes into new assemblages.[1] These lines and their blocks, checks and re-routings are for Deleuze the very stuff of any given society. In this chapter, I investigate poverty in Don Khiaw today: what it means and how it is experienced locally; what the aspirations are for change; and how people go about pursuing these aspirations. What processes of transformation are imagined and pursued in this context? What are their blocks? I focus first on what poverty meant for the women I became close to in rural Laos. I then turn to the fantasies that both women and men constructed in their attempts to re-fashion themselves and the blocks but also the triumphs they encountered within what were often extremely adverse conditions.

Becoming black, becoming white, becoming beauty

When I arrived in Laos for my first fieldwork, I was provided with a letter of research permission from the national office of the Ministry of Education. This stated that I was permitted to conduct anthropological fieldwork in any village I chose, and requested that government officials assist me. This letter was enough to deliver me through the Provincial level of the bureaucracy to the District level. At the District level, however, the letter lost some of its force. The District Chief was uneasy about my choice of fieldsite. He suggested something closer to the District capital, somewhere where it would be easier to "visit" me. At first I had thought this was a well-meaning but misplaced concern for my well-being. Eventually, in a conversation with some low-ranking officials over dinner, they explained that the authorities wanted me close so they could keep an eye on my activities. As one said, "this is not Thailand: foreigners cannot just go wherever they want. There is government."

As I learnt, there was not just one government. In this District, it was the word of the *cao muang* (District Chief) that trumped my letter of permission from the central authorities. I was forced to negotiate afresh for research permission, this time with the District Chief. I stayed in the care of District education staff for two weeks while these negotiations took place. These weeks were marked by a series of brief and rare meetings concerning my research plans, and long, directionless days filled with casual conversations with office staff. The office squatted in a muddy field of overgrown grass where cows grazed, their bells clanging. The office had no electricity and was too hot for comfort, so staff gathered on a wide bench under a broad shade tree outside for long streams of conversation, banter and debate. After my first five-minute meeting with the office head, I was invited over to the bench. "Oh you're beautiful," a chorus immediately began. Peng, a female staff member, was held up for comparison. "Hold your arm against hers," a man insisted, so we could compare the colour of our skins. "Oh you are very black," the man told Peng. Peng removed her arm very quickly, "I'm not beautiful!" she exclaimed, smiling, "I am so black!"

"Black is not beautiful," the man explained theatrically to me.

"Holly, what about him?" Peng motioned towards the man, "would you take him as a boyfriend? He's not beautiful. He's very black." The group laughed at Peng's rejoinder. "Not beautiful, not beautiful" they chorused.

I marvelled at their carefree banter about such topics—race, beauty, love. All were held in such reverence in the cultural milieu from which I had just emerged, that of urban Australia. In contrast to their relaxed banter, I was immediately awkward. I felt uncomfortable in my own skin. Suddenly, my body did not seem to mean to others what it meant for me. Those words, "white" and "black", denoted for me race, and in Australia, race had long since been dropped from everyday polite usage. Educated, urban Australians no longer talked about difference in terms of "black" or "white". This is not to say that there is now no discourse of difference, but this is framed now in terms of national or "cultural" origin. It is considered quite polite to ask, "what nationality are you?" but certainly not "what race are you?" There has been a proliferation of "multicultural" festivals and fairs, where food and dance form the acceptable and required modes of expressing difference, each national culture displayed in its distinct, cordoned-off stalls and performances.

Race, however, is unmentionable in everyday conversation. The very term now implies racism, and its use has been "carefully suppressed among modern, cosmopolitan citizens" (Cowlishaw 2004: 13). It would be uncouth in the extreme, in this context, to suggest that one race was beautiful, another not. Racist, even. Against racism, Martin Luther King expressed the dream that people "not be judged by the color of their skin but by the content of their character". In Dr King's statement, we see a strong correlation between race, skin and body—race is associated with the physical nature one is granted at birth, and over which one is thus more or less powerless. In this sense, race seemed only skin deep, an accident of birth, not an indicator of a person's worth.[2] The banter at the office confronted these sensibilities. The staff bluntly held that black and white were differences that mattered.[3] White skin was beautiful, black was not and, far from unmentionable, these were the subject of comparison, comment and ridicule.

Peng was assigned as my friend and companion for my stay in the capital, and shared my lodgings with me. That night in our rooms, she was happily rummaging through my possessions, trying on my clothes and cosmetics with an absorbed but light-hearted curiosity. My collection of sunscreens, moisturizers, and skin care products evoked particular interest. "What is this cream for?" she asked of each one, before applying a little. "For my eyes," "to make my skin soft," and "to stop the sun burning me," I replied to her queries.

"Oh," came Peng's satisfied reply. "This is why your skin is so white and beautiful. You can afford to buy all of these creams and stay inside all day. You have money."

"My skin is white because my parents' skin is white," I replied. I was taken aback at the implication that my skin was the result of manufacture rather than nature. I was a little taken aback too at my own reaction—I felt an unexpected surge of resentment at the thought that what I had taken to be bodily and given, my natural self, was perceived as the result of deliberate achievement and manipulation.

"You wait until you have lived in Laos for one year," said Peng, smirking, "you will be as black as me. Maybe more black, because you are going out to live in the countryside with the very poor people. If you harvest rice, you will be black." Peng used "black" and "white" here to indicate variability: for her, skin was open to manipulation and the key method of manipulation was wealth. She predicted, in a sense, that poverty would become me as my skin grew black, while her own aspirations were to become white, as a sign, consequence, and benefit of becoming wealthy. The colour of skin is a particularly good indicator in Laos of the constantly changing fortunes of the skin's inhabitant.

I have written elsewhere of how the Buddhist cosmology and the "cosmic hierarchy" through which individual people are thought to move, up or down, throughout their lives sheds some light on why it is that poverty is understood comparatively (local, regional and global comparisons are made in this highly hierarchical cosmology), and yet at the same time persons are thought to be capable of achieving movement through this hierarchy according to their own actions (High 2011a). Rather than emphasising skin as the immutable stuff with which you are born and should not be judged, everyday Lao usages of blackness and whiteness emphasized the skin's capacity for transformation. The changes in my own body during the course of my fieldwork were observed and were the source of frequent comment. A director from the District office shook his head when he saw me after six months: "you are so black," he said. "You are not beautiful anymore." In my home in a bamboo hut among rice fields, my body had registered a certain lifestyle, and this did not fail to attract notice, for these are the bodily indicators that Lao people read to gauge wealth and social status. Skins, as sites where both social distinctions *and* change are clearly written, are particularly dense symbols of the intensely hierarchical and yet mutable relationships in which Lao people imagine themselves.[4]

Lot, a friend I made in my eventual fieldsite, echoed Peng's sentiments. She said:

> Rural people are not beautiful: they are in the weather all the time, they come back black. People in the city, they are white, they are beautiful. They can look after their bodies, they have powder and lipstick and creams to wear. There's no shortage of things to buy to make yourself beautiful. All those things on Thai TV—things to make your skin white and your hair black. Those people on Thai TV are beautiful. They have noses like yours—foreign noses. They all get operations on their noses to look like that. Those people have money.

There is a generalized image of the rural impoverished body. The rural woman's gait—barefooted or in flip-flops, feet splayed and strides long and fast—is noticeably distinct from the urban middle-class woman's gait—hobbled and muted in ungainly platform or heeled shoes. Rural women's feet become flattened and hard against the soil of their rice paddies. Rural hands become rough and strong, adept with machete and hoe. Rural feminine mouths are stained red with betel nut, teeth stained black. It is often commented that transplanting and harvesting darkens the skin; that whitening

Figure 8. Beauty is bounty and bounty is beauty: this scene is an example of the over-abundance that is valued in displays of donations at Buddhist celebrations.

creams, moisturizers and hair dye are desired but not easily obtained in Don Khiaw; and that illness leaves its mark on the body. When I brought a Western magazine to Don Khiaw, I asked one woman if she thought the pictures of the models were beautiful. "Of course they are beautiful: they have never been injured or had a fever: ever," she replied. As one rural woman commented:

> …rural people are small, thin, dark, not beautiful. In the city, they are robust, white…they have soap and other things to look after themselves. The little children have white shirts and shoes for school. Here the children have no shoes, they are dirty.

The association of beauty with bounty pervades rural discourse. A bumper rice crop is described as *ngaam* (beautiful). Fields known to be fertile are described as *ngaam*. Hardy and fruitful vegetable strains are *ngaam*. At the Buddhist Holy Day during the rains retreat, the monks alms bowls overflow with excessive offerings of bananas and sweets. The monks are offered a multitude of miniature bowls crowded together and brimming: this overabundance is considered beautiful. The experience of poverty, as an experience of scarcity, is likewise understood as an experience of lacking beauty. Maew, sitting in the shade of her rural homestead, said, "I want beautiful things. But I don't see beauty here."

The moment when Peng argued that my skin was white because of my skin creams, instead of my birth right, I had been taken aback, somehow insulted at the insinuation that my skin was the result of effort rather than a natural given, as if, therefore, my skin was a lie and counterfeit. This was not how Peng had intended the comment at all. For her, an achieved skin was just as much a genuine indicator of my identity as a born skin, if not more so. When Peng commented on my skin and my cosmetics, she was commenting on my access to wealth and a particular lifestyle as telling attributes of my self. In this context, beauty products do not cover you up: they reveal you, your status, and your fortunes. They become you, just as poverty does.[5]

Becoming gold

Deng was in her late teens when we met, living with her older sister and brother-in-law. She had been born on Don Khiaw the youngest of six, but both her parents had died. By the time I met her, her older sisters lived one each in Paksong, Pakse, Vientiane, and in Don Khiaw and her older brother was a monk in the local temple. I first met Deng when she came to visit me at my house saying, "There is nothing to do in this village," by way of explanation, "all there is to do is walk and play. Go to visit people. So I came to visit you." It was the cool season, the rice harvest was in, and there was little work to do. Deng had been fainting at the sight of blood, and told me she would be seeking treatment for this weakness with the local spirit healer, Aacaan Coy. Aacaan Coy only treats his patients after nightfall. I was interested in this healing practice and she was afraid of the dark, so each evening for a few weeks she would collect me at sunset and we would walk through the darkening fields together to his house for her treatment, and then walk home again by torchlight. The dark felt close, private, and as we walked she would speak to me, her voice a smooth and high-pitched monologue behind me as we zig-zagged along the bunds of the rice fields.

One night Deng spoke to me of our mutual friend Lai. She said that Lai did not like her. Lai had never said a bad word to me about Deng, and in fact called her "*siaw*" (firm friend) and I told Deng this. Deng maintained that Lai did not want to be friends. Deng said, "I don't have any friends, because I am poor. My house is small. People don't come to visit me—I am lonely. I want to find money so that I can build a big house so that people will come to visit. Lai is richer—she has gold earrings. I have none. Lai has a living mother and father…mine are both dead. I have no one to help me find money." Deng explained her poverty to me in very personal terms: as a sense of shame, as immediately apparent in her appearance and her housing, and something that marked her off from her closest associates.

Her attention to housing is a common one. Houses, too, are described as *ngaam*, especially if they are large and lavishly decorated. There is a large range of houses in the south of Laos. The simplest are bamboo and grass thatch two-room shacks raised on wooden poles. More prestigious are the graceful hardwood houses with hinged shutters, elaborate staircases, raised on thick columns and roofed with corrugated iron. Deng lived in a house somewhere in between these categories, featuring some bamboo and some wood panels. The most lavish houses are the concrete and tile constructions, often painted bright white or colourfully. In Don Khiaw, the only house of this style was the one built for the abbot of the temple on the temple grounds with money from migrant remittances, but such houses are widely desired. Whatever the style, most people experienced their houses as continually unfinished projects, with more improvements and additions constantly planned. If you ask a rural Lao person if his or her home is finished, she will in all likelihood answer "*bo laew*" (not yet). Migrants often send home sums to be used for home improvements, such as balustrades, paint jobs and extensions, or upgrading sections to wood or concrete and tiles. The aspiration for home improvement extends well beyond an austere survival ethic. It encompasses aesthetic expressions of beauty, bounty and success and social expressions of hospitality and household composition. Houses, like their inhabitants, are experienced in a state of constant transformation.[6]

The night after Deng spoke to me of her sense of loneliness, she again collected me at dusk to walk to the spirit healer's house as the darkness gathered in. This time she spoke of her aspirations, "I want lots of money," she said. "I want gold all over my body—my ears, my neck, my wrists. If I have lots of money, lots of gold, I will have a boyfriend, and friends. Holly, if you were Lao, and poor like me, you would be alone like me too. Lao people don't like people who are poor. If you don't have money, you don't have friends, and you don't have boyfriends."

When we had walked some distance into the rice fields, quite alone in the brilliant moonlight, she halted on the path and turned to present me with a thin bracelet. She said it was a gift from a tourist she met while working in the kitchen of a guesthouse in Muang Khong. Deng studied primary school here and in a neighbouring village up to grade five. At age 12 she moved to the nearest urban centre, Muang Khong, where she lived and worked in a hotel for a year, cleaning and cooking for board and 20,000 *kip* (2 USD) per month. She then returned to her natal home to grow rice. The bracelet was a silver chain carrying a pendant that said "Laos". She spoke softly and told me not to tell anyone that she had given me the bracelet—absolutely no one.

"Why not?" I asked, admiring it. She replied that people will talk: they will assume that she is after my money. Reflecting on her apparent distrust of her neighbours, I asked her who she liked in the village, and she replied, "No one".

Like houses and skin, gold jewellery is common public display of relative fortune, and it is closely associated with beauty. Unlike houses, gold is an extremely liquid investment. The resale value of gold jewellery is thought to be strong, and in Laos holding wealth in the form of gold is widely considered to be superior to holding it in the form of currencies.[7] Marx described gold as "the universal equivalent" which could be almost magically metamorphosed into any of the infinity of other commodities. He wrote of the desire to hoard gold as the yearning to hold to oneself somehow that alchemy of exchange, "its gold chrysalis", because gold is the symbol of the freedom of the circulation of commodities (Marx 1976: 227–32). Gregory describes gold as "the supreme standard" of value in recent times (1997: 251).[8] Deng's fantasy of being bodily encased in gold can be thought of as a fantasy of encasing herself in this kind of chrysalis, a chrysalis that promises the unconstrained possibility purely of becoming something else, someone else. Her desire to be transformed in a chrysalis of gold seems confirmed by her identification with "no one" in this poor village. She identified herself explicitly not with her neighbours, but with an undefined otherwise.

Not long after we had established our friendship, Deng announced to me that she was going to join some friends of hers in Vientiane who worked in a garment factory there. They had come to visit their mother briefly, and had offered to take Deng back with them, saying that there was no shortage of jobs in the garment factory. She would leave with them in only a couple of days. Explaining her plans, she said, "I want to have lots of things. I want skirts, a denim skirt like yours. I want shirts. I want gold to wear." Aacaan Coy, however, who was still treating Deng for her affliction, prohibited her from crossing water while undergoing treatment. As a result, she could not leave the island when her friends left to return to the factory. Without them to guide her, Deng felt that she was not able to make her way to the factory. So she stayed.

During the daytime a few weeks later, Deng came to visit and we discussed the approaching village festival. Deng mused, "The festival will be fun, won't it? But I won't dance. I don't have anything to wear, I don't have a *sin* (traditional Lao skirt) or a beautiful shirt. I don't have any gold. I'm too shy to go." Her poverty was embarrassingly visible. Around this time, there was a rumour circulating that a young woman who had committed suicide in a nearby market town had done so because she had been unable to obtain one of the new baseball caps that had appeared in the markets. Deng would not take that path. She had plans, she explained:

> "That's why I'm leaving tomorrow, to Paksong. I will sell noodles for my sister who lives there, and ask her to buy me things. I want to wear gold. My sister here says I have to go tomorrow—either Vientiane or Paksong. I have to find money before the festival—if I don't, I won't come back. I won't go to the festival. I'm too shy to go without any gold. I like it here. I have always lived here. This is where I was born. If I move away, of course I would miss it here. But I have to go—I have to find money. I want so many things—shirts and skirts and gold. I want them so I have to find money. Today I got my papers to leave. I have to have a letter from the Village Chief, and from the deputy. I have to attach a photograph too—its expensive—20,000 *kip*! It's expensive isn't it? And a lot of work. But I need permission to move away from the village."

We sat in silence for a while—the only sound was the rustic murmur of chickens in the withered garden. Deng gazed at the chickens.

"It's not fun here. It's just not fun. In Paksong it is fun. They have motorcycles and cars and electricity. Here it's just not fun. I want to leave…You don't ever wear gold, Holly."

"I don't like it," I replied.

"And I like it so much! I want gold. I want gold for every part of my body…I guess we are different people…"

Deng left this time, and she did not return in time for the festival. She did return several weeks later, though, in April to visit for a few days during New Year. When I saw her, she had just arrived from Paksong, where she had been working with an elder sister who ran a noodle store near an army barracks there, and also has a coffee plantation. I noticed that she now wore a long denim skirt, a tight polyester t-shirt, an oversize windcheater emblazoned with "Adidas", platform shoes and her hair in a scrunchie. All this is new, very "Paksong" in style. We made arrangements to go to the temple to *haee dook may* (parade flowers) around the temple that night.

When darkness fell I met her at her house which she shared with her sister and her sister's husband and their infant. Deng was now wearing her familiar plain cotton *sin* (wrap around skirt), but on my arrival she slipped into the bedroom to change her clothes: a shiny blue *sin* she said that was usually worn by an ethnic minority—she saw them wearing them in Paksong. For her top she pulled on her Adidas jacket. She wanted a shirt she has seen me wearing, explaining, "I want a nice shirt to wear with my new *sin*. That is how Lao people dress—a nice shirt and a *sin*. I don't like to wear trousers.

I have never worn trousers. My sister won't let me. I must carry on the Lao rural tradition."

When I asked about Paksong she said, "I miss Paksong. I miss drinking beer. We would play karaoke every evening. It's so hot here—in Paksong it's cool…I am coming back to Don Khiaw to stay. I miss it here. I miss my little brother, my nephew. This is my village." She wanted to show me the new things she had learnt, such as how to serve Beer Lao in a glass of ice, so when we went to the festival I purchased a bottle, and she poured it for me as we sat by the river, this strange ritual that spoke of places that seemed so far off. She headed back to Paksong soon after.

Several months later, in the supposed wet-season of July (though no rains had fallen) Deng hailed me from her sister's house. I was not expecting to see her, as I had heard she had married a soldier up in Paksong. She was making charcoal, watching the smouldering makeshift oven stuffed with sticks. She was looking older somehow, her eyes and face were puffy. There was a new sadness about her. She said she had been back in Don Khiaw for two or three days. She said she had missed it here, missed her village. "I missed my nephew, my little brother, my older sister, my friends and you and everyone in the village. Cultivating rice is more fun than coffee. They are weeding the coffee plantations now—it's not pleasant." Her voice was hoarse.

I asked her about her future, what she wanted, and Deng replied with certainty,

> "I want to be rich. I want to have money, have a house, have buffalo. I must work hard, cultivate many fields. Because I am a farmer, you see. I have to grow rice. I have to cultivate a lot. Transplant a lot, grow a lot, harvest a lot. And when the harvest is in, I must distil alcohol. When it is distilled, I must go and sell it. And I must care for the chickens, the ducks and the pigs. When they are big, I must go and sell them. Use the money to buy wood and iron. And when I have enough, build a beautiful house. Then buy things to go in my house. But I don't have any of that yet—I have no funds. If I had funds, I'd raise pigs, plant orange trees, distil alcohol, look after chickens and ducks—take them and sell them. Each time I would have a little money, and I'd put it away in my house. Then it would be a lot. I'd build a big house with a shopfront. I'd buy things in and sell from the house. I'd still grow rice and eat in the house. I would do like those people do, like rich people do. The ones with money—they already have an inheritance and they can do this or that.
>
> "We are poor because we have no funds. We can only find fish and grow rice. My mother and father had nothing to give me. They had lots of children. What could we do to find money? We have to work hard—grow rice in both seasons, care for animals the way farmers do. But in our house we have no economy. If we had a mill machine, a motorboat to take fish to market, an electricity generator, then we could find some money. I want to do it, but I

can't. I want to make alcohol and sell it, find fish and sell them, look after lots and lots of pigs. Build a beautiful house. I want to but I can't."

"Here is my old village, I lived here with my mother and father. Here my sister says 'here at least we have rice to eat.' My sister won't let me go to another place—she says we are very poor here. We must live together. I want to go to Thailand—I want to earn lots of money and send it back home here. Buy a TV, a VCD and send it back here. But my sister won't let me go anywhere anymore. It's so hard to find money here—it's easier to find money in Vientiane or Thailand. There is no buying or selling here. Just farming rice and eating it, that's all. I want to have money, I want to buy beautiful things and wear beautiful clothes like them, like the Thai."

Deng, her sister and I descended to the rice fields to transplant the seedlings. Barefoot in the smooth, cooling mud of the field that they had irrigated with a seven-horsepower pump in a costly and desperate move against the drought, backs bent to the sun and faces turned to the mud, the conversation turned to banter about boyfriends and husbands. I realized that Deng's sister and Deng were trying, coyly, to ask me about contraception, why had I not become pregnant despite the visit from my Italian boyfriend? I realized, belatedly, that Deng had become pregnant to that soldier "husband" I had heard about. Thus those puffy eyes, the way tears always seemed about to brim lately. Yes, she was pregnant. "I will run away from my husband!" declared Deng with bravado, half mocking, half serious, "I am going to run away to Thailand! I will pay En to take me: 1,000 baht. My sister is afraid that if I go to Thailand I won't come back." She said, then, that she was afraid: she has a feeling she would not see me again. Then she said, "I want to go to America to live with my aunt, I want to earn lots of money and buy things to send back to my sister—send money to do the house and buy pigs and motors. I am about to get married and I have nothing for our house—no bowls or spoons. When I am finished with the harvest, I will take rice up to Paksong. We will grow cabbage there, I will live in the cabbage fields. You will be gone by then, won't you?"

Deng paused, straightening her back and fixing her gaze on the horizon, her hands idling with her handful of rice seedlings, her feet sunk deep in the ooze of her rice field.

I do not know, I have no way of knowing and I did not ask, how consensual, how loving, how pleasurable was the sex that had led to this pregnancy. Researchers have noted, and it is well-known in Laos, that noodle stores and beer cafes are the most common sites for prostitution there, but also that the distinction between prostitution and romantic sex is difficult to maintain in these settings: women will often only accept as their lover-clients men who can not only pay but also charm and persuade them (Lyttleton 1999). At any rate, Deng's move to such a store close by an army barracks was from the start overladen with such amorous-economic possibilities.

Years later Deng and her husband were still together and they had three children. I visited them once where they lived in the army barracks by the side of the road outside Paksong. I had met the husband before but he was always a quiet man, reserved and deferential, unlike his wife who was still familiar and expressive with me after all these years. The day I came by she had sent her two oldest children, who were in primary school, to pick coffee. The youngest one was just learning to speak, and stuck close by his mother, begging for sweets and showing off for us. The family had no agricultural land of their own, and got by mainly on the husband's monthly soldier salary. Deng used her talkative charm to sell lottery tickets on commission, but it did not bring in much. The family were in the process of building a house so she did not invite me upstairs. Instead, she, the youngest child and I went for noodle soup at a local store by the side of the road. There I met other people who live in the area: many of them were settlers from the Sii Phan Don region so the conversation revolved around the people and places we knew in common.

All of her desires had led her to this. Her fluttering attempts to break out of rural poverty had led to this enactment of its very familiar pattern: rice in Don Khiaw, coffee in the Bolaven Plateau, building and rebuilding a house, children. This pattern repeated itself through her desires and the way they had been blocked, diverted, constricted and narrowed. When I refer to Deng's "desire" I am not speaking here of the sex that made her pregnant, at least not only of that. All of Deng's ambitions were suffused with a sensual desire. The objects of her desire followed one another in quick succession: gold, clothes, pots and pans, USA, shirts, beer, money, travel. Her desire constantly generated these renewed demands.

These were often strikingly consumerist: one might think avaricious. Deng's desire did not express itself in a demand to be cut off from capitalism. Her dream was to be covered in gold, the very chrysalis of the kind of pure exchange that Marx observed capitalism promises. She wanted to be transformed by this exchange by immersing herself in it completely. Yet, this is a global system where the odds are stacked heavily against the likes of Deng. Here, then, was her dilemma: she could not stay on Don Khiaw. Her sister clearly wanted her to move on: too few rice fields, too many mouths. Deng imaginatively projected herself into a series of other circumstances. She tried to carve a path—the factory in Vientiane, the USA, Thailand, the noodle store in the Bolaven Plateau, and a soldier lover. She was looking for a line that would lead her beyond the inevitability of marginalization and would carve a new self: rich, beautiful, golden. However, in the pursuit of these, she became something else.

Deleuze and Guattari's notion of the "giganticism" of desire suggests the objects of desire are never simply things: a pot, a pan, a gold necklace, a shirt. They are "aggregates"—everything that that necklace stands in for, all the possibilities and fantasies that take off from such a thing: a pan with food cooking in it in a kitchen in a big house with a husband and friends coming to visit, not just a pan. Likewise her choice of a lover was a choice made in a whole social field composed of desire and the stops and gaps that cut off desire, or re-routed it.[9] As a result, love and sensuality have a "statistical" flavour. Our loves always have about them "something belonging to the laws of large numbers" (1983: 294). Sexual relationships are an "index of social relationships" via the libidinal investments of the social field (1983: 253). There was something of a patterned probability in Deng's object choice. There is also a "dwarfism" to desire, in that it resides in the smallest details, in the most routine of daily acts: "The truth is that sexuality is everywhere: the way a bureaucrat fondles his records, a judge administers justice, a businessman causes money to circulate; the way the bourgeoisie fucks the proletariat; and so on" (1983: 293). As with their intervention in the unconscious, when Deleuze and Guattari spoke of love, their aim was to unchain it from the stuffy confines of the familial, the personal or the private, and to understand it instead as located in (and a means of understanding) "connections, disjunctions, and conjunctions of flows that cross through a society, entering and leaving it" (1983: 252).

Anthropologists hardly need Deleuze and Guattari to remind us that love and material culture speak of social relationships.[10] However, the way they include love and material culture in a critical reworking of the basic insights of psychoanalysis is worth heeding. There was something delirious about Deng's desires. Some of them were wildly improbable—such as covering her body in gold or going to Thailand when she was already pregnant. For all of this apparent irrationality, they produced a kind of rationality that can be seen in the repetitious outcomes of lives lived in rural Laos. Rather than thinking of desires and love in terms of a concept like "cultural-symbolic schemes," with its emphasis on reproduction through the coherent meshing of cosmological meanings, an approach inspired by concepts like "delirium" points much more clearly to the productive power of missing parts, inconsistences, and contradictions. Unlike the culture concept, this approach does not require credulity in order to operate. I doubt that Deng ever naively believed she would be covered in gold or that she would finally join her relatives in the United States, but the desire and its impossibility was nonetheless central to the lines she did adopt. It is by attending to the holes, to the moments where "it's nuts" but also produces patterned rationalities, where what is impossible is just as important as what is present, that we can produce thicker descriptions of the way familiar patterns recur, sometimes despite themselves.

Taking flight

In mid-2005, I was visiting a friend on Don Khiaw when Father Hiang also dropped by. He had paddled his boat a few hundred metres upstream to Mother Ian's house next-door to collect some wooden planks for his house that he had bought from her. I asked after his daughter, Noy, who had left for Bangkok several months ago to work in a garment factory. To my surprise, he told me that yesterday she had returned home. This was all the more remarkable, because his son, Win, had returned only a few weeks earlier after seven years working in the fishing industry in Chonburi, Thailand. Father Hiang mentioned that both the returnees were going to the market town that day, and invited me to join them. Soon, I was perched atop the wooden planks on Father Hiang's boat as we floated down to his house.

I found Noy among a group chatting on the shore. She looked paler than the last time I saw her, and I commented on this. Others interjected that she looked fat. She smiled, taking these both as compliments. I heard that Noy had arrived home with a group of young migrants from the island, and the evidence was clear among the little brothers and sisters hanging out on the shore as they clutched bright new toys or wore new clothes. In Don Khiaw, the silty Mekong River water seems to wash everything into the same dull brown colour eventually, so these new things were striking, announcing in vivid hues that they were from elsewhere. Noy helped to carry in the planks from the boat to the house, and then reappeared in a new outfit, her hair thrown high in a scrunchie, platform flip flops, full-length denim jeans, and a white tee-shirt with pastel blue trim. Noy's brother Win showed up in a new-looking outfit, too: a bright pink shirt with dark denim jeans.

In this final section, I will outline how mobility, like that of Noy and Win, continues despite the regulations of migration outlined in the previous chapter. Wages are much higher in Thailand than in Laos. For instance, while Lai (in the last chapter) expected to earn 4,000 baht[11] a month as a domestic worker when we spoke in 2003, the coffee pickers of the Bolaven Plateau in the same year earned only 100,000 *kip* a month for arduous, dawn to dusk, physical labour. In exchange rates current at that time, 100,000 *kip* was the equivalent of 400 baht. In other words, Lai expected to earn ten times as much in Thailand as her age-mates were earning in the Plateau. Likewise, in 2003 the going rate for agricultural labourers working on the rice harvest or transplant on Don Khiaw was 10,000 *kip* (40 baht) a day. The minimum wage rate in Thailand was at that time reportedly 140 baht a day, and was even higher in the centres like Bangkok and Chonburi where Don Khiaw labourers typically are destined (184 and 166 baht a day respectively) (Ministry of Labour, Thailand 2006).[12] While I often met return migrants who had been arrested or had their earnings confiscated by Thai police, I never met anyone who had been unable to find work in Thailand. That is, the greatest hurdle faced by Lao labourers in Thailand was not finding work but avoiding the police and other predators. While Lao labourers were aware of the dangers that migrating to Thailand placed them in, they also recognized that the risks were difficult to avoid: their citizenship status combined with their poverty and aspirations left few other choices. Their exploitation must be considered in light of the alternatives, which are hardship and frustrated ambition in Don Khiaw, or lower wages in Laos' industries or commercial agriculture. Moreover, more than this simple calculation of profit versus risk, destination Thailand is firmly entrenched in a view of what is possible, desirable and expected in the future.

Daaw, Win, and Noy and I set off on the 20 minute ride to the nearest market town, Muang Seen. Their main purpose in going to the market town was to collect money, from what they called "the bank." Any visitor to Muang Seen will know that it houses no "bank" in the strict sense of the term. Its dusty, unpaved streets are lined with a series of open-air stores and a couple of guesthouses. It is not an administrative centre and does not house any branches of Laos' official financial institutions, so I was curious to visit this "bank". On our arrival, Daaw, Win, and Noy led me to what seemed from the outside like any of the other stores, complete with a selection of vegetables, tinned goods, sweets for donation on holy days and other basic supplies. However, inside was a wide space with a bench and mat for people to sit on. There were several people there when we arrived, most facing a large flat screen TV with remarkably good reception. Some metres back and to the left of the TV, the *maee khaa* (trader) presided, surrounded by telephones. She had one large landline telephone, and I counted at least seven mobile phones, each reclining in its own miniature deckchair. The trader handed me a business card, which listed the ten phone numbers on which she could be reached. She explained that part of her business was to allow people to place calls on her mobile phones. International calls were 8,000 *kip* per minute, regardless of destination. However, her main business was running a "bank": she passed on money that had been deposited in her account at the Agriculture Bank in Thailand on behalf of returning migrants.

Noy placed a call to her former employer in Thailand. At first no one answered, and we had to wait about an hour while she kept trying. When she did manage to make contact, she told the office to deposit her wages in the *maee khaa*'s bank account. We had to wait several hours for this to happen. The *maee khaa* was dealing with several customers at once. On the phone to the Agricultural Bank in Thailand at one point, she asked about Noy's money by saying: "Don Khiaw money, is there any money for Don Khiaw?" Noy's money had not gone through at that point, but the *maee khaa* learned that there was another deposit for Don Khiaw. The *maee khaa* asked Daaw "who is Phukhong?" "That's my little brother. That would be money for Suk. I'll collect it," Daaw replied. The *maee khaa* spoke on the phone for a moment to the bank, insisting to the person on the other end to "deposit the money with me."

Finally, the *maee khaa* heard on the telephone that Noy's money had been deposited. Win was also collecting money, although his had already been deposited and he simply needed to collect it. The *maee khaa* produced a large bag of baht and three envelopes. She wrote a name and an amount on each, and then slipped the money inside.[13] On the way home, Win and Noy bought some more wood for their parent's house extensions—carved balustrades for the veranda area. Daaw bought some ice-cream and put them in a cooler she had bought along and filled with ice. She also bought some soup, shoes for her daughter, and a new *sin* (wrap around skirt).

This "bank" was one of many partial remedies migrants continually develop to subvert some of the difficulties and dangers to which they are subjected. However, it too, was vulnerable and subject to regulation and change. It is notable that several years later when I went to revisit the "bank," it was gone along with the trader and all her mobile phones. I was directed instead to a man in a nearby petrol station who was said to be able to transfer money, but he was much more wary that the previous female trader had been and deflected my questions by saying that I should just use the Western Union money transfers if I was so interested in money traders. I gathered that there had been a crackdown, meaning my questions were unwelcome and the returned migrants had to find other means to transfer their money. This was another phase in the quiet tug-of-war between regulation and its subversion. Migrants tried many strategies to work with or around the regulatory regime that they confronted. Some purchased a Thai identification card clandestinely. Others were able to obtain one of the migrant worker cards offered by the Thai government to register undocumented workers. Each of these measures, however, represents an extra cost to Lao labourers who come from already poor backgrounds and earn already low wages. Since so many go undocumented, many Lao workers remain in vulnerable positions because of their citizenship status: afraid of arrest, unable to command higher wages in the workplace, and vulnerable to exploitation. Cross-border excursions seeking profit, beauty and personal transformation, then, continue among rural Lao, even in this era of heightened border regulation, but at the cost of new forms of vulnerability.

Some years later, when Father Hiang's children were once again working in Thailand, we used my mobile phone to call Noy at her work in Bangkok. At first a man answered, gruff. Surprised, and a little intimidated, I handed the phone to Noy's father to speak to him. When Noy came to the line I spoke to her briefly, but her voice was cracked with tears and she said, "I want to come home, I'm tired. I miss being there". I passed the phone to her aunt, who was with us, and the aunt urged Noy, "If you are tired, come home." We offered the phone to her mother, but she could not bring herself to talk to her daughter. I was not sure if it was pity or shame which left her wordless, or something else. When we had finished talking to Noy, we all sat subdued. I did not want to add to the sadness by asking if Noy was a prostitute, although it was clear that, in any case, to the extent that Noy's personal transformations and aspirations were being achieved, it was at a significant personal cost.

Conclusion

In this context of regulation and marginalization, Lao rural residents continue to attempt to carve out desired transformations, often against all odds, sometimes against all reason. This is an intensely hierarchical context where Lao people are well aware of the abundances elsewhere and their own marginal position in relation to these. They understand their poverty in "relative" rather than "absolute" terms in that sense,[14] but relative not to some national line of comparison (a fictional "poverty line"), but relative to a regional and even a global context. Despite this intense awareness of their marginal position, they maintain an understanding of poverty strikingly as a process of transformation, not a fixed identity. Poverty becomes you, physically, socially, and personally. This becoming betrays you, in that it is always visible, apparent to the public eye, an embarrassment and a social stigma. Yet it is not felt as a constant. Many of the people I came to know best undertook continual efforts at becoming otherwise: building or improving their homes, migrating to seek cash employment, experimenting with new strategies and working on their bodily appearance. Their commitment to these projects, in a context where so much was stacked against them, was at times overwhelming and humbling. They braved odds that were profoundly weighted against them, and managed to do so with a grace and optimism that I could only admire. These efforts often faltered against the checks and difficulties that blocked their desires, re-routed and refashioned it.

5

Stories of State

After dinner one night in August 2003, Cit sat on the step to the kitchen and lit a cigarette from the kerosene lamp. "This year, Laos is asking for rice from other countries. The whole country is in drought. Every single person is going to be affected. I'm not sure which donors are being approached: whoever has extra rice, Laos is asking for those foreign countries to send rice to help."

"Is it the World Food Program (*ongaan ahaan look*)?" I asked.

"Yes, I think so. Laos is asking them to send rice. But the foreigners should come themselves to distribute it. They should come and divide it in each village, give so much to each household. Otherwise, say our village is meant to get 10 tonnes, only 3 or 4 will actually arrive."

"Where will the other 6 or 7 go?"

"They sell it, in shops."

"Who? The *muang* (District and/or state)?" I asked.

"Yes, the *muang*. They sell it to stores. You can see the writing on the rice sacks, 'Assistance from Japan,' but they sell it in the store. One time some Japanese people saw the sacks being sold in the store and they took them back."

Mother Phong had been listening as she worked in another part of the kitchen, but this story was one that she knew well, that she had told me often, and she came then to sit with us by the lamp to tell it again. I knew, from previous tellings, that this story referred to the time just after the 1975 revolution, when she had been living in Pakse. There was a food shortage and some rice aid had been sent from Japan. She said, "We could see the name of the donor 'Japan' 'Japan' 'Japan' written on each bag. The government officials were selling the rice, but we knew that it was free assistance from overseas. But the government, they are not honest. Some Japanese people came to the market and saw the officials selling the rice, so the Japanese took it back again. Because the government was dishonest, the people obtained no rice, nothing to eat. But what can we do? *Khao pen cao pen naay* (They are the princes/ owners and the leaders). If they let us eat, we eat, if they don't, we don't."

Cit, seeming to take this as confirmation about his ruminations about the possibility of rice aid this year, continued, "They will only sell it…. If the donors distribute the rice themselves, then there will be no problem."

I pointed out that the current trend in development design was to foster capacity in recipient countries by employing local staff, so there was little chance that foreign staff would personally oversee the distribution of foreign rice aid. "The policy is that Lao people have to practice how to do this themselves," I said.

"They get to practice but we have to keep just sitting tight (*Khao aeeb heet hak hao tong yuu sue sue*)," Mother Phong commented with feeling.

I asked if the village had ever received any rice aid before. "Only one time, around 1997, but it wasn't free assistance. They made us dig for it, dig the road," said Cit. One meter earned 3 kilos of rice. However, payments had to be made for the sacks the rice came in, for the cost of the boat transporting the rice, and for the rice itself. "Anything that they could charge for, they did," Cit concluded. He seemed disgusted at these impositions. I asked about the rice aid distribution that I had seen on the account books of the District office recorded for 2001, but neither Mother Phong nor Cit had any recollection of it. "They must have sold it all," Mother Phong surmised.

Our conversation then turned to the road to nowhere (a World Bank project described in Chapter Seven). At this point of time, the road project had been decided upon at the District level, but no implementation had begun. Cit predicted that, like the earlier projects he had mentioned, the project would be scuttled by corruption:

> "They plan to steal the money—maybe not all of it. Just most of it. That's how civil servants are. They take the money meant for the people. I believe that the World Bank really wants to help us, but they give the money to the civil servants. If you give a million kip to a civil servant, maybe 200,000 will get to the people. I feel sorry but that's how it will be. Civil servants never used to have motorcycles, but today you see they all ride them. It is like the school they said they would build here."

He was referring now, I understood, to the time a group of Japanese development workers who had visited Don Khiaw to assess the need for a school building. The village leadership had been asked to prepare a detailed submission, but they had never heard back about it. Cit had been a deputy Village Chief at that time. He recalled:

> "It was going to be a full school with cement walls, toilet and water supply. They asked us to make a full plan and the Village Chief signed. But today,

you can see that the school was never built. We never heard back from them. What do you think happened? The civil servants took the money. The Japanese people wanted to help the Lao people, but they never came to see the true story for themselves. They just asked the civil servants, 'Is it built yet?' and the civil servants said 'yes'. And suppose the Japanese want to come and see, the civil servants won't let them come here. Or they will take them to the wrong place where there was already a school to deceive them into thinking it was built with their money."

"It is the same story as the food aid. New rice has already arrived to help those affected by the drought, but it has not arrived here. Where do you think it is? If you give rice to a civil servant for the people, the civil servant will certainly sell at least some of it. Even if you give it to the Village Chief, he will take some for himself."

Mother Phong leaned over to hold my arm and began telling me another story from the time when she had lived in Pakse, which again I had already heard several times before. She had established a trading business after bombing had driven her out of her market garden in the Bolaven Plateau in 1973. With the regime change in 1975, however, private trade was restricted. Furthermore, there were severe food shortages and Mother Phong worried about her aging mother who was living on Don Khiaw. She decided to relocate to Don Khiaw so that she could care for her and raise her five-year-old with the relative security of their own rice fields. On the cargo boat from Pakse, Mother Phong took out a container of cooked rice to feed her daughter. The other passengers snatched the food away from the child: her arm moved quickly in the light of the kerosene lamp to demonstrate the grabbing. "Everyone was so hungry, they forgot themselves".

In a choked voice, Cit quietly stated: "our Party and state are dishonest."

I had associated closely with this family for almost ten months by the time this conversation took place. When I first met them, the stories they told me had been quite different. Mother Phong had claimed that she had always lived on the island and Cit had claimed, parroting Party rhetoric, that the best solution to poverty was to follow the policies and directives of the Party-State. But over time, and as I became a part of their daily lives and a witness to unfolding political events, they began to share with me their more private stories of the state and their encounters with it. The sharing of these stories was a marker of our growing intimacy.

These stories were partly practical: they were not told idly, but as a means of conveying lessons about what the state is and how it operates. They show that the residents of Don Khiaw are experienced players in engaging with the state. These stories served in this intimate family setting as explanations, interpretative frames and predictive tools for their state relations. In the example above, these stories were used to predict accurately the non-arrival of famine relief and the dismal end of the road to nowhere saga (Chapter Seven).

Stories such as these form an important part of everyday state making in the south of Laos. They reify the state as an entity that time and again denies food, extracts, is violent, and selfish. These stories provide instructions about the known characteristics of this entity and give listeners the predictive tools necessary for interacting with it. When Mother Phong and Cit used these stories to explain to me why they thought the road to nowhere project would end in no tangible benefit they focused not on a critique of the approach or policy content of this particular project, its new "participatory" framework, the usefulness of a road, or the individual merits or flaws of the project. In fact, they did not mention the particularities of the project at all. Instead they spoke of the general characteristics perceived in the state and its officers as learnt from past experience. In their interpretation, it seemed to matter little if the road to nowhere project (which claimed to be an independent body partly funded by the World Bank) was participatory, pro-poor or all about empowerment. In their view, it was a state project, and like other state projects, it would end in coercion and extraction. Cit said, "they plan to steal the money" because that is how civil servants "are".

This conversation took place in the intimacy of the light flung from a single kerosene lamp after a shared meal among close associates, and it built on the knowledge that it was assumed we shared such views due to our long association. In more public realms, however, dissent in Laos at that time was severely curtailed.[1] I suspect that Cit's voice was choked in his final statement partly because, even in this intimate setting, critical statements about the Lao state carried the emotional charge of speaking that which must not be said but which, nonetheless, is said compulsively and repetitiously. Taussig[2] observed that a "regime of terror" will push stories of state into intimate realms: after meals, by lamplight and in intimate places. Circumscribed from the public sphere, these stories are divorced also from factual verification and resolution. Repressed, such stories of state in Laos became all the more important, taking on an almost mythological feel.

In them, fantasy and fact are difficult to distinguish. As I collected stories of state, I realized that the familiar distinction between corrupt state practices and so-called "legitimate" state activities (such as taxation and school fees) could not be assumed in these stories. Many times what I took to be state-as-usual such as road tolls, the collection of boat registration fees, interest on bank loans, and land tax were taken by my Lao friends as extraction-as-usual and as further proof of corruption. Unclear or difficult to discern situations were likewise offered as parables of corruption. Cit made reference to a

Japanese school that did not materialize, and he interpreted this non-provision as proof of Lao bureaucratic corruption. An alternative explanation is that the Japanese had asked for a number of proposals and selected only one: in this scenario, Don Khiaw did not make the cut, but not necessarily because of corruption. This explanation, however, failed to gain traction with Cit. Likewise with the food aid that Cit mentioned: while he pointed with disgust to the mandatory work and fees that came with the rice, meaning it was not free after all, another perspective is suggested when it is considered that the World Food Programme endorses and promotes "food for work" (*aahaan phuea ngaan*) programmes in Laos (see for instance World Food Programme 2005), and that it is standard for local contributions to be made as signs of "participation" and "ownership" by the receiving community. This is actually policy, not illicit corruption, although it might be disagreeable policy. Nevertheless, such mundane policies were often included in the intimate and extraordinary stories of state corruption related to me.

I suspect that there is barely a long-term visitor to Laos—including academic researchers, development workers, business people and bureaucrats—who has escaped exposure to such stories. Sooner or later, if he or she stays long enough, any visitor to Laos will be inducted into the "cultural intimacy" of nightmarish stories about the state in Laos. These stories form a kind of public secret. This secret is communicated to visitors in a way that shows that this knowledge is supposed to be unknown, but that it is necessary to know nevertheless if one is to have any operational efficacy politically or insider intimacy. Everybody in the know is supposed to know these supposed-unknowns. I have noted the repetition of these stories as they were told to me by Mother Phong and Cit: how many times did I hear the story of the Japanese rice, and always with that intensity? There is also a strange repetition in the reporting of such stories in the literature produced about Laos, especially in academic writing. Exposing these intimacies has become an expected part of academic writing about the Lao state. Yet on the other hand, in other forms of literature about Laos, such as official statements of the "grey" literature of the development industry and the bureaucracy, these intimacies are ignored altogether. So, in the literature about the state in Laos we have a case of repetition on the one hand and repression on the other.

An example from recent literature will help me make this point clear. Compare the following two items published in 2012. The first outlines the "known knowns" of Laos: this is the official story of the state in Laos at the time of writing. It is the Ministry of Foreign Affairs' summary of the "Lao Political Structure" available on its website. It states that Laos is a democratic and representative state run for and by the Lao people.

> The Constitution clearly established such a political system that the Lao PDR
> is a people's democratic state; all powers belong to the people, are exercised
> by the people and for the interests of the Lao multi-ethnic people. The rights
> of the Lao multi-ethnic people as masters of the country are exercised and
> guaranteed through the functioning of the political system which the Lao
> multi-ethnic people have chosen on the basis of the right to self-determination
> through the election of a body that represents their powers and interests
> called the National Assembly.[3]

Nothing special to see here, the website seems to claim: just another modern, multicultural democracy. How strikingly different this is from the second example, a description of Laos given by anthropologist Sarinda Singh. She describes Laos as "authoritarian," a political context where any criticism of the state is curtailed through fear, secrecy, and suspicion. She mentions almost in passing that there is "a lack of elections in Laos" (2012: 8). In one striking passage, she describes how in a private conversation among Lao friends, she casually criticized the Prime Minister of her own country. One of her Lao friends replied that such comments could not be made in Laos, at which point another shushed the conversation by miming the cutting of a throat (Singh 2012: 10). A longer quotation gives a fuller sense of Singh's assessment of the Lao state:

> An authoritarian state (that) actively demarcates and polices the bounds of
> public debate…What is certain is that all important decisions are the pur-
> view of elites; reasons for decisions and questioning of decisions are not for
> general discussion. Public questioning is limited by the state's intolerance of
> criticism and fear of this intolerance (Singh 2012: 9–10).

So, which one do we believe? The Ministry of Foreign Affairs website or the visiting anthropologist? Are there elections in Laos, or not? Are Lao people masters of their own land, or subordinate to ruling elites? Is this a representational democracy, or a secretive, silencing, authoritarian regime? I will argue that both representations hold interest for analysis as artefacts of contemporary Lao politics. Furthermore, these two styles of representing the Lao state are importantly linked to one another.

Scott (1990) has drawn a distinction between a "public transcript" and a "hidden" one. In conditions where there is a large disparity between dominant and subordinate groups, he argued, there will be a correspondingly large gap between the official, public version and that which takes place "off-stage" among subordinates beyond the gaze of power-holders. The dominant group effectively write the public transcript, often in terms flattering to themselves and furthermore in terms that rationalize their own rule through claims that they aid and assist subordinates. This provides subordinate groups with political weapons that can be used on-stage, such as demands that these rationalizations be realized (1990: 101). Yet for the most part, subordinates avoid conflict, confrontation and openly oppositional expression, pushing their own transcripts into more intimate realms. Building on this perspective, Herzfeld (1997) examined how these intimate expressions are in fact a way of participating, via discontent, in the nation-state as "the central legitimating authority in their lives" (1997: 2). He added that it might be bureaucrats as much as their disgruntled clients who participate in expressing this discontent which is at the same time a reification of the state as outside of themselves, a "shadowy power" (1997: 10). The clichés and ritualized aspects of the dominant transcript that Scott identified are used, Herzfeld points out, precisely because they work—they work by chiming into popular demands. Thus Herzfeld's approach builds on Scott's ideas while eroding the distinction between subordinates and dominant groups and their transcripts: even in highly oppositional contexts, the various actors must draw on shared symbols. This is what Herzfeld terms "cultural intimacy": the shared social, cultural and political grounding of even the most dry and formal formulations of power and knowledge.

This concept of "intimacy" is particularly useful for thinking through the state in Laos, especially because so many of the stories of state I have described, and the accounts written in the exposé style, such as Singh's above, rely on the idea of some kind of intimate moment. The concept of intimacy itself has a special relationship to the idea of truth. Intimate truths are not the superficial and plainly evident ones but the truths communicated in "calculated confidences" (Guégon 2006: 264): intimacies come as confessions and transgressions. They need to be disclosed or accidentally revealed in order to be known. Paradoxically, intimacies as revealed truths are also often seen as more true than that which is plainly visible. The word I am using for this orientation to knowledge, exposé, is thus particularly apposite for this register of representing the Lao state. We might think of the two knowledges of the Lao state contrasted above as two different claims to truth. The first is a claim to communicate knowledge that is already the dominant transcript. The second is a claim to communicate knowledge that is not readily known without exposure. The distinction, then, is between known knowns and known unknowns.

I am playing here on Zizek's mischievous use of Donald Rumsfeld's 2003 statement about the Iraq conflict.[4] Notoriously, Rumsfeld claimed that there were known knowns (things that we know we know), known unknowns (things that we know we do not know), and unknown unknowns (things that are simply beyond our ken). Zizek pointed out that Rumsfeld forgot to add the crucial fourth term: "the unknown knowns," the things we do not know that we know. Zizek's suggestion was that this is precisely the Freudian unconscious: "knowledge which does not know itself" (Zizek 2006b: 137). My modification here is that the second item mentioned by Rumsfeld, the known unknowns, can function, on a social level, as that knowledge that we know we are *not supposed to know*. It is a knowledge that is socially repressed. Socially repressed knowledge functions much like personally repressed thoughts in the way that repression provokes compulsive repetitions, pushing more forcefully towards exposure the more that it is denied. If known knowns are like the dominant transcript that Scott described, the known unknowns are like "hidden transcripts", but hidden in such a way that they provoke and insist upon an almost obsessive repetitive exposure.

Beyond both of these—beyond both the known knowns and the known unknowns—are the unknown knowns. This is the unconscious proper. This, Zizek suggests, is the appropriate field of enquiry for the intellectual. This is the area of the shared meanings that link the known knowns and the unknown knowns, the dominant and hidden transcripts, giving them their patterned, irrational rationality. This is what Herzfeld called "cultural intimacy," the shared cultural, symbolic and social terrain that links official and private narratives, and what I have been calling a political delirium. In this chapter I seek to trace out the unknown knowns in stories of state, both intimate and official. My interest is not to disentangle dream from reality, truth from fact. Rather, my aim is to interpret these stories as communicating this basic underlying political delirium.

This chapter takes as its example one striking period of state interventions in the countryside: the collectivization of agriculture. In the stories about collectivization that circulated in Don Khiaw, the state is objectified as a unified actor and imbued with a particular character. This was indicated in the common use of the term "they" (*phoen* or *khao*) to refer to the state and "us" (*hao*) to refer to ordinary people. Other terms, such as "the Party-state" (*phak lat*) or "the level above" reaffirmed this image of the state as separate from and above society. Even though social scientists have been enthusiastic to point out that the state is a human construct, and so ultimately indistinguishable from society, in everyday politics in Laos the state is often depicted in reified terms. My aim in this chapter is to take this reification seriously, rather than deconstructing it or putting it into question. I will adopt the ethnographic approach of methodological relativism, suspending my trained disbelief in the state for a moment to view the state in the terms through which it emerged in the stories told on Don Khiaw. I shall first summarize the framework of collectivization in Laos before turning to recollections of it and the characterizations of the state that they reveal. These characterizations,

I will argue, are charged with the ambivalences I outlined in Chapter Two: solidarity and exploitation, nurture and destruction, reciprocity and parasitism.

Rice collectivization in Laos

One of the first goals announced by the new regime in 1975 was to achieve national self-sufficiency in food (SWB FE/5090/C/1 20 Dec 75[5]). This was seen as a prerequisite to industrialization and a necessity for security and independence. This policy stance placed agriculture at the centre of the new regime's endeavours. The envisaged transformation of the countryside can be thought of in two stages: the first where the relations of ownership, production and trade were to be radically altered along socialist lines, the second where these alterations would lead to great prosperity and modernization. Some of the earliest decrees to emanate from the new regime concerned the transformation of the relations of ownership, production and trade. Directly after the regime change, the private trade in rice was banned: if rice was to be sold, it could only be sold to the state (SWB FE/W856/A/18 10 Dec 75). It was forbidden for any land to remain uncultivated (SWB FE/5090/C/4 20 Dec 75). In this array of policies aimed at total transformation and modernization, collectivization was the centrepiece.

The leader of the Lao People's Revolutionary Party, Kaysone Phomvihane, defined collectivization in the Lao context as "the collective way of life by means of collective ownership as a basis for production by first of all putting their land, cattle and agricultural tools under a collective ownership system" (Phomvihane 1979).[6] Collectives were to cultivate rice as a unit, and divide the crop based on work-points (after deductions for tax, welfare and investment). Collectives ideally were to be village-based. In a number of announcements, the regime encouraged villages of 30 to possibly 100 households to join together, though other announcements recognized that smaller collectives may be more suitable in the early stages of collectivization (SWB FE/6110/C/57 May 79). While the new regime described existing forms of rice production as individualistic, small-scale, short-sighted and private, the new programme was to transform the agriculture sector into a "collective, large-scale and centralized production..." (SWB FE/6110/C/4 7 May 79). The purpose of the collectivization of agriculture, then, was to radically transform the rural sector.

In a somewhat contradictory vein, the collectivization drive also suggested that the collective approach drew on a long-running rural tradition. Kaysone Phomvihane announced, "The new relationship constitutes the continuation and development of the tradition of mutual solidarity and assistance among our people" (1979). Another announcement suggested that collective agriculture "is adapted by our Party from the notion of 'asking a favour', which our Lao peasants of various nationalities have been acquainted with for a long time" (SWB FE/5554/B/2 5 Jul 77). Thus, according to the official story, collective agriculture was seen as both a massive transformation and as a continuance of agrarian custom.

This transformation/continuation was hoped to increase production, thereby contributing to self-sufficiency in food for the nation, and to the resources needed for national industrialization. However, the implications of this transformation, according to collectivization policy, were to extend far beyond mere rice production and distribution. The aim was to build a "new countryside": the changes wrought were to be economic, political and social. Collectives would provide taxes to the new government. They would also provision the sick, elderly, disabled and children with welfare. Some of the yield from collectives was to fund the collective's own public services. Other funds were to be saved for technical agricultural investment. In addition, the collectives would be able to support their own militia. It was suggested, too that the very existence of collectives would deter "enemies" and "bad people" from infiltrating villages. In the act of administering the collectives, it was hoped that the cadre would increase their skill and ability. Collectivization was planned to have far-reaching effects, and was absolutely central to the new regime's endeavours. On 24 June 1978, the radio announced that collectivization:

> ... aimed at building a new countryside, heightening socialist consciousness, raising the cultural, and scientific and technical standard of peasants, bringing into play their right to collective mastery, strengthening the worker-peasant alliance and the unity of all ethnic groups, reinforcing the people's democratic administration, mass organizations and people's armed forces and security forces, strengthening the Party's leadership over the countryside, leading to political, economic, cultural and social changes in the countryside (SWB FE/5847/C/1).

The transformation envisaged was immense.

The tools for this transformation, however, were tenuous. The regime openly admitted that the funds for the capital inputs necessary for large-scale agriculture were simply not available. In light of this, the regime suggested a reorganization of labour, and offered only advice, training and propaganda in support of the cooperatives. For instance, to further the collectivization drive in Champassak Province, Kaysone's four suggestions were 1) propaganda and education promoting collectivization, 2) guidance and advice to collectives regarding agriculture, 3) training sessions on the regulations of collectivization, and 4) improvement of leadership of collectives (SWB FE/5911/B/18 Sept 78). Nowhere in this list is mention made of investment. Even if the education and advice had been effective, it would have been inadequate because, as Evans (1990) has shown, large-scale agriculture cannot effectively be implemented without technical inputs.

Despite such shortcomings, Champassak Province was one of the most successful areas for the collectivization drive. Evans (1990), in his analysis of collectivization in Laos, gave special attention to Champassak Province, where Don Khiaw is located, noting the "unusually rapid pace of collectivization" there (1988: 38). By July 1978, it was reported that Champassak Province had 180 collectives, far outstripping any other province. So, why was collectivization so successful in Champassak? Kaysone, in an address in Champassak Province, suggested that the reason was that "the Provincial Party Committee has achieved a correct understanding and has urgently and positively made arrangements to publicize the resolutions of the political bureau", which in turn made the people enthusiastic to embrace the new policy (SWB FE/5911/B/18 Sept 78). Kaysone also credited the success to the people's "tradition of solidarity and mutual assistance. In this way, the people have accepted the policies of the Party and State as a result of their own wishes and knowledge…" (SWB FE/5911/B/18 Sept 78). The explanation given by Kaysone for the uptake of collectivization in Champassak Province, then, was the people's own desire to embrace it. Kaysone's pronouncements, if you like, formed the "known knowns" of collectivization, the dominant transcript. According to this version, desire stemmed partly from the attractiveness of government policy, once disseminated through education and publicity, and partly from a spontaneous and traditional predilection for "solidarity" in the tradition-laden countryside.

Evans proposed another explanation for the "success" of collectivization in Champassak. He described Champassak's unique position in Laos: historically an independent and right-wing principality, sympathetic to the Thai, the province shares a long land-border with Thailand, which was traversed by a persistent insurgency after 1975. Evans suggested that such security concerns meant that Champassak "tended to be administered along militaristic lines" (1988: 39). In the case of Champassak, Evans argued for a picture of forceful coercion. This was not a case of grassroots spontaneity, but the necessity of outward conformity in a context of extreme fear. Evans noted one official as saying that in Champassak there were only two good cooperatives out of 587—the rest he felt unable to classify (1990: 63). It is significant that, rather than explaining what these others were like, this official simply left them without a classification, as a gap. They were quite literally, then, known in terms of their unknown status. The official gestured to them as what could not be known in the official, "known known" Kaysone-esque picture: the known unknowns readily filled out the picture without having to be spoken.

Overall, the collectivization drive was a failure. Problems ranged from poor uptake to poor yields: the envisaged transformation of the countryside simply did not materialize. In an official announcement which effectively suspended the drive (SWB FE/W1044/A/22 15 Aug 79), the reasons hinted at by the regime were that: "Party committees at all levels have not yet studied and firmly grasped the Party Central Committee's line and policies as well as the specific points in their localities. They tackle problems carelessly," and furthermore, "The enemy or bad people have taken advantage of this weak point." The account offered by the regime was that failure of collectivization stemmed from incorrect or sabotaged implementation, rather than incorrect policy.

Evans, on the other hand, concluded that the drive failed due to a reason that was never officially acknowledged, but was nonetheless widely known. This was the inherent unsuitability of collectivization to the Lao peasantry, and the inability of the Lao government to enforce such unpalatable policies. Evans refuted the thesis that peasant society is somehow "naturally" predisposed to cooperative behaviour and therefore collectivization. He argued, in fact, that, "Peasant economy and society have their own irreducible logic and rationality" (1990: 123). This logic and rationality was, Evans argued, focused on the household, which functioned as a node of generalized reciprocity. Relationships extending further from the household were governed by stricter balanced reciprocity. Collectivization attempted a massive shift in these bases of reciprocity as:

> ... in true populist style, it asked the peasants to work together as one big, happy family. But these attempts threw together people who felt no natural affinity for or commitment to working together, and it led to feelings of injustice... (Evans 1990: 146).

Evans drew on Scott's argument that in the peasant economy, there is conservatism and resistance wherever the core production necessary to subsistence is threatened. The collectivization of agriculture represented just such a threat. Outside the special case of Champassak, Evans suggests the situation was "one of general confusion rather than general coercion" (1988: 43). The new state simply did not have the strength or capacity to impose such a policy. In the accounts we have of collectivization in Laos, then, we have two broad streams: an official account that presents the state as a wise leader seeking the betterment of rural people's lives, and a critical, unofficial assessment that views the collectivization drive as both sinister and foolish. I will now compare these two versions to the recollections of collectivization related to me in

Don Khiaw, in order to trace out the major themes and the interplay of these in stories of state.

Collectivization in Don Khiaw

Collectivization was first implemented in Don Khiaw in 1978. In that year, a milder version of collectivization in the form of labour exchange was undertaken, whereby three or four households were expected to pool their labour resources, working together on the respective land holdings during peak work periods. The harvest was then to be split equally on a household basis irrespective of land or labour inputs. Under this scheme, land was still held by the original owners, as were buffalo.

Father Dii remembered the labour exchange (1978) year with a laugh. He and two neighbouring houses cooperated that year, but the plan was not implemented strictly:

> They told us to work together. The civil servants would come every couple
> of weeks. And when they came, we would all rush to work together, so that
> there would be no trouble. But when they left, we just went back to normal,
> *phay heet phay man* (doing rice each to their own).

The harvest that year was damaged first by drought and then by flood. The flood of 1978 is one of the worst on record in Laos, and Champassak Province was hit particularly harshly. Most of the crop was lost, and the residents received some limited food aid.

In early 1979, the push for collectivization in Don Khiaw was intensified. Numerous gun-toting cadre held ten days of "educational" meetings in the temple hall. The cadre left after the "training" session, but they sent (armed) teams of representatives from their base on a neighbouring island every one or two days to oversee the collectivization. Father Khong recalled:

> They were civil servants but they had guns. They were civil servants and
> soldiers. They came often. There were always meetings. These days they don't
> come at all. But in those days they came every two or three days to inspect,
> Laven people, Lao people, but not people from around here. So many people.

The village was to operate as three separate collectives, called *cu*, each of about 15 to 20 families: one *cu* spanned the northern "head" of the island, another the south-eastern flank and a third the south-western flank. Each *cu* was to pool its labour, land, and tools for rice production, then divide the harvest between them based on labour inputs.

Each *cu* was assigned a leader. When I interviewed him, Father Khong was the only surviving *cu* leader. He remembered that he was responsible for making the others work. "If I didn't go out to the fields, then no one else would. I was always the first to work." Perhaps the most important responsibility of the *cu* leader was to record work points, or *khanaen*. The *khanaen* system designated three tiers, or *papheet*. *Papheet 1* were points earned by the strongest workers, and thus had the highest value. *Papheet 2* points were awarded to the other able workers. *Papheet 3* points were awarded to children and older people, who could contribute only slightly. A small allowance was made for those who could not work at all, such as the very old or very young.

The number of points awarded was based on work output. For instance, during transplant, output was measured by counting how many fields were ploughed, how many bunches of seedlings were collected, or how many bunches of seedlings were transplanted by a labourer. These were counted and noted down daily by the *cu* leader. Points were also awarded on a time basis—one full day's labour was from 8am to 12 noon, and 2pm to 4pm. Missing part or all of that time meant a loss of work points.

Land was pooled and had no bearing on the *papheet* or *khanaen* system. All fields which were owned by a *cu* member and located on the island were cultivated by that *cu*. Fields owned by *cu* members which were not on the island were not included. These were either left idle or worked by other cooperatives, without rent being paid. Residents of the island who had no rice fields, or whose rice fields were in another location, were included as equal members in their home *cu* for both work and rice division. Residents who owned land worked by the *cu* were not entitled to rent or compensation for the use of their land.

Buffalos were used cooperatively, but ownership and responsibility for their care remained with the original owners. The *cu* leader recorded work points for the buffalo, but when the rice was finally divided, these points were reportedly not considered. Workers were expected to supply their own tools and other equipment, but these remained the property of the original owners. Seed was provided by individual families, who used it for their own fields.

Cu members were required to work together in the fields. The method of farming rice together as a large group was a novel one in Don Khiaw, and the subject of much of the "education" given by cadre. Suaay remembered;

> ... the civil servants came from training in the cities, and they wanted the people to collectivise rice-farming. They wanted us to live together and eat together and work together. Solidarity! Not go our separate ways.

Aacaan Coy remembered this as one of the difficulties of the project:

> So many people were arguing and fighting. They did not get along well. Lots of arguments out in the hot sun. People coming late, having points deducted for lateness, or laziness. Lots of grumbling. We didn't want to do it—they made us do it.

Mother Kang, on the other hand, remembered the social aspects quite fondly:

> It was fun to work with lots of people. My fields were all transplanted in three days! It was very pleasant and the crop was beautiful. The fields were all beautiful for five or six years after the flood. We would all go to work in the morning together, the sounds of many people together, it was pleasant.

After harvest, the rice was carried to one area in each *cu*. The *cu* then worked to thresh the rice. This labour did not count for work points and was done "together" by the members of the *cu*. The paddy rice was then collected into a single pile. The enormous size of the rice harvest is frequently commented on when recalling collectivization. After the flood in 1978, the land was particularly fertile and the harvest was "beautiful". Two people each night were assigned to sleep at the pile, in an attempt to prevent thefts. At this point, cadre returned to the village to divide the rice. Father Khong hosted those assigned to his *cu*. He remembered that for his *cu* alone, there were representatives from "all" the departments, including four policemen, one teacher, one soldier, one from the industries office and several student volunteers. "My house was full of them," he stated. They stayed for over two weeks, arriving towards the end of the harvest and leaving after the rice had been divided. Since these people divided the rice, Father Khong said he did not know the ultimate division system.

During this same year, and apparently as part of the same project, the able-bodied men were required to spend part of the dry season in the Bolaven Plateau.[7] The village had been assigned an allotment, which was to be developed into a collective coffee plantation and market garden. Labour included clearing the land, weeding, growing vegetable crops and establishing the coffee plantation. Labour was organized through the *cu* system. Each household was to contribute one working age male to the *cu* workgroup. *Cu* workgroups were sent in alternating rotations, each rotation lasting two weeks. Those households which were unable or unwilling to send an able-bodied man were required to hire a man to send in his place. In addition, each household was required to contribute cash and rice for the living and travel expenses of their *cu* workgroup. The men stayed in rough huts in the forest. There was military supervision and organization. The system broke down after two rotations.

The universal memory of the 1979 collectivization is the ensuing shortage of rice. While everyone was short of rice, various reasons for the shortage were proffered. Father Khong recollected:

> The people didn't work diligently. They didn't have the desire to work. They didn't put their hearts into it. If they saw their friends not working, they would not work either! They didn't care. If we grow rice *phay heet phay man* (each to their own), the results are better…so we stopped.

This reason was commonly given for the rice shortage: people simply did not work as diligently when they were not working *phay heet phay man* (each to his or her own). Other reasons were remembered also. Another suggestion from Keng was that there were "just too many people. People who had no fields of their own were given rice just like those of us who do have fields. Usually the landless work on the mainland or rent land. But that year they all worked here—too many people." Keng counted off six landless families who were included in the cooperative "and each one of those families with eight or ten people! More people than land here." Many people also suspected their neighbours of stealing rice from the main pile, though no one had been "brave" enough to make a formal allegation. Whatever the causes, collectivisation resulted in severe rice shortages, and the people of Don Khiaw were forced to sell their stock or beg in order to survive. The shortage of rice was the reason given by participants for stopping the collectivization project after only one year. The ubiquitous statement was "we were short of rice, so we stopped."

Kaysone's official story that collectivization was embraced because it drew on traditional "solidarity" and a spontaneous predilection for village-based collective behaviour finds no support in these recollections: collectivization is remembered as a disastrous but temporary aberration from the more effective traditional production of rice through the usual *phay heet phay man* (each to his or her own) organization. Ethnographic data from Don Khiaw confirm Evans' rejection of the assumption of "spontaneous socialism" among the peasantry. Such compliance as there was to the collectivization policy did not spring from some traditional desire to cooperate. These recollections instead show a willingness to try collectivization—not as a tradition but as an innovation.

In their memories of collectivization many people claim that they participated partly because they thought it might work. Father Tui explained: "We saw it was their plan, to solve our difficulties. We had never tried it before. It looked like it would work. So we tried it. But it didn't work." Keng recalled; "The civil servants told us that if we worked together, we would have more to eat. So we tried it out. But it didn't work, so now they have given us the irrigation machines—another plan! Try again!" Collectivization is remembered as one of a series of government plans intended to increase rice production, although this was a plan that ultimately failed to achieve this goal. This apparent experimentalism hints at the desires that underwrite local engagements with the state, even in apparently coercive instances such as collectivization: these are the desires that the state will bring or can be prodded to provide the resources needed for personal transformations, such as wealth, education or health care.

Kaysone presented only a partial truth, the official story, the known knowns about collectivization. But, these have a force that is not simply that of ideology or lies. Known knowns have a convincingness of their own because they tell a certain truth. While it might have been widely known that many other, officially unknown elements were at play in the implementation and then failure of collectivization, that is no reason to altogether dismiss the official story. The dominant transcript had currency and effects, especially to the extent that it tapped into the rationalization of the state as a potential provider.

Coercion remains alongside this as a central motif in recollections of collectivization. One resident of Don Khiaw remembered:

> They were always telling us what to do, and we were so afraid. We are very close to Cambodia. People would come across from Cambodia: mother dead, father dead, children dead. We were afraid it would be the same in Laos.

Mother Kang suggested that fear was the main reason for adoption of collectivization:

> …nobody wanted to do it, they made us do it (*hay heet*), just like irrigated rice. The brothers and sisters (the LPRP) had us do it (*hay heet*), you could not refuse to do it. They had us be together, cooperate, be unified. But we were afraid. They said we should not cross our friends.

The rationalization of state as provider coexists with a sense of fear, so that in the reminiscences of participants, the two were often difficult to separate. The Village Chief during collectivization was Father Hian. He stated:

> In those days, the plan was to cooperate—*loong boeng* (try it out and see). But it didn't work. Now the plan is to get enough to eat. No one wanted to do it. We just did it to *thuea loong* (try one time). But there were no results, no benefits, so we threw it away. I was very afraid of the civil servants—I was afraid of dying. If you argued with the state you could die. I was afraid to complain or disagree. I was afraid to tell them we would not do cooperative rice farming. That was impossible. Of 200 people, could you be the only one not to participate? They came to teach us, from every department, to do collectives. More than ten days, raise our awareness. I was afraid of dying. But afterwards, when we didn't have enough to eat, I asked the government if we could stop, do rice *suaan tuaa* (individually) *phay heet phay man* (each to their own) like before, so that we would have enough to eat. So they let us work the fields like we do today.

This recollection of political change evidences an ambivalence: the state emerges as a source of possible nurture (in the form of more rice) and destruction. When Father Hian sought to de-collectivize, he sought to portray this political action as legitimate, not rebellious, by appealing to the virtue of the state as a wise leader, interested in the well-being of the populace in the face of rice shortages. Father Khong, the *cu* leader, likewise explained:

> It wasn't that the public servants let us stop. We just stopped. The harvest was poor, so we stopped. I wasn't afraid to stop. We tried collectivisation, but there was not enough to eat. My house had never been short of rice, but we were short that year. I was afraid of being hungry. I don't know why they made us to do it—it was orders from above. I followed the orders because I had never tried collectivisation before, and I was scared of them. I was the leader of the *cu*—how could I refuse to do it? If I didn't do it, I would be resisting them, resisting their thoughts.

These statements indicate that the shortage of rice is remembered as justifying and legitimating farmer-led policy change even in a context of extreme fear. Both these local leaders assert that they were too afraid to openly resist the scheme, but that the evidence of food shortage, the failure of an effort at state nurturance, legitimated their eventual relinquishment of the policy. Fear is not denied here: it is still mentioned. However, the relinquishment of collectivization is remembered as a legitimate act, not resistance.[8]

Conclusion

Recollections of collectivization reveal a fundamental ambivalence in understandings of what the state is and what it is capable of. The ambivalence is similar to that of eating, which can both give life and destroy it (Chapter Two). The state emerges in stories of collectivization both as a potential source of benefit and as a potential source of destruction.

In Chapter Two, I noted that the state is said to "eat with the people" in ways that breach reciprocal norms and are considered exploitative. Likewise, at the opening of this chapter, Mother Phong's stories of the Japanese rice, the story of the snatching of the rice and Cit's story of the missing Japanese school were offered as examples of such parasitic state behaviour. These stories also offered pragmatic instructions about dealing with the state: Cit used these stories to accurately predict the dismal outcome of the road to nowhere project, based on his assessment of the state and its projects as parasitic. These stories warned that the state immorally leaves people hungry and unnourished: as Mother Phong put it, "*Khao pen cao pen naay* (They are the princes/owners and the leaders). If they let us eat, we eat, if they don't, we don't." These stories also instruct listeners that the state is to be feared: it is known to be violent. In recollections of collectivization, it was repeatedly stated that opposing or refusing state demands was not an option: "we could not *not* do it". The state in these stories is a controller of resources—money, rice, taxes, development funds, and people themselves. There are seized, lied about, wasted, hidden, and hoarded. The state emerges much like the dog-father: rapacious, dangerous, and powerful.

Given the character traits of this perceived entity and its known past behaviours, many of its current actions are interpreted through the frame of corruption. Corruption is seen as the system itself, as part of the moral make-up of this reified entity, the Lao state. I do not wish to claim here that corruption is only a myth and not a reality in Laos. Corruption is one of the expectations of office now.[9] It is also the case that the central government is trying to distance itself from the image of corruption. A number of inter-national conventions, announcements and even public disciplinings have identified corruption as illegitimate.[10] Corruption has been identified by the centre as another battle it sees itself engaged in, another common enemy (like poverty) that state and society fight against, side by side, for the common good. Accusations of corruption have thus become something of a political weapon, and at the central level, such accusations are scandals that can bring projects into disrepute or ostracize personalities. So, corruption is far from an accepted "cultural norm" in Laos. In the stories of speculation and suspicion that form the mythology of the state in rural Laos, rather, corruption is another of its damning characteristics.

Given the strength of this distrustful orientation towards the reified state, it is all the more surprising that it still manages to capture desire. This is the everyday contradiction of petty politics in Laos. For all its shabby appearance as corrupt, violent and extractive, the state is still found at the centre of many —though not all—of the aspirations of rural residents. The people of Don Khiaw did not imagine a stateless future. What constituted the good life in their imaginary was importantly facilitated by a good state, one that would provide and nurture. When speaking about what they wanted for their chil-dren, people listed a good, state-sponsored education and an off-farm future, perhaps working for the state. When speaking of the desired future for the village, they spoke of joining the electricity grid, the road network and re-ceiving more generous development projects. When they migrated to improve their lives, it was overwhelmingly to places better connected to wider net-works of state and markets. It is not that the ideas of state and incorporation into wider structures were rejected, but that these simply have not been forthcoming in ways that match expectations so far. The state promises, but does not deliver. This was the rationality that underpinned their explanations of why they engaged with collectivization to begin with, and why they subse-quently stopped.

The state emerges as a reified, transcendental character from the stories of state that rural Lao share with one another and report in retrospective narratives, and this character is imbued with a particularly compelling kind of ambivalence. In telling the known knowns and the known unknowns, Don Khiaw residents are also communicating the unknown knowns: the shared political rationalities where the compelling valences are those of nurture and destruction, largesse and extraction, eating and being eaten. For all the apparent fear, then, there is always also this element of seduction. Part of the ongoing energetic engagement with the state was to denounce it and comment with passion on its deceit, its extractions, its non-provision of services. Another part of this engagement was to hold the actually existing state as illegitimate in relation to an image of what a legitimate state would look like. Just as the dog myth allowed for two kinds of power—destructive and nurturing—so too do these stories of state allow for two guises of power. The actually existing state extracts and oppresses (like the dog-man) and is denounced. However, the implicit contrast is with the hoped-for ideal state that would provide, nurture, and protect (like the mother). This ambivalence makes the state a particularly absorbing topic for impassioned—although often private—discussion. Despite the apparent loathing for the behaviour of this beast, the state remains the most common forum for political engagement. The state is reified as the repository of not only disillusion and distrust, but also hopes for a better future. It is from this perspective that the state can be understood as emerging from an intensely passionate, intimate engagement.

6

Resurrecting the State
"The will and desire of the people"

When the Village Chief, Siinuk died, there were rumours. There were rumours that he had stolen the money I had donated for the school project, and that the worry had put so much strain on his brain that he died bleeding from the nose. There were rumours, that, to the contrary, he had simply contracted TB and in his obstinacy had left it untreated, which caused him to die. There were rumours that he had embezzled the fees householders had paid for their Household Registration Census Booklets, and the debt was still owed by the village to the District for these in the months and years afterwards. There were rumours that some of the three million kip that had been paid from the Village Chief pension fund to his widow would be claimed back to cover this, but this was controversial. So, we spoke of Siinuk often after his death. In the rainy season of 2003, the rain did not come as expected in June and July and the rice seedlings struggled pitifully in the drought-stricken paddy fields. If the rain did not come soon, the seedlings could not be transplanted and the crops would fail. In desperation, Don Khiaw residents turned to the old irrigation pump. This pump had originally been part of a government-sponsored mechanized irrigation project, designed to let farmers raise at least two crops a year. However, the pump had fallen out of use and was sunk in the mud on the lee of the island. In July 2003, the men strained and worked in the heat of the day to lift it from the mud and clear the pipes that were choked with soil. They spent precious cash to obtain diesel so that they could start it, hoping against hope to get water to those seedlings. But the pump jumped to life, ran hot, spluttered out and would not start again.

There was speculation that Siinuk had haunted the pump. The irrigation pump, now abandoned, had arrived during his term in office. When he was alive he had spoken to me of his frustrations with this project. He had presented me with a terse, telling analysis of the project's faults: the inadequate technical training and maintenance, the debt that accrued to those villagers who had experimented with irrigated rice, and the subsequent frequent visits from bank staff seeking repayments, then the threats from the bank to seize people's fields, buffalo, even their bicycles. The dramas and disappointments surrounding this project had harried his term in office. It had haunted him. Now, I was told, he haunted it.

In the previous chapter I drew attention to the everyday reifications that are made of the state in Laos. I attempted to take these reifications at their word, as serious, indeed world-making, symbolic engagements with some of the most important forces my interlocutors had experienced. It would be easy to argue, now, that in fact these reifications do not hold up, that in reality state and society are impossible to distinguish, that after all the state is a human construction and thus only a part of the social relations that it seems to stand apart from. Some time ago, Abrams influentially wrote that, "The state is not the reality which stands behind the mask of political practice. It is itself the mask which prevents our seeing political practice as it is." He argued that therefore, "The task of the sociologist is to demystify; and in this context that means attending to the senses in which the state does not exist rather than those in which it does" (1988: 58). This influential essay sparked a trend for demystifying the state, taking off the mask to show the state as actually non-existent, exposing to us that the reifications are all in our heads.

Demystification might be the task of sociology, but it is not the task of anthropology. The anthropological approach that I follow is one that wilfully lets itself be "caught" by the meanings that are powerful for the people one encounters in the field. Jeanne Favret-Saada, a champion of this approach, suggested that the word "belief" itself is problematic as it implies already the analyst's disbelief: it is only things that we already disbelieve that we describe as "beliefs". This presents a methodological problem for the anthropologist: to adopt a dis-believing stance from the outset, and yet to try to participate and observe in the manner of classic ethnographic fieldwork, produces only a scoffing position in the fieldworker. The fieldworker can then only collect a series of disconnected facts and examples about the foolish credulity of the people she works with. The connecting thread between these disparate absurdities will elude her, because the only one she can grasp is the one she brought with her: her belief in them as "believers" and her faith that *they* "believe" while *we*, writer and reader, remain demystified. She cannot enter their stories, and she cannot take part in the series of events, because these will be linked together by interpretations that "catch"[1] people and produce their own, gripping, absorbing and sensical way of seeing things as they unfold (Favret-Saada 1980). To enter this, a "methodological relativism" is needed (Brown 2008). What relativism means in this context is not some kind of abstract philosophical or moral orientation, but a practical approach to the very real challenge presented by ethnographic fieldwork: if we are to enter as fully and as humanly as possible into other's lives in order to learn, how else can we do this than by allowing ourselves to be caught by the dramas, interpretations and dreams that catch them?

If stories of state are to be approached ethnographically, then, they must be allowed to catch us. It is from within mystified moments that we can start the process of taking people and their worlds seriously. In the previous chapter, I showed how stories construct the state as an entity in order to decry it. They endow the state with extraordinary powers—powers at times over life and death, the power to influence whether there will be rice to eat, or help delivered in a crisis. This entity is then condemned as illegitimate: the stories of state I described depicted it as dangerous, feared and exploitative. Yet I also suggested that the state is read as "intimate", in that it is associated with possible assistance and nurture. Is this not a contradiction? How can the state be both reified and intimate, associated with both exploitation and nurture? In this chapter, I will explore the tension between these through the concept of "extimacy"—the intimate incorporation of an external entity. This concept, drawn from psychoanalysis, provides a footing for a reformulation in broader terms of the anthropological insight that state formations, where they are found, often trace their beginnings to a mythological stranger-king and a moment of original violence. Conversely, states that trace their beginnings to such bloody origins are also often self-cast as utopian projects, promising prosperity and protection. I develop this theme by examining mechanized irrigation, a development programme that was at first experimented with, then rejected, then returned to by the residents of Don Khiaw. I use this series of events and interpretations to examine the desiring return to the state and its promises. States operate not only through a monopoly on force, but also through their utopian promises, the appeal of which persists and sometimes even becomes stronger the more they fail to be realized. I argue that the desiring return to such promises is much more than simply play-acting along with some dominant transcript or credulous enslavement to ideology. While it is true that the state is viewed with suspicion and fear, there is an extimacy with this feared entity.

Resurrecting irrigation

The irrigation programme had been abandoned for months by the time the attempt was made to resurrect the old pump during the drought. When I had first asked about the irrigation project, village residents had explained to me, very convincingly, why they had eventually deliberately found a way to avoid the national push for dry-season irrigated rice production. I had been struck by the conciliatory yet firm manner in which they said they had negotiated away from this state project without giving a hint of open opposition. The dry season directly preceding my fieldwork was the first dry season in which no irrigated rice at all had been cultivated on the island since the commencement of the scheme four years earlier. So, this was a very particular moment for them, and I had busied myself collecting the many conversations that circulated that year as locals were justifying this farmer-led policy reversal to themselves, to each other, to local agriculture officers, to the bank representatives that still came calling for previous years' debts, as well as to me.

The rationalization that they employed appealed to the practical over the political. Dry season irrigated rice just did not work, particularly in this area. There was no electricity on the island so all the pumps required the purchase of fuel as well as fertilizer. No investment was made in adequate canals: instead, dirt canals were dug with requisitioned village labour, so water was lost to seepage. Also, there were problems with maintenance of the pumps. This all meant that the pumps did not irrigate the fields as efficiently as hoped, and ended up using a lot of costly diesel. The costs of fertilizer, pesticides and diesel for the pump were initially covered by loans taken out with the Agricultural Promotion Bank at interest, adding an extra expense. Some farmers were even driven into debt when problems such as uneven water supply or pests damaged the crop, leaving farmers with no means to repay the original loans. Those who experimented with dry season rice production in the first three years found that it did not turn a profit that could compete with other activities, such as fishing, raising other crops or leaving to work on the coffee harvest in the highlands. For those households already sufficient in rice the question was one of profit: *naa saeng* (irrigated dry-season rice) was simply not competitive and was possibly costly.

For poorer householders, the problems with the project were even more profound. These farmers often had to factor in the additional costs of hiring land and buffalo, as they often did not own these themselves. They were also more prone to eat rather than sell their dry season rice crop. Poor householders are by local definition those whose wet-season crop is not sufficient to feed the household throughout the entire year. So, with *naa saeng* they began eating the dry season crop as it ripened, then had nothing to sell to pay back their debts, which were calculated in cash. They also told me that agriculture office workers and local leaders had put special pressure on the poorest farmers in the village to experiment with dry season cropping, because the irrigation programme was intended, after all, to reduce poverty and help the poorest of the poor. Thus, it was especially poorer householders who took part in the project, due to either (by their accounts) their fear of officials and leaders, or the desire to take advantage of development aid. It was then they, the poorest, who found themselves most indebted to the Agricultural Promotion Bank. This debt often came packaged along with blame. One Provincial employee (the deputy director of the Champasak Agriculture Office) said, exasperated:

> I think the government has been too kind. They gave the machines to the people for free. Do they do that in your country? Just give machines to farmers? No. But our government is very kind, so they gave machines to the people. Then they lent them money—for the diesel and the fertilizer. The village has still not paid them back. For Don Khiaw it has been four years now and they still haven't paid them back. What would happen in your country? If you owe money to the bank and you don't pay it back? They will come and repossess your house and your things. Maybe that's what they should do in Don Khiaw—I saw all the people have television sets. They sit and watch television comfortably. Maybe the government should come and take their televisions. The large diesel pump is like a bus—riding the bus is cheaper than driving your own car, because lots of people go together. This makes the price low, so the bus is efficient. But the people do not want to use the big machine, because they don't want to work together. They think only of themselves and their own house.

These comments reflect the collectivist assumptions that many officials hold about how poverty can be addressed in rural Laos, and the way this is linked to a language of failure, and then blame and retribution. Fortunately, other employees of the office were much more understanding of the difficulties faced by small farmers in attempting to undertake irrigated rice. Nonetheless, this official's viewpoint was far from rare, and indeed there *were* moves to record personal possessions, such as television sets, of those who remained indebted in Don Khiaw, with the idea that these might be collected in lieu.

As I enquired more about the irrigation project, I learnt that these lessons about the unsuitability of irrigation for the area and for the local economy had only emerged slowly, over time. At first there had been some scepticism but also some willingness to try it out, with a tentative hope that irrigation would at last deliver the long-held promises of prosperity through modernization.[2] I have argued elsewhere that the appeal of the irrigation project could be seen in local engagements with it, where the approach they took was "experimental". Both the irrigation office and farmers seemed to be feeling their way along under the pretext of the shared goals of poverty reduction and rural development. Of course, this apparent consensus on these laudable goals concealed many differences and difficulties which became apparent as the project wore on, not least of them the inappropriateness of the irrigation idea for the local environment, its unprofitability, and its inability to compete with other livelihood options (High 2013a).

Nevertheless, mechanized irrigation had strong backing from the central government, even after these difficulties became very apparent. The abandonment of the irrigation project in 2002–2003 was an act of some assertiveness for these marginal village residents as it required going against the will of officials and leaders. I recorded then how it was executed with subtlety, avoiding outright contestation. Locals, especially the poorest, needed courage to go against continuing pressure from bank officials and local leaders who sought the continuance of the project through—especially—the participation of the very poorest. I recorded and reflected that year on the way these marginal village residents manoeuvred to this political outcome despite their fear of the consequences of open political dissent. I described their adroit manoeuvrings as a political modality of "experimental consensus" (High, 2013a).

The large pump that lay abandoned on the side of the island stood as a symbol and reminder for me of this failed experiment. Writing more generally of the fascination that decaying modernist structures hold to the Western eye, Buck-Morss has noted "because these decaying structures no longer hold sway over the collective imagination, it is possible to recognize them as the illusory dream images they always were" (cited in Gordillo 2011a: 142). For me, the abandoned pump revealed all that had been hoped for, and had failed, in the irrigation project. Its rusting decay and clogged up conclusion was a reminder of what had happened to that ambitious, utopian modernist undertaking: the futility, waste and destruction. I will admit it—the pump imparted to me a sense of hopelessness and lost dreams.

However, the people on Don Khiaw, I was soon to realize, saw the abandoned pumps differently. What I witnessed only a couple of months further on suggested that they saw at least some seeds of hope in that abandoned edifice. After all these months of quietly assassinating the irrigation project, there now came this attempted resurrection. People were caught in the idea that the pump could be revived just in time to save the annual rice crop and ensure the core subsistence of the village. The abandoned pump, which Siinuk had assured me never worked efficiently anyway, was lifted from the mud by nothing more than the strength and commitment of a determined group of volunteers. This was not a response to official pressure, but to a local initiative. Beasley-Murray has noted that the surprising thing about ruins is not so much that they speak of ruination, but also (and perhaps more importantly) that they speak of persistence. Ruins are what remain even after failure, destruction or abandonment. They are "surplus, excessive, surprising evidence of what endures despite the odds" (2011: 160).[3] The abandoned pump was a ruin in this sense—a reminder of what had drawn people to irrigation in the first place. The group who gathered that day to lift the pump out of the mud were motivated by this revitalized hope. However, they met with no luck: the pump was useless, perhaps haunted.

Some days later, Bunmii, who was the only Party member in the village, and had been acting as Village Chief since Siinuk's death in the absence of a new appointment, called a village meeting. He sounded out the idea of requesting another large pump from the government. He asked the assembled residents "*Naa saeng* (dry season rice): do you want another motor?" I heard one man call out "*ao*" (want), confirming that he, at least, did. Laughing, Bunmii continued by, asking, "Just one person, or together?" The sole voice from the back of the meeting continued, "My rice is dead this year—I'm going to be short of rice." While Bunmii had specified that the pump would be requested under the title of "*naa saeng*" (meaning dry season rice, which policy demanded be cultivated and arranged by the cooperative "Water User's Groups") the voice at the back of the room was clearly interested not in these collectivist policies for the dry season but in his personal wet season crop that was currently under threat.

The idea that coalesced in the meeting was to use the government's known nation-wide commitment to investment in dry-season irrigation to gain just enough support to ensure the survival of this wet-season crop. During the meeting, other people eventually contributed to the discussion, and it was resolved to put in a request as a group for another large motor from the government. This decision won out over an alternative idea of requesting a series of seven-horsepower pumps given to individuals on loan contracts. Bunmii explained to the meeting that, to make this kind of joint application on behalf of the village, it would be necessary to pull together some information about land holdings and yields in the village, how severe the drought had been that year, how much land had already been transplanted, and how much could not be because of lack of rain. With this in hand, he would make an application (*sanoe*) to the District office to request a further pump.

After the meeting, I asked Bunmii why he was going through all of this, despite the failure of irrigated rice in the past, despite the way the irrigation project had haunted his predecessor, despite the debts incurred in the past because of irrigation and despite the way the previous irrigation project had caused so much anti-government disgruntlement. He explained: "*Cit cay yak day pasaason*" (it is the will and desire of the people). They see their crops destroyed, they want to do *naa saeng*, so they are asking the government to help."

I had by this stage been hearing the problems and flaws with *naa saeng* for months, and had been told flat out that "no one wanted to do it. They (*khao*, the civil servants) made us do it." Now I was told that *naa saeng* was "The will and desire of the people." The phrasing is similar to Kaysone's claim, in the previous chapter, that collectivization arose from some kind of autochthonous, traditional desire. Perhaps Bunmii was just giving me a short gloss, trying to explain a complex issue simply, for my benefit. Surely Bunmii's position as the only Party member of the village, and his long association with local government, must be taken into account: he had been heavily involved with the Youth Union when he was younger, leading to a post in the District office which he held for some time before returning to his natal village, and by Don Khiaw standards that made him particularly well-integrated into the state apparatus. He continued to be prominent in village-level state activities, especially those related to health: it was he who was custodian of the village buffalo medicine kit, and it was he who was later also the person-in-charge of the emergency anti-malarial medicines that were provided to the village in an aid programme. Bunmii was, compared to his neighbours, a state man. That said, Bunmii worked vigorously to avoid being posted in an on-going role as Village Chief, accepting only to take it on in the interim after Siinuk's death, while another man was sought. He explained that being Village Chief was too much work and he was not interested.

Villagers, such as Bunmii and many others, are called on to embody the state through the roles they play. While this has been interpreted by some as another piece of evidence that the line between state and society is only a misleading "effect" that must be seen through and demystified,[4] my approach is to take the way people play at the state seriously, as an extimate engagement.

Playing at the state

Within Don Khiaw, there are ample opportunities, indeed demands, that "the people" become functionaries of the state. Bunmii was an exceptional example of someone who had taken many of these. Most people will take on less than Bunmii but will at one time take on at least one of these roles. Don Khiaw, composed of only 66 households or just over 300 people (including about 60 schoolchildren), required the following roles to be filled: the Village Chief and two deputies, a secretary for the local Party cell, the heads of each of the village neighbourhood divisions (five in total), three representatives each for the Youth Union, Women's Union, and National Front representatives, village and neighbourhood members of the militia, the police, the tax collector, and the two school teachers. The *cat tang baan* (village organization), then, consisted of over 30 people at any one time. Since these posts were generally unpopular (I never met a person in Don Khiaw who *wanted* to be Village Chief for instance—one man even threatened to move away when the possibility was raised) these official roles tend to be circulated among the men of village aged between 25 and 50, although some roles are specific precisely in that they are not to be filled by such men (the Women's Union, for instance, demands female representatives, the Youth Union, younger men, the National Front, older men). Most village men and some women, then, are likely to have a taste of a variety of official roles throughout their lives. There are also a number of ceremonial roles, such as the chief layperson at the temple, the *ca* who addresses the local territory spirit (High 2006a) and the *luuk khii* (funeral specialist): these, too, were distributed typically among the men, although the ritual leaders tended to be older than those that took on strictly state roles.

Father Lot was elderly when I met him, and told me about the various roles he had played in the village, explaining:

> If they told me to do it, I'd do it. If there was work to do, I'd be the one to do it. *Heet nam phoen* (Do it with them, i.e. the state). The truth is, everyone in the village does something with "them" (*phoen*). There are lots of jobs. If you are not Village Chief, you are a police or soldier. And they change it often. I was Village Chief for two years, then they changed it, then I was Village Chief again. *Heet pen cang san* (it is done that way).

In addition, people without an official role such as these were often expected to attend village meetings: the norm was to send one adult from each household. In my records, meetings were held approximately monthly with attendance as high as 52 and as low as 23.

The Head of the Women's Union during my first fieldwork was a young, unmarried woman called Daw. When I interviewed her about her work with the union, she at first claimed not to be the head of the union, though others there quickly affirmed that she was. She then seemed not to make too much of it: "We don't do much," she replied diffidently, "it is just *wiak baan kaan muang* (village political work). At festivals we do the rice collection drives, cook food and count the gifts. I wait for the District to send orders." I asked her why she was doing it and she replied: "they arranged it that way. They assigned me."

Who?

"The village committee. Siinuk, you know, when he was still alive. The *muang* and those people. They arrange the Women's Union. Whatever they say we follow, whatever comes out we do, we do their work. It is not a lot of work, but only sometimes. If people from outside come here because they have work in the village, the Women's Union boils water for them, makes them food."

She imparted to me a sense that there was only a surface conformity with the requirement from the centre to have a Women's Union at all.[5] This was a recurring pattern in how people discussed their participation in the state in Don Khiaw: they conformed, they played their part, but they maintained a barely concealed oppositional mind-set at the same time. While on the one hand, it was necessary to enact these roles, boiling the water and collecting rice dues for festivals, in the case of the Women's Union, there was also the insistence that this was not really oneself—it was the will of another external agency acting through and in oneself. Thus, even when people "became" the state as they took on these numerous small official roles, they maintained the oppositional consciousness that I outlined in the previous chapter. The state remained "they" even when the self was taking part directly in its activities.

When I was collecting basic information on poverty reduction, asking people what the state did in the way of assisting people, Father Di told me that, before I came, he heard in a meeting that the policy of the government now was to have national sufficiency in food:

> But it isn't a reality because of a lack of funds. *Wao sue sue, tee patibat bo mii* (they just say that, but there is no action). Now they just *book* (tell) the Village Chief and have him *book* the people. You see Bunmii has been to a lot of meetings, received a lot of information. I don't know what to say, I don't know because the government, our government—you know—it's up to the Village Chief to know and to say. They *nam phaa* (guide) and we *patibat* (do it) their way. That's all.

There is an explicit split here where "they" direct and "the people" are expected to follow. The fact that the self is not subsumed by the reified state is confirmed by the self's capacity to lie. Indeed, the lies go both ways. For instance, the requirement for "*phantha*," conscription, was a major bone of contention in the village: the village balked at the idea of sending young men away for months or years on end to act as soldiers. Bunmii was acting as Village Chief at the time and reported afterward, quite openly, to the village meeting on how he had lied to officials in order to avoid it. He said that he had under-reported some (left out three men, the really young ones), exaggerated the family commitments of others (he claimed Laay already had a child with Khum, when in fact the couple were childless, and claimed others had old and frail parents), and reported that still others were busily engaged in higher education. This was met with approval and even some pride at the meeting—Bunmii, it was agreed, had done a good job representing the village. Lying, pretence and play-acting are key elements of how the state is enacted in daily village life, revealing not only the intimate, everyday presence of the state but also the way that, through such everyday engagements, it is externalized.

A politics of survival

Later, in August, Bunmii and Phet were on their way to a meeting in the temple called by Agricultural Promotion Bank officials aiming to collect on irrigation debts. Phet was one of the poorest residents in the village. She owed significant debts to the bank due to her past involvement with the project. "I've got nothing to give them," Phet explained to me. "I don't even have rice to eat each day." Bunmii, the acting Village Chief, listened to her lament then simply echoed her sentiment: *"Bo mii khao kin khu mue"* (no rice to eat each day). They were stopping by at Cit's house to collect him, as he would attend the meeting too, as he was acting as second deputy Village Chief that year, and in that capacity (only) was involved in the irrigated rice saga.

Cit was a relatively well-off villager, in that he was one of only three households on the island that had produced enough rice in the previous year to meet his own household's consumption needs (although not enough to sell, and his household was still extremely cash poor). He had not attempted irrigated rice, although he had been keenly following it. Since he was relatively well off, he had been spared much of the pressure from officials to adopt it right away, so he had been able to wait and observe how the poorer households went with it before committing himself. He asked, speculatively, of Phet, "Will they make you do *naa saeng* again?" The two discussed the possibility that the bank officials would force Phet to continue with irrigated rice so that she would have a possible income stream with which to pay her debts. Including me in the conversation, he said, "If you are poor you should not do irrigated rice in the first place, *bo mii bo heet* (if you have nothing, do nothing), isn't that so, Holly? If you already have nothing, you won't have any money to repay the debts."

The three of them discussed strategies for the meeting. What to do if the bank employees demanded repayments? What to do if the bank employees demanded that people take even more loans by encouraging yet more irrigated rice? Suuay, Cit's wife, offered advice to Phet: "Tell them '*khooy bo mii* (I have nothing.') Say 'I still have nothing to eat. I can't do *naa saeng* again. I can't repay you.' The government won't take the money from you then." Cit then expounded his own theory again, that poor people should not do *naa saeng* because they only get into debt. However, Phet objected to his interpretation this time: "but *phuu mii* (people who have, more well off people) got into debt also." Cit said that Phet did not do *naa saeng* correctly (*bo thuek*) so therefore she was not "*kum kin*" (she did not achieve rice sufficiency). Phet defended herself by saying, to the contrary, that irrigated rice was unsuccessful for a lot of people, and not just due to her lack of skills. The conversation had turned from a strategic one sharing tips on how to deflect state demands to one that showed the fractures within the village between rice-sufficient and rice-insufficient households: this year, sufficient in rice, Cit felt able to speculate liberally that it was a lack of skill or finesse in rice production that rendered other householders to fall short of rice production.

Phet, Cit, Bunmii and I headed to the temple where we gathered under the monk's house. There was a single bank representative there. Against my expectations, he had arrived on time. He was extremely civil and helpful, not only taking the time to explain things to me, but also working carefully and gently with the indebted farmers who attended the meeting. When we arrived, he was filling out a form for each indebted individual, which recorded the *cu* (group) in which an individual had borrowed, the years and seasons (wet or dry) that they took out loans, the debt accrued and repaid in each period, and also their *phapheet* ranking, either one, two or three, where one means they are well off, and three means they are poorly off. When this form was complete for each individual, he asked each to sign on the bottom left. After filling out the one for Phet in front of her, he said quietly, "If you do find any money, it is important that you pay the loan back…the loans are supposed to be only for six months. Our interest rate is low compared to other lenders—only 12 percent." He attempted to be gentle and persuasive, but there was a kind of abrupt exposure in his words as well. Individual loans, not only Phet's, were being discussed openly in front of all people present at the meeting, regardless of their involvement. This was very convenient for the visiting anthropologist, but I also felt awkward at this casual airing of Phet's personal affairs.

Cit and Father Di (the head of the village National Front) did not seem to feel so embarrassed and indeed actively participated in the conversation even though they themselves were not indebted. Seeing the total of Phet's debt, Cit weighed in to say: "Go to the bank and pay it, that would be really good." Cit continued to expound on his theory that one should not do dry-season irrigated rice unless one has one's own funds, as loans were too dangerous for the poor. He found wide agreement at the meeting: in this context it came across as an indirect criticism of the bank official's presence. This was a widely recognized flaw in the project and thus a challenge to the legitimacy of the project in the first place, so it could be interpreted as a way of defending the heavily indebted members from demands for repayments. However, it was also a critique of the decision-making process of people like Phet.

By the end of the meeting, only eight indebted households had shown up out of 25. The original call to the meeting stipulated clearly that there should be "no absences" but no one seemed very surprised that this order was not strictly followed. When a form had been filled for each of the indebted people there, the meeting turned to a discussion of these absences. The conversation was casual, more of a rumination than a report on the absentees. I heard that some were absent because they had left the village to move to a new, government funded "development village" to the west (described in High 2008). Another family had reportedly moved to Savanakhet. We were discussing where Deng might be when she arrived late. A teenager, she had inherited the debt from her parents who had died. She sat next to me, turned and whispered, "scary, isn't it?" Conversation then continued about other missing debtors. People seemed quite cooperative in offering information. Kong was apparently in another village for the day, the teachers were in school, teaching. "Where is Hia?" people laughed—no one knew.

I asked the civil servant about the bank's policy towards people who moved away: how will the debts be administered and collected, especially if borrowers move to a different district (and thus a different branch of the bank)? He explained that he would tell his supervisors about these relocations, but if even one family member remained in this village, he would collect the debt from that person. In policy the *cu* (group) are meant to guarantee loans, so if an individual or family moves away the remaining wider group should in theory be responsible for the loan. However, in practice this was not enforced and the loans are managed individually. He told me, as I already knew, that the bank had the right to seize assets. He explained: "the bank officials will talk to the person in debt and say—OK well in 15 or 25 days, we will come and get the money, or we will take whatever things you might have and sell it at market price." He said he has done this before. "That is why the *phaphet* "levels" are so important. *Phapheet* three have nothing to sell, so with them they have to find a plan to find money instead".

Phet was recognized as firmly in *phapheet* three. She ran out of her annual wet season rice in the 5th month that year and the previous year it had been in the 7th or 8th month. This year was a drought, so she feared she would harvest no rice at all. I walked home with her from the meeting, picking our way between the dry and cracking rice fields. I wanted to hear her speak more about irrigation. Curious about the role played by state functionaries, I asked "what did Siinuk do for you when he was *hua naa cu naa saeng* (leader of the irrigation group)?" She replied: "*bo day heet nyang, ao way kin* (He did nothing: he took it, kept it, ate it)." What about help from other quarters? I asked her; neighbours or family for instance? The bank loans say that borrowers are meant to act as a group. Despite the *cu* (group) organisation, she replied, all the irrigated rice work was done "*phay heet phay man* (working each on his or her own)" and "*khong phay khong man* (keeping one's own things for one's self)." People did not assist one another with the labour: when one person had done their own harvest, they were done. Phet seemed to want to convince me, at this moment, of how alone she was in her poverty, how unsupported she was, even by her neighbours.

"*Uk laay khooy* (I am very worried)." Phet said, "I'm so in debt, how will I find the money to repay them?" She explained that she had sent her 17 year old son to Thailand through the migration agents. She believed he was working in sea fishing, but he had been gone a month and she had still not heard any news from him. She hoped that he would send money home eventually, but the agents would take their 2,000 baht commission first, because she had been able to pay nothing to them up front. Speaking of her own plans for the coming year, she said that she had some wet rice fields inland—she had farmed there once before and got a good harvest that year, but then it flooded the next and she got nothing, so she abandoned them. She was reluctant to go back there—so remote and uncertain—so she would look again for fields to rent on Don Khiaw.

"Does your country have very poor people like this?" she asked. I replied that there are a small number of very poor people there. "Of course only a few" she says "because your country do not *heet naa* (grow wet rice). *Heet naa ko ued ko nyaark* (if you grow wet rice, you will experience shortages and be poor)."

The next day she planned to make and sell *khaopun* (a kind of noodle soup) to try to make money. The bank staff said they would come in a month's time to collect the debt. "What can I do to find that cash?" she asked rhetorically. She had made a couple of repayments, but she said the debt keeps "running up and up" with interest. One of her sons was at that time living in the temple in Nadii: she had sent him there so that he would have the chance to study grade five of primary school. Her other son and daughter were in first and third grade respectively here on Don Khiaw. "It is just me and my husband now, farming just the two of us."

Phetsamon, her daughter, led a game with the younger children outside my house. Two boys had long bamboo poles with wheels attached and a crossbar as handle. They ran from my sitting bench to another one further down the path. They had one passenger, Phetsamon, who wore a crumpled hat, green leaves as money, a broken bucket and banana leaf as a bag. She said to one, "I'm off *haa ngoen* (find money)." The boy ran her over to my bench. She paid him two leaves: one leaf is 4,000 kip she told him. He joyfully called "I made money!" (*khooy day ngoen!*). "What will you buy with it?" Phetsamon asked. "Sweets" replied the little boy. Phetsamon, then in third grade, had been transplanting rice for years by that time: I remember seeing her in the transplant the year before, mud head to toe and wearing a big old t-shirt worn knotted around her waist as a skirt. This year there was no water for the transplant, and the children played in the dust instead.

The extimate state

As it turned out, Bunmii's request for a further irrigation pump met no success that year, and despite this and many other village-level efforts to ease the crisis, many peoples' rice crops suffered terribly in the drought. The following year, all but four households fell into the category of "not enough rice to eat," indicating a dramatic increase over the previous years in the number of households locally considered to be poor. The drought that year, and the futility of the efforts to ask for aid in this crisis, and the way previous projects, such as irrigation, wound up landing the poor in debt and more desperate than ever, are just some examples of the "stealthy violence that consigns large numbers of people to lead short and limited lives" (Li 2009: 67). Pointing out that large numbers of people appear to be superfluous to the needs of the current economy (their land is needed, but the people are not), Li argues that what is needed is a positive politics of states that "make live" through support rather than "let die" through neglect. Hers is a positive valuation of the potential "biopolitics" of state interventions. The term "biopolitics" indicates the state's involvement in the intimacy of the bodily survival of the population, but it has often carried negative overtones of sinister-seeming state control of private functions. Li suggests a positive reading here instead in terms of the promise of bodily survival. Without it, "Who, then, would act to keep these people alive, and why should they act?" (Li 2009: 66).

The original irrigation project had been a clear example of what drives Lao rural residents away from state projects, and what has taught them caution and distrust in their dealings with it: the poor planning, inadequate maintenance, the coercion, pressure brought to bear on the very poorest, and the resulting debt. Put quite simply, the irrigation project claimed to help but ended up hurting, leaving many of the poorest worse off than they had been before. Yet, even in this case, the utopian promises of this state intervention, the hope that it might hold some possibility of relief during this drought, returned and led to its attempted resurrection. Desire for state intervention in the politics of survival flowed back in just as it had seemed at its lowest ebb. The desire expressed in the meeting that resolved to request *more* pumps was the desire for the state to assist in the maintenance of life, to exercise the biopower to make live when the core rice crop was under threat. As this desire flowed back, it tilted local politics away from disgruntled disengagement and disillusionment with the emptiness of aid back once again towards engagement based on a plea for assistance, a plea for the state to help directly by giving rural residents the tools they needed to grow the grain they associate so profoundly with life itself.

Where does this demand for the state come from, anthropologically speaking? Furthermore, in a context of such disillusionment, where the state is reified often only in order to be demolished as illegitimate, why is it then resurrected?

Li's positive reading of biopolitics provides us with a useful corrective to those views of state intervention which have focused on its limits and failings, and on coercion and violence: "A biopolitics of the population, when it succeeds in securing life and wellbeing, is surely worth having" (Li 2009: 66) she reaffirms. Certainly, the sense that the state in its guise as nurturer and protector of life is "worth having" is an ethnographic fact in Laos, but much more broadly, too.

Graeber has argued that anthropology provides a wealth of resources for thinking through this allure of states, of how it is that in a remarkable array of contexts states have come to be thought of as "worth having" even when they are associated with violence and exploitation. States are not universal in the human condition, but they are a particularly common formation, especially today. His reading of the ethnographic record of these suggests that states are always at least two things: a form of institutionalized raiding and a utopian project. How, and why, are they both these rather opposed things at the same time? If we could answer that, it might be clearer why biopolitics has come to have such ominous overtones, when the intentions seem—as Li points out—so important, even laudable. Examining the institutions of divine and sacred kingship in Africa, Graeber argues that sovereign states are internalized enemies. The logic of sovereignty is the logic of war—a war between rulers and the ruled. The violence captured by rulers is arbitrary, meaning that it is essentially meaningless. It occurs outside of and often in violation of existing norms. It is impossible to represent and through that very characteristic, it provokes attempts at representation. One of the common attempts to represent this power is to represent it as divine, not only destructive but also life-generating and enhancing. The identification with this divine force shared among a population becomes the basis for a joint political identity: "Their war with the sovereign becomes the ground of their being, and thus, paradoxically, the ground of a certain notion of perfection—even peace" (Graeber 2011: 55).

Likewise, anthropologist Marshall Sahlins has investigated why it is so common to find examples in the ethnographic literature of stranger-kings. The reason kings are so often mythologized as originally strangers, he argues, is the power associated with externality. An actual stranger or an element experienced as fundamentally foreign stands for all those forces that lie beyond our control and yet to which we are all ultimately subjected: the brute fact of death, the uncontrollability of the weather on which livelihoods often depend, the unsettling unknowability even of those people who are closest to us. Sahlins' argument is that this experience of alterity is also an experience of raw power. One way of capturing power and its productive potentials is to capture this strangeness, to make intimate that which is initially external.[6] The archetype of this is the marriage between a stranger-king and an autochthonous princess, but he argues that all marriages contain this element of the incorporation of external reproductive powers by making the strange familiar.

Sahlins originally traced out this pattern in the Pacific (1981), but he drew inspiration from the ethnography of Africa (Heusch 1982) and Europe (Dumezil 1988). Subsequent scholarship has shown how relevant this concept is for thinking through the indigenous politics of the Austronesians (see the collection edited by Caldwell and Henley 2008) and Sahlins has been pursuing the concept into Southeast Asia (2012, 2010, 2008). The pattern he identifies is certainly common in Laos. I have already mentioned in Chapter Three the example of the chronicles of the Kingdom of Champassak, which record that the realm was originally ruled by a queen in the 1600s. Queen Phao was the beautiful daughter of a commoner. The annals claimed that she became pregnant during an illicit affair with a visiting nobleman in 1638. Internal conflicts moved her to hand the throne over to a monk, but his vows prevented him from acting with sufficient authority to quell the strife. He in turn handed power over to a Prince descended from the kings of Vientiane (Archaimbault 1971: 2). This storyline makes little sense unless understood against the larger thematic in the political story telling of the region which repeatedly draws on a stranger-king motif: the stranger who manages to bring order to a disorderly, and often feminine, local realm. It is well known that the people now considered uplanders or ethnic minorities in Laos (formerly known as *khaa* or *Lao thoeng*) are widely said to have been the original inhabitants of the land, and myths tell of how they were "trick or cheated" out of their lands by incoming settlers who are now the dominant ethnic group (Sachchidanand 2005: 31). Myths tell of even older occupants of the land, the often-female water-spirits and nagas, who had been subdued through force or marriage by incoming settlers. Sahlins himself begins one of his expositions on the stranger-king with an example drawn from Angkor Wat. A Chinese traveller in the late 13th century reported that each night, before the king at Angkor could sleep with his own wives, he would need to mount a tower and mate with Soma, a naga spirit. The traveller reports that she was a snake with nine heads who would transform into a woman. She was the autochthonous owner of the kingdom, the very same naga who had been startled, overcome and married by the founder of the Khmer dynasty. If she failed to appear for the king, he would die (2008: 177).

There are many more regional examples of the stranger-king theme, and I will consider these and their implications in my conclusion. For now, I want to reflect on just one part of that much larger argument. Sahlin's point is that many things that we depend on are beyond our control, and this experience gives us the symbolic tools to think about power in terms of its foreignness but also its intimacy. He demonstrates that this understanding of power has been enshrined in the stories people have told, again and again and in many parts of the world, about where political authorities came from and how they embedded themselves locally. Sahlins suggests that if we submit such stories of state to historical testing (was there *really* a naga-queen?) we will miss the point. He writes of "a small industry in historical debunking, if not just pooh-poohing, on the part of western scholars—too often at the expense of ethno-logical understanding" (2008: 190). In this chapter, I have argued that the same could be said for the studies of the state which pooh-pooh, debunk and demystify the everyday reifications of the state that people make. In fact, the state is mystified and mystical because it taps into a larger cosmology of power. It is this cosmology that we must take seriously if we wish to engage with the state, ethnographically.

I withhold, however, from tagging the state in Don Khiaw a "stranger-king". While I admire the work Sahlins has done in drawing this pattern out of the ethnographic record and developing the concept, ultimately the struc-tural dynamic that Sahlins is interested in pushes beyond the stranger-king alone: the stranger-king is but one example of a much larger pattern which Sahlins himself calls "a more general condition of human political order" (2008: 179). I am wary of how his chosen term implies both masculinity and royalty in a structural dynamic that does not necessarily involve either. I pre-fer the more neutral term coined by Lacan of "extimacy" (*extimité*). Although Lacan did not fully develop the concept,[7] the term has been used to point to the general psychoanalytic insight that at the most intimate, the most interior, the most fundamental parts of the subject lies a kernel of strangeness. For Lacan, the unconscious was a continuous surface, like a Möebius strip or Klein bottle, meaning that the distinction between outside and inside did not apply: thus his aphorism that "the unconscious is on the surface." This was a rejection of the depth-psychology idea that the "true" self lay somewhere at the "core" waiting to be revealed through analysis. More than this, Lacan argued that the most intimate part of the self, the fundamental fantasy, actually remains profoundly inaccessible to the subject. This is what Freud called *das Ding* (the Thing), a foreign, traumatic element essential to the subject that cannot be symbolized. Although it is at the kernel of the subject, unique and essential to it, it is also utterly foreign. This is known through *l'extimité*—the intimacy of the originally external (Zizek 1986: 147).

Conclusion

The state in Laos can be thought of as extimate. It is reified as external and even dangerous and yet is intimately engaged with. Its very foreignness, its status as "they" (*phoen, khao*), an other, an outside force, its shadowy unknowability, its association with violence and rapaciousness, its arbitrary action, endows it with a kind of power that is truly extraordinary. The state can capture desire, perhaps even utopian fantasies about the improvements it promises to deliver, because it stands for this kind of raw power. The source of its terror and its reification is also the source of its attraction. In this way, this most external entity becomes the most intimate. It becomes not only an affair of "they" but a matter of "us," imagined as holding power in the most essential parts of being, in the spare politics of bodily survival. The reification of the state as a stranger is central to the perception of the kind of power it holds, and thus is part of its intimacy.

Perhaps Bunmii was obfuscating or simplifying for my sake when he characterized the request for another large pump as emerging from "the will and desire of the people." Even so, lies are telling. The lie he chose was revealing of something very true about state relations: the will (*cit cay*) and desire (*yaak day*) of the people, their most intimate aspirations, their struggles against poverty and their struggles to stay alive and maybe one day to prosper, these are at once most intimate and yet also engage them with that reified entity, the state. These are shaped by the possibilities and promises offered by the state, and they are an important part of what makes Lao rural residents keep coming back to the state despite their distrust of it. Here, the intimacy of the state has the intimacy of care. Care ceded by an external agent involves a particular kind of humility, humiliation and risk. Phet's loans were exposed in the meeting, open for examination, as were her skills and capacities and possessions. Understanding this extimacy might go some way to explaining why, in the south of Laos, the state is constantly resurrected despite the demolitions it is subjected to in everyday disgruntlement, distrust and suspicion. Even when demands for state largesse remaining often unfulfilled, and themselves become the source of disgruntlement, the fantasy remains, and is indeed intensified. The state haunts even those who reject it most forcibly—and this capacity for resurrection and return is one of the key characteristics of desire itself.

7

The Participatory Poverty Reduction Project

The first I heard of what I came to call "the road to nowhere" was when my neighbour, returning from a meeting one day, called out to me through the thin bamboo walls of the house I was renting: "The World Bank is coming tomorrow!" It was 3 May 2003, 11 months into my fieldwork. I was excited then at the news. At that time, the island had a run down, two-room dirt-floored school, no electricity and no running water. The closest market was over half an hour away by motorboat, but petrol was prohibitively expensive for most people. In the months that I had lived there, I had seen children die of malaria in their parents' arms, adults grow thin through the lean months when they had no rice to eat, and the persistent efforts at earning cash hindered by regulations and lack of services. So, I responded enthusiastically: "That is so good! I wonder what the village will get—maybe a school. Or rice?" My neighbour simply replied, *"bo laew"* (no already) and told me again about his experience with the Japanese school (Chapter Five). He was already predicting a similar outcome for this World Bank project.

Over the ensuing months, a joint World Bank and Government of Laos project called "The Poverty Reduction Fund" unfolded. The key idea of the project was that funds would be spent on sub-projects designed and executed by village residents themselves. The purpose was to decentralize decision making about poverty reduction to "the people". In practice this involved a lot of meetings, starting at the village level then working up to the District.

The so-called "road" that resulted in Don Khiaw from these meetings almost a year later was really only a strip of overturned soil indistinguishable from other footpaths already on the island: no money was spent on materials or equipment for serious road building. Instead, people's labour had been requisitioned: wages were promised, but when these were less than the amount expected by village residents, they stopped work and the "road" remained unfinished. During my fieldwork there were no cars, motorcycles or even carts on the island anyway: watercraft are the main form of transport in this region. The road, then, was unfinished, unused and almost invisible. However, residents remembered it with injustice. There was a drought that year and many households were short of rice. They had interpreted the road scheme as similar to "food-for-work" relief programmes, in which it was a routine requirement to labour in order to obtain disaster relief. They complained bitterly when the "wages" for work on the road did not meet their expectations for food aid during the drought, and the road became another vivid example for them of the corruption, extraction, and lack of assistance perceived as characteristic of the Lao state. However, in 2008 the PRF central office maintained that the sub-project in Don Khiaw was officially a success: it had been completed, they said, all funds had been allocated, and importantly the people had "participated" and demonstrated their "ownership" of the project. The road *as a road* did not eventuate, although by the conclusion of the project, this seemed at most a side issue to almost everyone involved.

I have written elsewhere about the question of the wages and corruption in this project, pursuing the question "where did the money go?" (High 2009). In this chapter, I return to the road to nowhere to tell a longer, more complex story about sustained political contestation. This project was subjected to wildly differing interpretations not only in the acrimonious conclusion over the wages, but throughout its execution. A close look at how this project unfolded shows how different actors understood, employed and manipulated the political terrain. I change gears textually here to a narrative style. As with any story worth telling, this one lends itself to many interpretations. However, I have described my interpretations as part of the narrative as these developed and changed throughout the events, and were indeed part of them. I will save my final conclusions for Chapter Nine. In its rawness this story provides an illustration of the political delirium I have been outlining in previous chapters —the fear, the disillusionment, the recriminations, but also the aspiration and fantasy that drive engagements again and again, the intimacies and extimacies with this loved and feared state.

4th May

The temple bell rang at 8am, calling the people to the meeting. The day was fresh and clear after a full night of rain. It was strange but pleasant to see bright green grass pushing through the darkened soil after all these months of dry white earth. At the temple there was, unusually, a table decorated with fake flowers. Four visiting officials gathered around it. One of them I recognized as Sasii Sampeng, the administrator responsible for Sub-District Eight, of which Don Khiaw was a part. The other three were new to me and each wore a white t-shirt emblazoned with the motto "poverty reduction is everybody's work". The three Don Khiaw Village Chiefs joined them.

Sasii commenced proceedings with a discussion of the national policy priority to reduce poverty and graduate from Least Developed Country status by 2020 because "the people" were the only ones who really knew about their lives, he noted, ultimately it would be they who would identify the problems of poverty and manage solutions to them. The project starting today would collect information from the people about their problems and the possible solutions.

Then, one of the men wearing a white t-shirt was introduced: Sisanuk, an employee of the Poverty Reduction Fund. He marked himself as a dynamic speaker by moving out from behind the table and presenting while standing in the middle of the circle of people seated on the ground, speaking to all of the parts of the assembly. He had materials: jumbo-sized sheets of paper stuck on a board, markers, and a laminated flipbook of pictures. The purpose today, he said, was to identify suitable sub-projects. To be suitable, projects needed to be grassroots, small-scale, jointly enacted, jointly managed, and to yield joint benefits. Any proposal must be within the capacity of the village to execute itself, there must be participation from the people (this would create "ownership"), and everyone in the village must share in the results.

He raised his flipbook. The emblem on the cover was a circle: yellow on the top to represent poverty and green on the bottom to represent wealth. The middle was blue, representing the peace and stability needed for development. A man and a woman were pictured carrying agricultural produce, representing work. The woman, he observed, was carrying less than the man to symbolize the reduction of women's heavy labour. Below them, a boy and a girl in school uniform were depicted reading a book to symbolize the importance of education. The first page pictured a group of people sitting under a tree, all raising one arm each. This, he said, was a village meeting. He flipped through many more pictures, stopping when he got to one of some men and women digging. He said that this were people working together. He then showed a picture of some men and women looking at a noticeboard. This, he said, represented the transparency that would be an important part of the project. Holding up a picture of a bridge with a tollway, he said that the people should try to collect users fees for any projects they undertake, to cover costs of repair and maintenance, as these will be the responsibility of the village. He held aloft an A4 sheet of paper with a circular diagram:

Background of the PRF

Among other innovative efforts, the Lao Government has established the Poverty Reduction Fund by the Prime Minister's Decree PM/073 on May 31 2002 in order to support one of the primary goals of the national socio-economic development plan and policy to eradicate poverty in the country and to quit the status of a Least Developed Country by the year 2020.

The PRF will deliver development resources at the village level targeted at the poorest districts in the country, and mediated through strong participatory and decentralized decision-making processes.

The objectives of the PRF

The main objectives of the Fund are as follows:

- build capacity and empower poor villages in poor districts to plan, manage and implement their own public investments in a decentralized and transparent manner;
- strengthen local institutions to support participatory decision-making and conflict resolution processes at the village, *khet*, and district levels, involving a broad range of villagers, including women, the poor and ethnic minorities.
- assist villagers to develop community infrastructure and gain improved access to services;

The principles of the PRF

The PRF Project has 7 very important principles :

1. *Simplicity* : Methods and techniques used in the sub-projects should be simple. The villagers should able to do things themselves and to maintain everything, according to the needs and potentials of the villagers.

2. *Village choice* : Many things/different kinds of sub-projects are possible, but some are prohibited.

3. *Participation* : Villagers should make decisions together and cooperate with each other to implement the sub-project. Villagers can make contributions of local materials, labour, etc., if they are able to do so, and they

should be willingly work with the PRF Project.

4. *Ownership* : The people will plan, implement, manage and maintain the sub-project.

5. *Transparency and accountability* - Among other things, regular meetings, will be held and an information board will be used to publish information about the project, so that the people can follow what is going on and avoid corruption in the project.

6. *Wise investment* : Allocate funds properly for real needs. Make sure that poor villagers benefit from the project, and that the outputs of the project are sustainable.

7. *Empathy* : Siding with the poor and disadvantaged. The poorest people in the village should get help.

Figure 9. PRF promotional pamphlet circulated in 2003.

I recognized it instantly as a "project cycle" complete with planning, action, review, stages, leading back to the planning stage again, although I wondered what the people of Don Khiaw would make of it. In the "review" corner were two very dull looking Western men sitting at a desk—the symbol of the World Bank, Sisanuk explained, and their right to scrutinize projects. He told the people that the government of Laos had become indebted to the World Bank to support this project, and had done so because it wanted to help the people ease poverty.

He then listed more rules about what was not allowed as a sub-project: diesel pumps or electricity generators, dangerous or poisonous projects, and buying or renting land were barred. He stressed again that the project would only pay for schemes that have widespread community support and benefit everyone. Among all these restrictions, the example he came up with again and again in attempting to explain what would be "suitable" was the village school.

He stopped and asked for questions. Schoolteacher Thong wanted to know if the money was available only to groups or to individuals as well, perhaps as private loans or microcredit. Sisanuk replied that the money could only be used for the village as a whole on community projects, not for private loans. He used the example of the school again, saying that if the school is nice, the children will want to study, and they will be able to get good jobs.

Schoolteacher Thong responded: "our village has had a school now for many years, and still the people are poor. I don't see how more work on the school will fix poverty." Sisanuk replied that this was the kind of thing to be discussed in smaller groups.

The next question was from Mii. He wanted to know if the money would be incurred as a debt to the village. The concern—widespread—was that like the irrigation project, this attempt to "help" the poor would end up leaving them in debt. Sisanuk explained that the village would not have to repay any funds provided under this scheme.

Sisanuk turned to the women: "the women are very quiet—do you have any questions? Do you understand? Why don't you speak up?"

"Because they can't," replied Grandmother Bunnaa. She was one of the oldest women in the village, well into her eighties, and also one of the most talkative people I have ever met.

"What?" he asked, taken aback by her characteristic forthrightness.

"They can't. They don't know. If you want to do it the women will do it with you. That's how it is."

"We have to have women's participation. Women are very important."

"Of course women are important. You can't do anything without women. If it was just men nothing would get done. Nothing would be possible. There wouldn't even be any people."

There was laughter at Grandmother Bunnaa's rejoinder, then the men left for other parts of the temple grounds, while the women formed one discussion group remaining in the temple hall.

"What are we doing?" Grandmother Bunnaa asked.

"We're going to talk together" Sisanuk replied.

"Who will talk? None of us will say anything. We don't know. Tell us and we'll do it. Whatever they want to do, I'll go along." The women giggled their agreement. "Who will speak?" Grandmother Bunnaa asked them, but no one replied.

Sisanuk asked, "Where are the Women's Union leaders?" Daw and Viaw were at that moment fulfilling their Women's Union duties by preparing the food for the visiting officials, so they were unable to come to the actual meeting. I saw Maew and Peng, also members of the union, but they did not identify themselves to Sisanuk. Maew shrank behind a column.

Grandmother Bunnaa asked again, "What are we doing?"

"We want to know what problems there are in the village, what can be fixed in the village," Sisanuk explained, again.

"The school!" exclaimed Grandmother Bunnaa, "It's in a terrible state. It's falling apart. The people are too poor to fix it. Oh, we are so poor ... help us ... go on! Help us! *Sooy nae* ..." she leant forward, pulling that last syllable out in a crone-like drone and fixing him with a beady eyed stare. The women around her laughed. Sisanuk seemed to change the topic. He asked how the temple hall was built, particularly where those massive columns that held up the temple roof aloft came from. Grandmother Bunnaa told him that people did it together: a great mass of people joined together and went to the forest to cut the trees, carted them here, and raised the columns together. He then told her again to ask the other women what they think the problems are and how they can reduce poverty. He then left to look at the men's discussion groups.

The women asked me for ideas. I replied that I did not have any. Grandmother Bunnaa said, "we could raise chickens and ducks." Grandmother Nyot had an idea: weaving. They could purchase some looms, and the older women could teach the younger ones. Many women picked up the idea, chipping in to say that they could weave, even though they had not for years now. There was excitement in the air. Sisanuk and the other officials had withdrawn, but two of the Village Chiefs, Bunmii and Kong were observing. Bunmii handed Peng a pad and pen and asked her to write down the women's three ideas.

"But I can't write!" protested Peng. She moved to sit next to Duk, who was very enthusiastic about the weaving, handing her the pen and paper. Duk asked, "what do you have to write?"

"You have to write the things you like, what you want to do," explained Peng.

"Weaving" said Duk with certainty. The idea was echoed from several women, but most were not listening at this point: most were resting or chatting. There was just a small hub around the pen and paper. I joined them and found the list complete:

1. Weaving
2. School
3. Road

Sisanuk came back and read it. "Have you ever done weaving before?" he asked. Most women were silent, but a few affirmative answers were offered tentatively. "But have you ever done it to sell?" No one replied. "It's completely different, weaving for market. You have to have knowledge of the market. You have to know how to sell. You don't have the knowledge for this. Suppose everyone does weaving—who will buy it? You don't know about weaving for the market."

Duk spoke into the disappointed silence: "we could raise animals."

"You don't know how to. Do you have special knowledge about animals? About all the diseases they could get? How to make them healthy and strong? Have you ever raised animals before? How will you get the information you need? You can't study because you don't know how to read."

"You want us to do the whole thing again then?" Duk asked, bravely I thought.

"Yes. Do it again."

Sisanuk walked off. Duk refused to write anymore. She asked me to be the scribe and told me to write:

1. School
2. Latrine
3. Well

Sisanuk came back and took the sheet from my hand: "A latrine? The project has to benefit everyone. Will you build a latrine so big that the whole island can use it?"

"No." It was Duk who replied again.

"Well it has to be for the whole village."

"What if the latrine was in the school?"

"That would be OK."

Duk told me to add the phrase "in the school" after "latrine" and after "well". Sisanuk came and took the paper again.

"Is that right?" Duk asked.

"Yes, it is correct." Sisanuk accepted the list.

The gong in the temple was struck and the men's groups returned to the hall. The women's and men's lists were written in small letters in the top left-hand corner of the jumbo paper. I walked over so that I could read it, and found that the men's list was almost identical to the women's:

1. School
2. Road
3. Latrine in school

It took very little discussion to merge the lists. The final village priority list for Don Khiaw was:

1. School
2. Road
3. Well in school
4. Latrine in school

The final step was to choose the "village representatives" from Don Khiaw. In an effort to circumvent perceived entrenched hierarchies, the Poverty Reduction Fund required that each village be represented in its meetings not by the Village Chiefs, as is usual, but by elected representatives. These were selected quickly—the two women representatives were Daw and Viaw, of the Women's Union, who were not present because they were preparing food for the visiting officials. The two men selected were both businessmen and among the most wealthy householders in the village: Dee ran the cargo boat to and from Pakse and Nyueang was a money lender and rice trader.

Sisanuk closed the meeting with a comment about the importance of village-wide agreement: the ability to reach an agreement is essential. Finally, he observed: "Education is important, isn't it? You all chose to promote education." Daw and Viaw arrived with the food they had been preparing, and the officials sat down for a joint meal with local leaders.

5th May

The following day, my neighbour Khum dropped in to visit as I was washing my clothes. "Did you understand the meeting yesterday?" she asked.

"Most of it," I said, thinking she was asking if my language skills had kept pace.

"I didn't," she said. "I did not understand them. They talked a lot but I didn't understand. They are going to build a school, right?" I replied that I did not know. We sat for a while speculating about what the priority list had meant. Khum was already suspicious.

I called on a few key figures that day to gauge their reactions. Mii explained that in the men's discussion group, several men had put forward their own small business plans: some wanted to set up as carpenters, others in handicraft production, others wanted to plant an orchard. However, he said "they" (meaning the officials) "said the project had to be something done all together. They only let us say 'school' or 'road'. They said that people's ideas were *suan tua* (individual) or household initiatives, but the project required *suan huam* (collective) ideas." His own preference was that whatever money there was in the Fund should be split between householders on the basis of wealth. Each could then pursue their own business ideas, perhaps with guidance and support from development workers.

When I called on Duk (the woman who had spoken up so bravely in the village meeting on behalf of the women) she seemed dispirited: "I thought the project was to help poor people—to see which families were really in poverty and help them specifically to find money or work. But they didn't let us. They made us do the school. They didn't let us do anything individually or as a household."

My neighbour Cit was strongly against the idea of building a school because he said it contradicted the project's claim of addressing poverty. He said:

> Take Bii's son (Bii had recently died). Maybe he will be able to study for one
> more year, but I think that he will probably have to stop. He has to look

after his mother and his little brothers and sisters. He has to farm and find food and money. Who will promote his education? No one. He will not be able to study no matter what the school is like. If we build a nice school, it still doesn't change the situation that some children have parents who can help them, and some don't. I think building the school will only help the five richest families in the village—and they are not in poverty anyway.

What we need to do is find a way that each house can benefit. The thing is that they want us to do everything together, as a village. But it is hard to think of something for the whole village that is useful, so we just said the school and left it at that. The best thing would be to divide the money up and give a section to each household. But the government doesn't want to give money to families or households. They are scared that we would just take and waste it. I think that we should take the money and invest it in a bank with high interest rates, or invest it in a business. The interest or profits could pay for things like repairs on the school, or roads, or we could just divide it between each household each year—even a little bit would help. Or we could take the money and make it into scholarships for 50 children—one child from each household could be supported to study all the way through primary school. Perhaps even overseas. That way you can be sure that each household gets some benefit and it would solve poverty too, because the children would be able to find good jobs and send money home.

The problem is that in our country, you cannot say that there is a problem because in our country, there is only one Party. If you complain or speak up too much, ohh, it's dangerous. It's against the law. The people don't want any trouble, so they go along with what the government says.

7th May

I arrived flustered and afraid that the village representatives had left for the Poverty Reduction Fund Sub-District meeting without me. The previous day I had heard that the village representatives from this and the other villages in the local Sub-District were to meet for the next round of meetings. I had made arrangements with Dee, one of the representatives, to accompany him to the meeting but when I arrived at his house I learnt that he had gone with his cargo boat to Pakse instead. I then had to walk hurried and hot down the long hook of the island to the Village Chief's house. Bunmii did not look too pleased to see me. I offered pleasantries but he only grunted in response while he changed into his long pants, belt, and white button up shirt: his meeting clothes. His sister, Viang the mad, finished her breakfast and came outside to wash her face. Her mother called out after her asking what she planned to do that day and she replied, "watch the men make fireworks." I caught her eye and asked, "Do you ever make fireworks?"

"No," she said.

"Why is it that women never make fireworks?" I asked, tossing around for a conversation.

"I'm going to take a shit," she replied, heading off to the trees.

Her mother came out, asking politely, "What did you have for breakfast?"

"Banana," I replied.

"Bananas!" she seized on the topic. "It is so hard to find them these days." I had two in my bag and I offered them to her. "Fantastic," she said. "I will feed my bird!" The household kept a parakeet that has been trained to say *"pay thay"* (gone to Thailand). "I went yesterday to find some, but I couldn't find any …" the mother continued discussing bananas as she moved out of earshot.

Daw, one of the female representatives, arrived looking pretty and fresh in a crisp pale blue shirt and an austere, mainly black, business-like *sin*. Bunmii, Daw and I headed off by boat, picking up Nyueang further south. He, too, was looking dapper with slicked combed hair, shirt and trousers. We headed to a neighbouring island. Pulling up at one village, we were surprised to be hailed by Cit, my neighbour. He told us we had come to the wrong village: there was no meeting here. This village was instead hosting a wedding. All last night I had heard the sound system blaring loud music across the river: a soundtrack to my insomnia. It had stopped five minutes after my alarm went off in the morning. Now I learnt the music was coming from the bride's home. There were few ribald jokes about the young couple and the kinds of meetings they might be having, and we moved off again, heading south on the river.

We found the Sub-District meeting at the temple of the next village we tried. We were late, but not the last to arrive. Attendees were given 10,000 kip (1 USD) each on arrival as payment for their time, and petrol costs were covered as well. I recognized most of the officials this time: Sisanuk, Bunloet from the District fund office, and Sasii Sampeng the District advisor to this Sub-District. The priority lists from all the villages in the Sub-District had been posted on a board in the temple hall. There were requests for noodle making equipment, ploughing machines, a health centre, solar electricity, and horticulture training, but by far the most common projects listed across all the villages were schools and roads.

The officials explained that the purpose of the meeting was to choose six projects from among all of these ideas put forward, and prioritize these. First, though, the meeting had to choose from among the assembled representatives four people who would act as Sub-District representatives at the District meeting: two women and two men. The officials wrote the names of the six nominees on the board. The board was then rotated so that the body of the meeting could not see them. People were asked to walk around to that side of the board and make a mark next to a name to indicate their vote. The officials were seated where they could (and did) watch each vote. Sisanuk even made a note in his exercise book with each one. The first male and the first female on the official nomination list each won by a landslide. The winning two men were bought out the front for applause, and their female counterparts—at the insistence of the officials—reluctantly emerged from the audience too, crouching, too modest to even stand up, their faces cringing.

The officials seemed buoyed by this completed task, and said that there was just one item of business left: to choose the project priorities. Unfortunately, this Sub-District had eight villages and 24 sub-project ideas, but the meeting needed to select just six priorities from these to send on to the next meeting. Sisanuk advised, "You must agree and reach consensus. Talk together to see what the real needs and problems are. You have to work together to choose." The officials at first stood directing the meeting with the men sitting at their feet responding, and the women some way behind mostly silent. The party from Don Khiaw were all silent. The only person who championed the idea of a school in Don Khiaw was Sisanuk. He drew up a priority list on the chalkboard, which included four roads projects, and a school for another small village and a school for Don Khiaw. He asked, "do you agree?" Most of the men at his feet did not. One man from a large village suggested just building roads, no schools. He pointed out that the other villagers had built their own schools, why couldn't these two? Roads may well reduce poverty whereas schools have certainly failed to do so. Such dissenting voices grew louder, and the meeting became acrimonious. The officials withdrew outside accompanied by about half the women. In their absence, the Village Chief of the large village grew even more outspoken. The group from Don Khiaw remained utterly silent.

The officials came back in, and the meeting became quieter. Sasii Sampeng made an apologetic speech offering to seek an extra sub-project or two for this Sub-District. He reminded them that there would be more opportunities next year and that the selection criteria should be need, not greed: Don Khiaw and the other small village really needed schools.

Sisanuk suggested combining some of the different road projects into one large road project. He sat down near the Chief of the largest village and some of the other more outspoken men. They formed a circle of quiet but intense discussion. Sasii joined them. The conversation was earnest and then smiling. Heads nodded. Sisanuk rose to write a new list on the board. The schools were still on the list as the last two priorities, but the road projects were coordinated into one continuous road linking several villages on one of the larger islands. There was applause when the "consensus" was announced. People seemed relieved to go. The officials closed the meeting without saying when they would be back so on my way out I asked about the next stage of the process, but I could not get any answers. By the time I had finished asking these brief questions, my Don Khiaw friends had already fled. I caught up to them waiting in the boat, impatient to be gone. They hoped to make it to the wedding, while I hoped to take a rest.

Later, when I was resting under Suay's house I told her husband Cit about the meeting. I had donated some money towards building the school and I told him that now, since the officials seem so dead set on building the school in Don Khiaw, it would be best if we kept my donation separate to use for school books or uniforms, and let the Poverty Reduction Fund shoulder the responsibility for the construction. He responded vehemently: "No, we will build the school ourselves. We can't wait for them. Did they say when they would do it? Will they do it? We can't know. No. It is best that we take your money and build it ourselves. We'll do it all ourselves."

Nyueang, who had also been at the meeting representing Don Khiaw, walked past, returning from the wedding. Suay called jokingly: "Come and sit down Mr Head of the Fund. Show us the money. Where are the millions of dollars they have promised us? Show us!" Nyueang laughed, joining us; "there's no money, just talk. All the talk you could want." Nyueang, like Cit, did not believe that the meeting meant a school would be built. He pointed out that the officials left without saying when they would be back or when the projects would go ahead. None of the projects were discussed in any detail: they said "build a road", but not how long it would be, "build a school", but not what type of materials or how many rooms. Not even a vague budget had been offered. His simmering distrust was evident. He added that the representatives from the other villages had been very heavy handed campaigning against Don Khiaw: he said it was only because of my presence that the school project had been prioritized at all. Finally, he added that he felt the officials had not wanted me there. He pointed out that originally we were told to meet on the 8th, but a subsequent message was sent to the committee to shift this to the 7th. Nyueang, Mother Phong, Suay and Cit agreed that the officials had been trying to manoeuvre so that I would miss the meeting.

"But why?" I asked, surprised. The officials had always been friendly and cooperative in my interactions with them.

"Because they are going to do wrong, to poison (*phit*) the project," said Nyueang. The others helped to explain: because I do research, I go to the District and Province and Vientiane and ask questions, I read documents and I ask about things like projects and policies. "Suppose," said Suay, "the international donor has said it will provide a certain amount per project, and our project receives less. Where has the money gone? The officials don't want anyone asking such questions."

Nyueang was soberingly serious. He warned me that the officials were trying to control and manipulate me. He asked me not to mention this to them, especially to Mr Bunloet, who had been more friendly to me than almost any other official. I promised not to. He offered to explain things to me, one day when I had time. "You saw us," said Nyueang, "I am too scared to speak to officials. They frighten me. I wasn't bold enough to speak."

Mother Phong added that when the District asks for fees and levies, the village can usually only pay some of it. The officials then think poorly of the village, so the leaders of the village were shy and circumspect with the officials. They were not bold enough to push for the village's advantage. I told Nyueang that I would go to Muang Mounlapamok in a few days time any-way, so while I was there I would try to find out more about the project. He approved, and commented that, after all, I was able to research into facts in a way the people of Don Khiaw simply could not. Mother Phong and Nyueang came to the earnestly held conclusion that from now on, any action on the Poverty Reduction Fund must include me. They said that while I was here, the officials would be too afraid to disadvantage Don Khiaw. They would have to act honestly, and do the project in a timely manner, because I would be watching.

Nyueang left saying on his way out that he would cooperate with Father Di to find where my donation to the school had gone (at that time we thought it might have been embezzled by Bii before he died). He echoed Cit's earlier strong determination for us to carry on alone on the school building project, to find the money in the village, and manage it ourselves because he doubted that the government would ever help.

19th May

I tried to catch the cargo boat to the District capital, but it chugged its way north without stopping, apparently not noticing my attempts to hail it. I was due to give my monthly report to the District Education Office, though, so I convinced my neighbour to take me by boat south to Muang Seen, the market town. From there I caught a Russian truck that had been converted into a bus by hammering on some boards for seats. These were now falling off. Everything was falling off that bus. I arrived at the District capital with parts of the bus in my hair. Once there, I found that I could not get a room in the government guesthouse as I usually did. All the rooms were full, I learnt, because the Poverty Reduction Fund District consultative meeting was about to take place.

After my report at the Education Office I left my things with a friend who lived in the government boarding house. I was surprised to find an

English man sitting in the familiar old hammock by her house. He was employed by the Poverty Reduction Fund in Vientiane. After these weeks of fruitless speculation in Don Khiaw I had the sudden luxury of a friendly and informative English-speaking authority. He, for instance, was able to tell me that the District budget for the PRF (which no one on Don Khiaw had been able ascertain) was 68,000 USD, based on the calculation of 5 USD per "poor" person. The definition of "poor" was based on a set of criteria provided by the Lao government, namely, village access to health care, water supply, education and road plus an assessment of income. This was a pilot of a larger planned national rollout of the programme, I heard. This, the first District consultative meeting ever attempted by the project in Laos, was to select a list of top priority projects from among all of those put forward by the various Sub-Districts in the District. The top project would be funded, moving through the priority list until all the funds had been allocated. He emphasized that the choice of project priorities would be up to the representatives from the Sub-Districts. They could choose "anything they want" he said.

For the remainder of the day, I sought out Lao PRF workers and asked them to help me understand the project. Usefully, one project worker was able to explain some of the interesting translation choices I had observed between the English and Lao versions of project documents. When the English documents stated "community", for instance, the Lao documents stated "*saaw baan*" (villagers). He explained that he thought there was no direct translation for community, and his best approximation for it in Lao was "people in the area." As shorthand, he used "villager" in its place. Likewise, there was apparently no easy translation for "participation". The term used instead was "*khwaam suan huam*" (togetherness, the common good). This overlaps somewhat with the English term "participation" but to my mind carried a lot of additional collectivist ideals with it. The small District capital was alive with the bustle of so many new officials. I found a room to share with a friend and settled in, resolving to stay to witness the long-awaited District PRF meeting.

20th May

I was supposed to meet the District PRF head at 11am for an interview, but he was not in his office when I arrived. I took a walk through the government guesthouse and found him and many other PRF workers gathered in a preparatory meeting for the District meeting the next day. I asked to observe, and they agreed. The PRF workers were seated around a long dining table under two slow moving overhead fans. Bret, the English PRF consultant I had met the day before, sat opposite his translator.

Bret stressed that the 68,000 USD allocated for this district was entirely in the people's hands. However, sub-projects would be assessed for success on two criteria: "Has it helped the poor?" and "Did they absorb all the money?" He noted that if a sub-project did not spend its entire budget, then "obviously" this would impact on its eligibility in the next accounting year.

Bret stressed that the budget was very limited. Not every village would be funded this year. From 68,000 USD, perhaps one school and two dispensaries could be completed in the District. As he spoke, the examples he used to illustrate were always government services such as a school, health service, or road. Bret introduced the selection criteria that were to be used to choose the sub-project: he stressed that these were "only a suggestion" designed in order to "to help them choose", "not imposed—the final choice is their choice." Yet I knew that the project guidelines were more than suggestions—I had seen in Don Khiaw how the selection criteria had already directly reduced the potential project proposals to a handful of ideas: school, road, latrine in school.

Perhaps influenced by Nyueang's simmering distrust, I perceived an emerging pattern of non-provision: First, the definition of "poverty" used by the project, where four of the five criteria were government services, meant that the existing lack of government services was rewritten as "poverty" rather than simply poor governance. Then people demanding these services were rewritten as poor people begging for help rather than citizens demanding their due. The next step was that the delivery of this "help" was offered as a form of charity where the poor had to prove themselves worthy poor. The final absurdity was that the criteria for proving themselves worthy and obtaining funding again was by providing their own government services. I wrote in my fieldnotes that day that it was an incredibly inefficient way of providing services. A prodigious amount of hours had already been consumed in meetings, from the village to District level, which seemed excessive given the prospect of "maybe one school and two dispensaries". These meetings, I was starting to suspect, were not about easing poverty and they were not even about providing government services. These were an elaborate statement in how, by and large, services were *not* going to be provided. At the meetings, rural residents were asked to participate in this non-provision and indeed were held responsible for it.

While my mind ran along this track, the planning meeting continued. Bret was explaining what it meant to help the poorest of the poor. He gave the example of two competing proposals: a water supply and a community hall. The water supply, he explained, would more immediately help the poorest of the poor, so it should be preferred ("preferred by whom?" I wondered, privately, "I thought it was meant to be the people's choice?"). What was needed in a sub-project, he said, was "direct impact, direct help". They were looking for big impact on small budgets. He told the officials "If it doesn't make sense, then you have to question more…it is for us to use our common sense." Bret was training the staff in how to guide the selection of sub-projects based on the PRF's own particular logic: apparently the people's participation required such expert guidance.

As the sun was setting after the meeting I went to shower but the shower was occupied. Bret was waiting there too, so I settled in for a chat. I mentioned my inkling that the work considered in this project was not "the people's choice" but simply government work, because all of the allowable sub-projects seemed to be government services like roads and schools. He rejected this, saying again, "that is what the people want. The people choose those things…so…" I asked him again if this was government or an international aid project, and he said that it was an independent body: the staff on the Poverty Fund are not public servants, so they do not have wage problems that so many Lao public servants have. As our conversation drifted on, he said at one point: "The government has taken a risk. They have borrowed 20 million dollars from the Bank. They want to be able to collect tax." I pointed out that that is exactly what the rural people suspect: that this project is simply a vehicle for making further extractions from the populace. He said it was very true—the government wants a tax generating population so that they can fund government services. He called it a vicious cycle—the government does not have enough money for services, so the people are poor and do not want to pay tax to a government whom they do not see providing any services. I realized that, from our differing experiences in Laos, Bret and I saw the situation in much the same way, but with a very different moral interpretation.

21st May

I attended the District level meeting. Don Khiaw was represented by the four representatives "elected" from their Sub-District. At this meeting the budget was at last announced: 68,000 USD for the entire district of 66 villages. Representatives were asked to decide which sub-projects to fund from the proposals of all the Sub-Districts. They were told that they could decide on one District-wide project, such as a major road, or divide the money among a few smaller projects such as a couple of schools and a health centre in the district.

The representatives decided to split the money evenly between each of the ten Sub-Districts: 6,800 USD per Sub-District. The Sub-District that

Don Khiaw was part of decided that the fairest thing to do would be to make sure that each village obtained some of this money. Their top priority, a road project, turned out to be supremely appropriate for achieving this sort of equality. Unlike a school or a health clinic, a road can be split into kilometres and metres, and these distributed to each village and indeed each household. Don Khiaw was allocated two kilometres of road improvements out of a total of 18 kilometres for the Sub-District as a whole. In Don Khiaw, the eventual road works were further split by the metre so that each household would benefit from the wages attached to the work. No money was allocated for materials. Calculations were made at the District meeting this day with the assistance of Bret confirming that the budget *would not be sufficient* to pay for labour planned. Knowing this, the project nevertheless pushed on: the stage was set for the road to nowhere.

After the meeting I met Khamphat, the Lao head of the Fund usually based in Vientiane, and Sarah Broome, the second foreign advisor on the project. Sarah was wearing a dust mask against cigarette smoke. She told me she had worked with bilateral and NGO organizations in Laos on previous projects. She described one where she had, heroically and against all odds, provided every village in one District with a school and water ("they said I was crazy!"). She started with the PRF a few months earlier and said when she first arrived, Khamphat kept telling her that she was "making trouble… but he doesn't say that any more. I think he's learning, he's seeing that these things need to be considered." She asked for my observations but before I could reply she observed that the project was moving too fast: people were ill-informed, creating false expectations. She felt that the solution was more community education using media campaigns and meetings. She wanted people in the village to scale down their ambitions. "They need to do things that they can do themselves," she said. For instance if they wanted a school, they should work for a wooden one rather than a cement and brick one. I wanted to say "but they already *do* do everything themselves. They already *do* have a shabby bamboo school. They don't want another one." Instead, I told her that I did not think people wanted to scale down their ambitions. She responded that maybe they are not "that poor" here after all. She returned to her main interest, which was perfecting knowledge of the project. She saw imperfect knowledge as a problem in the project from Vientiane to the village level. Today one staff had apparently told village representatives the wrong thing at the meeting: that person had now been "moved to another area of the project". During the meeting Sarah had seen that many staff did not understand the project themselves, and from my cautious criticisms, she made out one take home message: the villagers did not understand the project either. She embarrassed Khamphat and me by posing this as a challenge to him.

She observed that all the sub-project proposals so far had been flawed by vagueness—"a school" they said—but how big? What materials? I pointed out that this was due to the people having no idea of the budget or scale of the project. Khamphat responded that he had not wanted to release the budget during the planning stage because he wanted a snapshot of village needs in general. Sarah said that at least the District budget should have been released. The frustration between the two was evident. I asked her if this was a government project and she said adamantly that, yes, it was: she was just as adamant in this as Bret had been in his claim that it was not. She said that the PRF was meant to cooperate with all parts of the government, but remain separate from them, but she said it was the World Bank that wanted this separateness. The project was peppered with rifts: between Lao and foreign staff, between different levels of staff, between government and non-government workers and it was unclear even to employees what its relationship to the government was. This was compounded by the newness, the experimental nature of this project. There was a frontier nature to it: the PRF had the flavour of a kind of wild social experiment.

I went home to Don Khiaw on the cargo boat the following day. When I told my neighbours roughly about the District meeting, they took delight in adjudicating on the various disagreements I had observed. They sided firmly with Sarah on the question of whether it was a government project. Father Khong said, "that woman's clever…she knows the true story. It's definitely government business…believe the woman".

4th June

I was in Vientiane to renew my visa. I contacted an applied anthropologist there who is well known for his considerable work and expertise in Laos. I wanted to discuss the PRF with him. We met in one of those downtown bakeries that cater for the expatriates and tourists of the city. He stated plainly that he thought the Poverty Reduction Fund was chaos. His understanding was that the project was set up as an adjunct to the controversial Nam Theun 2 hydropower project. The government had encountered difficulties funding and executing the scheme because of environmental and social concerns. The World Bank got involved demanding another round of assessments. One of the problems identified was that the project gave no indication of how any of the potential profits would be used in any meaningful way for the nation rather than simply embezzled. The government was asked to show how they would handle the new funds in the national budget ensuring that some of it got to the grassroots. The Poverty Reduction Fund was initiated to demonstrate an ability to use the money to impact poverty. It is something they can "point to", he explained. Also he said pragmatically, "there are so many careers riding on this. The World Bank is so committed now—it has to go through." I, in turn, gave him my observations of the project.

My critical views apparently got back to Sarah and Bret. I had arranged to meet them in the same café the next day for an interview, and they had been friendly and cooperative. However, by the time we met, the mood had soured. Sarah wanted to hear about my research. When I told her my preliminary findings in general about Don Khiaw, she said "but that's not like the rest of Laos. Not all of Laos has repatriated funds. You can't make a judgment about all of Laos based on that village." I responded that my sense of the strength of the ethnographic method was deep knowledge of one place rather than shallow knowledge of many places.

She countered that this project was a poor example of the dynamics I wanted to study. In many ways the Lao government had been forced to do and say things in this project just to get donor money. This was a strange beast, she argued, not representative of any one particular will. It was created from a modular pattern initiated by the World Bank in Indonesia and then replicated here.[1] She warned, ominously, that I had to be "very careful," although she did not explain why. Finally, she said that she personally was only doing the project because she felt that there was a lot of good that could come from it. Taking the chance to include Bret, who had been very quiet, I asked him why he was doing it. He said it was a "challenge" and that he was "trying to do the best with a project that was set up by the World Bank". Sarah pointed out the high amount of staff turnover—she was the fourth foreigner hired so far. The project had unfolded very quickly, with inadequate time for training. She wanted me to know that they were only feeling their way: "you can't Holly! You can't judge the results of this now!" She said that she felt that there were lots of eyes on them, and that I was one more set of eyes. She was evasive about providing the documents I had requested when we initially set up the meeting, claiming that they would not be "completed yet"—even though these were the documents that I had seen being used to guide the meeting in the District prioritization process. She gave me a hopelessly brief paper she had prepared called "Introducing the Poverty Reduction Fund".

She changed topic to the general principle of participatory development. She used the example of a failed project she knew of where latrines were built which were never used because they had no water. "The people would never have chosen that. The people laughed." Sarah made large hand movements as she said, "the people can do anything. It's completely up to them." She poured out story after story of mismanaged projects, their simple solutions in participatory planning. "And it works, Holly, it works."

25th September

I returned to Don Khiaw with news of the District meeting and my unsettling encounters in Vientiane. Residents, I learnt, had heard no official news from the PRF since the Sub-District meeting. They continued to speculate that the school project may go ahead, and that alternatively perhaps nothing at all would eventuate. Then, in September 2003, a letter arrived summoning the village representatives plus the Village Chiefs to a meeting, though the letter did not state the purpose of the meeting. All four of the village PRF representatives claimed that they were too busy to go this time, so only the Village Chiefs and I went along.

It was unseasonably hot, unseasonably dry that September, and the sun cruelly baked on struggling rice seedlings as the deputy Village Chief, Cit, and I walked swiftly through the parched fields to the head Chief's house. We found the head Chief, Bunmii, with conjunctivitis in both eyes. "Since the war," remarked Cit, "the Americans dropped all those chemicals, and now conjunctivitis is everywhere." Cit took Bunmii's face in his hands, muttered, and blew a short, sharp burst into each eye, a *pao* or "blowing" cure. "Let's see if it clears up in one or two days," Cit said. Bunmii, Cit and I headed off by boat to the meeting.

Sisanuk, again in a white Poverty Reduction Fund shirt, met us and the other attendees at the temple hall. He was worried because of the meagre turnout. Of the 17 people attending the meeting, most were Village Chiefs, not the supposedly more neutral PRF elected representatives. Sisanuk was concerned that the meeting would not appear participatory enough. Nevertheless, he addressed the gathering, stating that today's meeting would plan in detail how to implement the sub-project. The Don Khiaw Chiefs heard for the first time officially that Don Khiaw's proposal for a school was rejected at the District meeting and that they instead had been allocated two kilometres of road improvements. Moving swiftly along to the main purpose of the meeting, Sisanuk explained:

> The aim of today is that the people, together, decide how to do it. The people must make a detailed plan for the proposed road. The people must care for and manage the project. We have to follow the policy of the Fund. We (the project officials) are not the heads. We are only here to help. The people must decide. Every activity must be done together and the people must be the owners of the activity. We want the bank to smile, not be angry. So we need women to come. That's according to their policy. The World Bank has told the government to do it this way: the people must make the decisions. That's the way the project goes.

The people heard that today they must decide on: a technical design for the road construction; the nature and source of materials and labour; a budget, including the voluntary donations of "the people"; and then compare the total costs to the total beneficiaries. One of the few village representatives there said, "I want a specialist engineer to do this proposal. We don't know how to."

Sisanuk replied, "an engineer can't decide. It must be the people who decide. If we get an engineer in here, next thing you know the World Bank will come and inspect the project and the whole thing will be scrapped (*siia*)."

The participants were required to complete a "Sub-project proposal form." It provided a large area where the village donations—in labour or necessary items such as sand or gravel—could be itemized and evaluated. The English version stated, "Communities only decide the amount and nature of free contributions they wish to provide—they may wish NOT to contribute at no cost. <u>The allocation of Sub-project grants is NOT subject to free contribution from participating communities</u>" (emphasis in original). However, the officials stated (in Lao), "we have only a little money, but we want to do a lot. So how will we make the road? Will we use the people's labour? Have them bring the sand and the gravel for the road, and dig the road." The budget was 6,800 USD. The official PRF estimate for the cost of road improvements was 15,000 *kip* per metre (1.5 USD), which placed the cost at 270,000,000 *kip* (27,000 USD). It was quickly realized by all participants, as indeed it had been realized at the District meeting, that the budget was not anywhere near sufficient for the road project. A significant element of voluntary labour and donations, it seemed, would be necessary if the project was to proceed.

A woman representative dismissed the call for voluntary donation of labour, stating, "the people won't do it—they'll go and find fish instead. We should give them a reward for their work. People won't build the road up high, they will be lazy and dig it only a little so it is low—like the road we already have." Her statements reflected the general sentiment among the representatives and Village Chiefs at the meeting.

Deadlocked, the meeting broke for lunch. I crossed the river with Bunmii and Cit for noodle soup at Muang Seen. We laughed about the idea of the two kilometres of road on the island—what would we do with it? With no bridge to the mainland and no other roads, the two kilometres on offer would just connect nowhere to nothing. We were all tired. Cit wanted to continue digging his fishpond. Bunmii said his eyes felt a little better thanks to Cit's *pao*, but they were still badly inflamed. The men had been given 10,000 *kip* (1 USD) each to cover the costs of today, but after buying lunch and subsidising the inadequate petrol allowance both had made a loss. We all just wanted to go home.

We joked that I should complain of a sore stomach—that would allow us to leave the interminable meeting. I thought they were just messing about until we returned and Bunmii addressed Sisanuk with some urgency, "Holly is sick, really ill. We need to take her home." Sisanuk did not let us go immediately. He was worried, I suppose, about the already low attendance at the meeting. He stated that today's work was very important and offered me some mysterious medicine. I refused to take it, and learned against a column in the temple hall, piqued that my bogus illness had been treated so lightly.

Cit and Bunmii remained silent, too. Hours slid by, and in the sticky heat of the late afternoon, I slid off to sleep. I suddenly woke to the sound of Bunmii saying with urgency, "look how ill she is, we must take her home." Cit, Bunmii and I left, with Sisanuk's surprised half permission. Once in the boat, the three of us released a loud burst of conspiratorial giggles. "Oh, what a meeting!" exclaimed Cit. "Would it ever end?" The darkness was gathering in by the time Cit and I picked our way in the half light back across the parched rice fields to our neighbouring homes. Approaching Cit's homestead, he called to his wife: "Holly lied! What a clever liar. If she hadn't lied, we would still be at that meeting."

His wife laughed—"if everyone else lies, you have to lie along with them, isn't that so?"

Relaxing at last, glad to be home, I asked Cit why the meeting was so long and so deadlocked. Unlike his silence at the meeting, he was talkative now: "They want us to work for free—then where is all the money going? The road is to be built from plain dirt—they don't have to buy any materials. And they want the people to put in their labour for free. Where is the money going?"

"Why didn't you ask them that?" I ask.

"I was brave enough to say so, but I didn't need to, as everybody else was saying the same thing. Everyone who spoke said the same thing—if the labour is free, where is the money going? Did you see that they didn't want you there? It was when you were asleep. They said that you were not part of the project that you really shouldn't be there. That's because they don't want you to see."

"They don't want me to see what?"

"They plan to steal the money! I wish I could tell the World Bank exactly what is happening here. I wish I could write them a letter to let them know the real story—I think they would be happy to hear it. They need to come and see for themselves. They need to come to the village and see—then they will do it honestly. In foreign countries there is no corruption, right? Foreign people are not so dishonest."

I told him that there is indeed corruption in Australia, although people are afraid of getting caught. I then told them that it was the foreign consultants in Vientiane who had tried to dissuade me from my research. "It is they who didn't want me asking any questions. They said they don't want my eyes on them. But the Lao government staff have never asked me to stop doing my research," I pointed out.

"Well if the World Bank is also dishonest, I don't know what to say. There are so many problems." I told him that I did not think that the World Bank was dishonest, exactly, but that they misunderstood. The pressure to work for free was a case in point.

"Who wants to work for free?" he agreed, "Digging is hot, heavy work. Why would we do this if we don't have enough food to eat? We have to go out and find food! This project is supposed to help reduce poverty—but instead they want poor people to work for free. This will not help the poor— if we have to work for free, it will not be done in a year, or even two. We must find money and find food. If you don't go to find money, money will not go to find you! If they offered pay, say 20,000 kip a day, I would do it. There are 60 workers in the village and they would all do it. That is 120,000,000 *kip* a day. They don't have enough money. The money is too little to achieve what they want."

Conclusion

When I returned to visit Don Khiaw almost a year later, I interviewed Duk again. Always so forthright, she told me that the road project had been partially implemented: the people had begun to dig the road, but when no remuneration for their labour had arrived, they abandoned it. Due to the drought the previous year, all but four households in the village were short of rice. "Oh I am so short of rice!" commented Duk when I spoke to her, "I wanted money to buy rice, so I went to dig the road. I'm very poor so I arranged to dig more than my friends, to earn more wages. But then they didn't pay us." Following her directions, I located the road on the east flank of the island. It was a long strip of soil carved through the vegetation, about three metres wide and built of soil dug up from a gutter dug on each side. The vegetation had been cut back, but it was already rapidly returning: with no motorcycles or carts on the island, there was no traffic on the "road".

Bunmii, the Village Chief at the time, found me there. He said energetically, "They still have not paid the wages—people here are short of rice to eat, more short this year than any other year because of the drought. We wait for that money." He described his efforts to work through the District officers he

Figure 10. This was one of the best areas of footpath that resulted on Don Khiaw from the "road to nowhere" project.

knew to try to obtain wages for those who had dug the road. The project was left unfinished, he told me, because the village residents had called a halt to the work in protest. He was preoccupied with how to use the road project to obtain rice or money to relieve the very real food shortage arising from the drought. I was struck at how irrelevant the road's presence as a road had become. The long mound of dirt trailed to nowhere, petering out in the new growth as if it could not recall its destination or purpose.

In 2008, I asked the PRF central national office to respond to the suggestion that corruption might have been at play in the road to nowhere. They vigorously defended the project, and I was able to spend several days in the Vientiane office examining financial records related to the Don Khiaw project. In this way, I found documentation indicating that some wages *had* eventually been paid in Don Khiaw. According to these, the wages had originally been delayed because the wider Sub-District road project had gone over budget: the more assertive neighbouring villages had claimed their wages first, and by the time it was Don Khiaw's turn the project had predictably run out of money. As the work continued without the means to pay wages, the project effectively became indebted to village labourers. In the internal review prompted by my research, this was identified by PRF staff as a serious flaw, and staff assured me that they were working to make sure it did not happen again. Now, however, PRF staff explained, the project had been completed and all the wages had been paid. The project was considered by them to be a success. The people had "participated" and demonstrated their "capacity". From 2009, furthermore, PRF officers announced that it would be formal policy that no wages could be allowed to be paid for unskilled village labour, such as digging road works. Furthermore, they had decided to cease operations in this area in the south of Laos after this first trial year.

My admittedly amateur audit of the financial documentation at the head office revealed no significant discrepancies, other than what appeared to be some rather dull examples of administrative incompetence. Rather than corruption, it seemed to me that something more mundane, but altogether more unsettling had taken place in the road to nowhere project. Policies had been adhered to, the project cycle had been completed and the budget acquitted. However, the result had nonetheless been absurd and unjust.

I returned to Don Khiaw in 2008 and asked again about the wages, this time prompting with figures obtained in the PRF office. Some clarified that they *had* obtained some amount of wages (ranging between 100,000 *kip*/ 10 USD and 140,000 *kip*/14 USD per household), but that in their view this was only a *partial* payment: they had done much more work that this and thus expected much more money. The Village Chiefs confirmed that they had been involved in the distribution of these wages, but claimed to have lost the paperwork relating to this distribution. All residents that I consulted continued to express dissatisfaction with the wages, claiming that even if some wages had been paid, these were not adequate.

The road to nowhere saga was enlivened by the familiar elements of political rationalities in Laos. It pivoted on the idea of aid: it claimed that it would reduce poverty by providing aid directly to the poor, but its method was to achieve this via village cooperation that would, ideally, end with villagers helping themselves. However, this did not conform to local norms of productivity, based on *phay heet phay man* (each to their own). It also jarred with local forms of mutual aid which insist on a person at the centre to give and receive debts of virtue (as I will explain in Chapter Eight). Furthermore, by asking villagers to help themselves, the PRF breached the political rationality that conceives of a legitimate state as one which extends aid in times of dire need, such as the drought that year. Since the project did not extend aid, but instead was effectively a project of non-provision of government services, it was interpreted as illegitimate. It slotted into a more general reified picture of the state as corrupt, non-providing and exploitative. While PRF staff, such as Sarah, blamed the project's failings on technical issues such as a lack of knowledge and administrative hiccups, Lao rural residents interpreted them through the lens of this politicized reification of the state as corrupt. Through its failings, and particularly the bitter dispute over the wages, the PRF took its place in the long list of stories of state that locals tell each other as warnings and proof of the state's cruelty.

Yet none of this was assured from the outset. While village residents were able to predict the project's failure from the very day the World Bank came to Don Khiaw, they nonetheless continued to engage with the project with an appraising eye. The questions and ideas they presented at the village meeting indicated that villagers continued to probe the project to see where and how they could extract some benefit from it. Ultimately, this took the form of demanding wages, and this is where the most protracted dispute occurred. All of this probing and assertion of claims took place in a context, remarkably, where people felt extremely fearful and intimidated: I hope that this narration has given some sense of just how afraid many Lao rural residents are to ask direct questions about policies and to speak out in situations that they associate with the state, even when the issues at stake effect them directly. However, I hope this narrative has also shown that, despite this widespread fear, they nonetheless continue to go forward to meet the state. People really did dig the road, because they really were expecting wages, and they really did go to the interminable meetings. They even dressed up for these dreaded meetings. This cannot be explained simply through fear but requires an understanding also of the desiring resurrection of the state even in a context of disillusionment. In the next chapter, I take a more schematic look at the idea of aid that played such a prominent role in the political rationalizations of this and the previous two interventions described.

8

Mutual Aid
Delirium and the Political Field

Sisanuk's rather saccharine reference to the massive columns in the temple hall during the village meeting in the previous chapter, and his use of this example to suggest that the people should think of how to "work together" to ease their own poverty, indicates a more pervasive tendency to see village-based cooperation as a traditional characteristic of rural Laos that can be tapped by development projects. The logic of mutual aid was one of the key rules implicit in the Poverty Reduction Fund. A latrine was not permissible. A latrine in the school was. A personal business plan was not permissible. A community-built school made of local materials was. The legitimating factor here that distinguished a valid from an invalid suggestion was the imagined presence of a community working together to construct their own public goods like roads and schools to be shared among themselves for common benefit. Yet Don Khiaw's definitions of community do not fit easily into the idea of the collective village imagined in the road to nowhere project. Lao rural residents do refer to village residence as an important indicator of identity, but in economic action they cultivate person-centred networks that are diverse and widely dispersed. A resident of Don Khiaw is likely to count as closely-cultivated kin people in Thailand, the Bolaven Plateau, urban centres, the USA and Australia. In many ways, the idea of the village-community pursued by the Poverty Reduction Fund was a fantasy. By "fantasy" I mean not that it was false or made-up. I mean that it was one of the possible answers generated to that compelling question promoted by desire, which is "What do others want from me? What do they see in me? What am I for others?" (Zizek 1996: 117). This is fantasy in the psychoanalytic sense: an

151

unstable answer generated in response to both the impossibility and yet importance of formulating ourselves in the eyes of others. In this chapter I propose to take the fantasy of mutual aid seriously as part of the shared delirium born of desire that shapes the Lao political field.

Cuing from Deleuze's concept of delirium, I argue that mutual aid recurs in Laos like a compulsion. It generates its own rationalities that guide or make sense of action, even when the people who get caught up in these rationalities do not necessarily believe in them. Mutual aid is everywhere throughout the political field in Laos. Yet it is often conspicuous by its absence. In the preceding three chapters, I looked at three different policy processes: collectivization, irrigation, and the road to nowhere. It is striking that the concept of mutual aid returned in each of these, each time dressed up in the costume of its particular era (socialist collectives, irrigation management transfer, and participatory planning). Each of these initiatives was particular, influenced by trending international buzz words and the latest set of foreign advisors of the time, yet still they came to be spoken of in this very familiar framework of mutual aid. Think, for instance, of the official mentioned in the last chapter charged with translating the PRF documents into Lao, and how he struggled to find a translation for "participation", settling at last on *suan huam* (the common good). This term much predates the participatory turn in development policy and points well beyond it. When he struggled to think of a translation for "community", he just used the Lao word for "village." In doing so, this translator was tapping into a very long-running pattern in Lao political practice: imagining an autarkic village complete unto itself due to internal cooperation and then imagining that this cooperative unit can, counter-intuitively, serve the purposes of the latest state policy. The fault of this kind of thinking should be obvious: how can mutual aid, imagined as pre-existing and a mode of autarky, also be the mode through which the state and development is enacted? Why are the state and development industry even necessary if mutual aid is already so natively effective at achieving these ends? If this "mistake" had happened once, we might accept it as such, but that it occurs again and again, and is still occurring, requires a larger explanation. Projects come and go, it seems, but mutual aid remains the obsession of rural policy in Laos.

I am not arguing that time and again dominant discourses have been ground down into an eternal peasant logic. There is something more intimate at work here than that. In Scott's discussion of nonrevolt among the post-peasantry, he recommended "asking directly whether the values embodied in peasant culture do in fact accord with the dominant myths of the social order" (1976: 240). Scott predicts that in times of dissatisfaction dominant myths will be subjected to "symbolic reversal", turned upside down as dominant narratives are used to subversive ends (1976: 236). This does apply to mutual aid, yet Scott has not gone far enough. The symbolic reversals occur in all directions like a hall of mirrors. Mutual aid, if we think of it for a moment as a "dominant myth of the social order", has a local reality (there really is mutual aid that occurs in Don Khiaw) but this is "reversed" into state policy. Through an apparent sleight of hand again and again Lao peasants are held responsible for their own (non-)provision of services: if they cannot cooperate to build a road, said Bret, then "obviously" this would lessen their chances of receiving funding in the next round. It does not stop there: mutual aid is reappropriated in rural evaluations of this state non-provision. The state itself is deemed guilty and thus illegitimate when it does not offer any or enough aid. Recall the Village Chief, standing on the road to nowhere, telling me with such passion that he would try to extract some aid from the state in light of the drought that year, under the guise of wages for the road and as charity. The reversals involved are repeated as echoes of each other. Mutual aid is dispersed throughout political action at all levels, dominant and non-dominant, in policy and private evaluations, personal and general, not as a reality but as a particular kind of rationality on which people build their recriminations, expectations and assessments and tear down those of others. Mutual aid is a grand narrative in Laos in the making of the nation-state, but is also peppered throughout daily interactions in the most unlikely and intimate places.

Mutual Aid in Policy

The Lao state demands that Lao peasants cooperate, but this is a confused message. It includes elements both of censure (complaining that Lao peasants do not cooperate enough), reinforcement (idealizing Lao peasants for their traditional cooperation) and utopia (if we all cooperate then development will be achieved). The flip side of mutual aid, of course, is non-mutuality. Mutual aid is thus closely tied to perceptions of social decay including divisiveness, corruption, betrayal and mistrust.

A few examples will illustrate this. The first is from a newspaper article written in 1941, in Laos' first newspaper, *Au Lao Nyay*, a publication associated with the small, elite circle of Lao nationalists. In an article entitled *Pathet Lao* ("Lao land") an unnamed author wrote: "Among all things that we lack first, it must be noted that the most important of them is cohesion and solidarity. The Laotian is an individualist, even a bit anarchist" (cited in Ivarsson 2008: 159). In order to build a nation, the article went on to explain, it would be necessary to overcome what the author described as the *sue sue* nature of Lao peasants, that is, their happy-go-lucky, easy-going, unambitious nature. The *sue sue* character was thought to be a rather self-centred individualist, interested in at most his or her own immediate family and oblivious to, or resentful of, wider associations and authority. The urban nationalists aimed to modify this parochial figure to create a modern citizen inspired by "solidarity, sacrifice, and the revival of a Patrie" (Ivarsson 2008: 168–70). Mutual aid was conspicuous by its absence and had to be invented in order to create the Lao nation.

As discussed in previous chapters, mutual aid has been a long-running preoccupation of the Lao People's Revolutionary Party (LPRP). Evans (1990) concluded that a major reason for the failure of the collectivization of agriculture in Laos was that the policies assumed a proclivity for collective endeavour when in fact Lao peasants are motivated by household-based strategies. The LPRP, in the collectivization drive, engaged in a contradictory effort, both proclaiming the naturalness of collective endeavours for Lao peasants, and demanding that they be created through revolution. Despite the failure of this drive, requirements that rural residents act collectively have been a persistent part of subsequent policies, particularly those that aim at poverty reduction and development. During the push for mechanized irrigation in the 1990s, farmers were required to form "Water User's Groups" to cooperate to manage loans and fund a communal Village Development Fund. In the previous chapter, it was evident how collectivist ideals underlay the "Poverty Reduction Fund" where every sub-project had to be planned and executed collectively, and in a manner whereby "everyone" would benefit. Collectivist ideals are also evident in the move since 2003 to place "the village as the implementing body" for all poverty reduction policies (High 2006b). During my fieldwork, I observed that labour was regularly requisitioned from the rural populace for state schemes, such as maintenance on roads, schools and irrigation, and that these orders were phrased in the language of mutual aid. I should note that these orders were often received with a great deal of cynicism and the kinds of everyday resistance Scott has described: evasion, foot-dragging, and off-stage complaint. As recently as 2010, a new decree was passed enabling and encouraging Lao peasants to form collectives for the purposes of poverty reduction, confirming again that the national goal of eradicating poverty by 2020 is being pursued by the LPRP still through the encouragement of collective endeavours. Throughout these diverse interventions—which were each as much a sign of the times as they were of continuity—there is a curious repetition. Again and again, mutual aid makes its return.

The contradiction of these policies is that they both assume mutual aid for the common good as a pre-existing village resource waiting to be exploited *and* require it to be brought into existence in response to a state order. Strictly speaking, if mutual aid was such a genuinely local and spontaneous phenomenon in the village to begin with, then the orders to cooperate would not have been required in the first place.

This "now-you-see-it, now-you-don't" quality of mutual aid can also be seen in some of the scholarship of the region. Ireson, an anthropologist who worked extensively with development agencies in Laos before publishing several academic articles in the 1990s, argued that Lao peasants are characterized by mutual aid because it is economically necessary for survival in remote, rural areas, as mutualism was the only insurance Lao peasants had against calamity. Furthermore, mutual aid was a leveller, reducing social stratification. Ireson goes on to note that:

> …labor exchange and other forms of mutual assistance express and reinforce an ethic of village solidarity and cooperation…. This solidarity acts as a buffer against outside political and economic forces, and has resisted the tendency to develop capitalist relations at the village under either capitalist or socialist governments (1992: 71).

Thus for Ireson, mutual aid exists and has always existed in the Lao village because it is necessary for subsistence agriculture, and it furthermore serves to insulate the village from economic change or the encroachment of the state. Ireson interprets this quality in a positive light. Compare this to Rehbein, a sociologist. He agrees with Ireson that Lao peasants are primarily subsistence orientated even in this century (2005: 34) and that they achieve this via mutual aid and reciprocity, but he asserts that the Lao and other ethnic Tai:

> …accord a much higher value to the nuclear family, however, than most of Scott's peasants. In a way, this is very modern and Western but it also means that Tai are not very good at collective endeavours. As coordination and cooperation are necessary for the functioning of any market economy, this cultural trait is a big stumbling block for development projects (2005: 37).

Thus for Rehbein, economic development in Laos is hindered by a cultural deficit of mutual aid, much like the stubborn individualists described 60 years earlier in *Lao Nhay*. The recurring theme is that Lao peasants have mutual aid, or they do not, and that either way this is hindering economic or national development. It would be easy to leave our analysis here and interpret mutual aid as a characteristically clumsy nationalist or state-sanctioned ideology that some academics have obediently reproduced. However, it would be a mistake to lurch too far in this direction, to interpret mutual aid as nothing but the result of a dominating discourse.

The stone left unturned here is the valence of mutual aid among Lao rural residents themselves. Ireson and Rehbein's contradictory statements do not just emerge from a parroting of development ideology but also, I suspect, from the frequency and passion with which mutual aid is discussed in Laos by the targets of these policies themselves. I am thinking here of the conversations I had during my own fieldwork, especially in the first initial months, as rural Lao residents made sense of themselves to me. I heard that Don Khiaw was a village with a "natural economy" (*seetthakhit thamasaat*), where people helped and gave instead of using money to buy or hire. It was separate and distinct from wider structures such as the national economy or state, they told me. While most households used their own labour for the majority of the work in the fields, days of mutual aid where friends and family would come to help for a day or an evening on a particular task were paraded before me explicitly as a pleasant and important part of people's lives, although people claimed that these were more common and more spectacular in the past. The Lao have many local idioms for mutual aid, such as *sooy kan, hak phaeng, bung yaeng, saamakhii, suan huam* and so on. I witnessed some very large events of cooperation.

I was being presented with the smooth exterior of Lao mutual aid, but also, inevitably, its fractures and contradictions, the private life of these public norms. Despite (and indeed because of) the passionate investment in mutual aid, mutual aid events are also a frequent source of disappointment and criticism. In village meetings, for instance, a common refrain heard from Village Chiefs was that not enough "solidarity" or sacrifice had been evident, and meetings often featured sessions where mutual aid was explicitly explained and exhorted to village residents by the Village Chiefs. This was often in response to the lack of success of state projects that relied on corvée labour garnered under the idiom of mutual aid.

We have seen in previous chapters that mutualism recurs in state discourse: contemporary and past Lao policy *requires* that Lao peasants cooperate, often as a vehicle for the non-provision of services and the incorporation of rural residents into some of the lowest rungs of an increasingly unequal society. However, it would be a mistake to interpret mutual aid as therefore a hegemonic imposition in the service of some elites: in my fieldwork I was a witness to forms of spontaneous mutual aid that would be hard to interpret in such terms. But nor is mutual aid a spontaneous act of moral autarky. Rather, I suggest that mutual aid traverses realms, from central offices to dusty District quarters to the village meeting, as an enduring obsession and a delirium. Below, as a counterpoint to the previous examples I have provided of state requirements for mutual aid, I will describe one of the grandest successful enactments of mutual aid I had witnessed: the *caeek khao*. I will then compare this with other, often less successful attempts at mutual aid in response to state policies, in order to draw out the features of mutual aid as a delirium.

Caeek Khao

The *caeek khao* is a festival (*bun*) held in a private homestead to generate large amounts of merit through donations to visiting monks and to transmit this merit to a particular deceased person. This often takes place at the time when the bones remaining after cremation are interred in their final resting place (such as inside a temple, if the family can afford to buy a plot). More or less from the moment of death, plans begin. Money is put aside and saving can continue for years. Young animals might be purchased with an eye to raising them for slaughter at the *caeek*. Coconuts are horded and rice is stockpiled. A date must be requested from the senior monk who coordinates such events so that they do not clash. Under normal circumstances, the *caeek* is held in the dry season after the end of the monks' rains retreat because during this period monks are able to travel and lay people have more time to join in the work and festivities.

Once the date is obtained, invitations are prepared. In the *caeeks* I observed, these were verbal. Members of the household hosting the *caeek* call on specific people, in person, if possible, or these days by telephone. Each invitation is tailored to a particular invitee, listing the work and ritual observations requested of that individual. Often hundreds of people are invited including neighbours, friends and relatives from the region and further afield, so this stage of preparations can take weeks or months. Etiquette demands that only people specifically invited may attend, and once invited, one is obliged to accept and attend unless one has a very serious excuse. As a result, usually not all members of a household are invited because it is generally agreed that it is not wise to leave a household unattended altogether.

Invitations are also lyrical. I have translated one below, delivered to a father and daughter pair (the mother and son of the same household were not invited).

> *Hay Nang Lai pay soot pay sooy yuem sing yuem khoong*
> (Miss Lai, come join in come assist, borrow things borrow items)
> *Taaween hok khum ho khaotom*
> (on the day of the 6th night of the moon wrap rice sweets)

Toon laeng hay cao noon phuun
(In the evening, sleep over there)
Cet khum hay say baat say wat
(On the 7th night of the moon, make religious donations)
Phoo Di pay cat pay caeng
(Father Di, come organise and come arrange)
Say baat say phok
(Place donations in the bowls of the monks, in their alms bowls)
Pay yuu pay noon
(go to be there, go to sleep there)
Fang thet fang thum
(listen to the sermons, listen to the teachings of the Buddha).

The correct response to such an invitation is to *"Pay, yuu dii mii haeng ko pay"* (I will go—if I live well and have my health, I will go).

This particular set of invitations was delivered by a woman, Peng, who was arranging a *caeek* for her deceased father. Peng arrived at Lai and Father Di's house in high spirits but tired: she had invited numerous people that day and her words now came out fast and with a sing-song quality from repetition. Teasing her, Lai and another woman who was visiting kept asking Peng to say it again for different reasons: "sorry I didn't hear…what night of the moon is it again?…I forgot already…what was I supposed to do?" Peng reeled the spiel off again and again.

What is notable in this invitation, and this was common in all *caeek* invitations, is how specific it was. Lai was invited to cook, borrow things, and participate in the rituals. Her father Di, meanwhile, was invited to oversee the event generally, as well as take part in the rituals. Peng invited me to her *caeek* as well, but not at this moment. Instead, she waited for when she could visit me in my own home, and she delivered an invitation specifically tailored to my capabilities: I was asked to wrap sweets and sleep over, as well as take part in the rituals, perhaps because my capacities were considered quite few. Young men were invited to go on large parties to catch fish, young women were asked to help shred the great mounds of coconuts. Other able-bodied and skillful people were asked to construct the temporary outdoor shelters (*phaam*) in which the monks would sit and eat.

At the *caeek* the monks are offered an elaborate meal. Preparing this requires the assembly of a small army of cooks, as well as helping hands to gather the food and equipment. Large amounts of firewood, charcoal, food-stuffs (rice, fresh fish, coconuts and so forth) and cooking equipment (such as borrowed pots, serving trays and rice containers) must be assembled. All the cooks and helpers need to be fed, as do the elderly guests who are invited to preside over the ritual events and who often work on making the gifts to

Figure 11. Wrapping rice sweets in preparation for a merit-making donation.

Figure 12. Monk's begging bowls piled high with rice, sweets, and bananas.

the monks appropriately beautiful—and for this they require banana leaves, beeswax, flowers and so on which also must be collected. The *caeek*, then, is a festival of work. The work, in turn, is achieved through the assembly of assistance from a network of friends and family. Mutual aid is what makes a *caeek* possible.

Observing the *caeek* in action shows how incredibly specific these assemblages of mutual aid were. It was not that "people" in general helped one another, but that specific people (the hosts) called on specific forms of assistance from among their personal network of neighbours, relatives and friends: Peng specifically asked Di and Lai directly and personally to help. She did not ask Lai's mother or brother, or the other two people who happened to be there and heard the invite. She asked Lai and Di based on her personal relationship with them, her knowledge of their particular capacities and characteristics. Helping was vital to the *caeek*, but it was based on particularities, rather than a generalized (and generalising) mutual aid ethic.

Usually, relatives and friends start arriving weeks beforehand to stay over and help the hosts. Flocks of them can be seen roaming the village borrowing cooking utensils (such as coconut shredders), sleeping mats (for the guests who will sleep over) and sheets of corrugated iron (for the *phaam* outdoor shelter). Youths would gather to shred coconuts on a hastily constructed platform under a tree, jostling in close to each other and engaging in banter, word play and teasing. The work parties that ventured out to collect firewood and haul in large catches of fish were likewise often convivial and high-spirited. This was not like the usual work of the homestead (often alone and subdued): it was festive and done closely, even intimately, with familiar neighbours and visiting strangers. Other tasks in the lead up to a *caeek* included setting up the large outdoor cooking area and washing and soaking the rice for making noodles (*khao pun*).

The day before the main event, the majority of lay guests arrive. They bring gifts for the hosts: usually about a kilo of rice, an additional item of food, tobacco or betel nut, and a few thousand *kip*. These are presented on arrival to the head of the household. Gifts are carefully noted down in a jotting book for future reference. Older guests gather in this receiving area as they arrive, surrounding the senior host, many of them becoming engaged in making decorations from banana leaves and beeswax for the donations the next day. The donations intended for the monks were assembled in the *phaam*: these usually included highly decorative single beds covered in items such as pillows, kitchen items and decorations (the number of beds indicated the amount of merit to be made—I saw a range from three to eight).

Younger adults meanwhile were organized into work stations for each stage of food preparation. The shredded coconut was processed into coconut milk and oil. In another area, rice was soaked in the oil. In another, soaked rice was wrapped carefully into small banana leaf packages. In the outdoor kitchen, these little bundles were boiled to make rice sweets. Some of these were barbequed until crispy and enjoyed on the spot, or diverted into women's handbags to take home for children, but the majority were stockpiled for the next day's large donation. A similar pattern was held for noodle production: preparations had been going on for days, soaking and pounding the rice (often by gaggles of teenage girls working on the huge wooden foot-powered pestle). The paste was then boiled in the outdoor kitchen, softened, then strained into strings through a perforated frame into boiling water. In the outdoor kitchen, working over wood fires stoked in earthen trenches under large pots, groups of primarily women undertook the hot work of making meals for the masses of workers, such as fried noodles, stir-fried vegetables with tiny meat morsels, and noodle soup. Most of the meat from the slaughtered animals was reserved for the monks the next day, but meals emerged from the kitchen in a continuous stream, delivered on communal trays of little bowls to the workers at their stations.

Despite this factory-style organization of work, activities were fairly slow-paced. There were frequent delays and breaks caused by hold ups at some previous point on the line, or by the decision to stop and eat. While it was clear that there was a job to do, it was equally clear that everybody should enjoy the experience: alcohol was passed around; some women were wearing make-up; food was enjoyed. Despite this emphasis on fun, one and all said that they were there primarily in attendance to "help" with the work required for making this amount of merit. Yet, it was often unclear who was helping whom. In addition to being fed generously on the day, workers took noodles, great armloads of boiled rice sweets, and barbequed noodle paste home at the end of the day to give to other members of their household.

In the evening people gathered again to eat and "sleep" at the hosting homestead. I have put "sleep" in quotation marks because the bustle and noise of events often made sleep impossible. A large sound system and VCD/TV, is typically hired to boom out Thai or Chinese movies, musicals or comedy shows. In the household grounds, entrepreneurs may set up improvised stalls offering iced drinks, ice-creams, alcohol, balloons and sweets for sale. Work continues through the night, as well, with animals being slaughtered in the cool wee hours for the morning meal.

Early the following morning the monks arrive to receive the donations and meals that have been prepared for them. The monks hail not only from the local temple, but surrounding ones as well. A photograph of the deceased person is typically displayed. When the sutras have been chanted and the monks have departed, the laypeople then share a meal. The rest of that day and the next few days are absorbed with the work of packing up: returning borrowed items to their owners, deconstructing the temporary shelters, and cleaning.

A person at the centre

I have discussed the *caeek* here at length because it is one of the most obvious and grand examples of actually existing mutual aid in the south of Laos. These events are planned—often over the course of years—and eagerly anticipated as profound achievements of merit making. Their execution is often spectacular, coordinating resources on a large scale and typically with great success. It is worth, then, paying some attention to how these feats of co-operation are achieved.

The most notable feature is their *personalistic* nature. Invitations to help in this "work" are based on the particular relationship between host and invitee, and the specific characteristics of the invitee: invitations were individually tailored, and the notebook on the day recorded individual attendance and gifts. These events work, in sum, because there is a person at the centre giving and receiving gifts with specific and known persons as part of an ongoing personal relationship. This means that the particular group of people rallied for a particular occasion is always specific to the persons who are doing the rallying and to the occasion. The "communities" that are created through these efforts are one-offs, unique assemblages, not enduring groups.

There was often a *super-abundance* of efficacy in these groups: more sweets were produced that could be consumed by the monks, more people were ready to shred coconuts than there were coconut-shredders, so many noodles were produced that they far exceeded need and were pressed into the hands of departing guests. Beauty is bounty and bounty is beauty: this super abundance was a key part of the aesthetics of success. The aim was not just to meet the goal of providing a lavish meal and gifts for the monks, but to do so with an over-flowing of abundance and capacity to spare.

This is an indication of the *task-specific but not task-exclusive* nature of these occasions. These were not simply matters of getting a job done in the most efficient way. There was a job to be done, true, but these were quite literally work-parties. While the work was extensive and often difficult, much of the activity also involved meeting new people, catching up on news, passing the time waiting, and enjoying food and alcohol. These events were aimed not just at getting a job done, but getting it done in a way that exceeded the bare bones of the work at hand. The contrast with the PRF's insistence on maximising "beneficiaries" per dollar spent could not be starker. The logic of the *caeek* was quite the opposite of the PRF: it was not at all to get the work done at the greatest "impact" for the lowest price, but to complete the task elegantly, with beauty and bounty.

This pattern is observable in other forms of cooperation as well. For instance, when a new house is built, or an existing house is extended or moved, it is common to call on a person-centred network of neighbours, friends and family to come for a day's work, and to offer in return a joint meal (which is cooked by friends and family who have come to help). The meal, and indeed the whole event, is typically accompanied by alcohol and conviviality. Often there are more labourers present than are actually needed to complete the work (and this is deemed a good thing), and it is not uncommon for whole groups of people who have come to "help" to gather and chat, apparently idly, at these work events.

I do not wish to romanticize rural mutual aid: my point is not that mutual aid always works, or that it is always the best method, but that given how important mutual aid is in the political morality of Laos it is worth paying attention to those instances of mutual aid that do actually work. In Don Khiaw, mutual aid works when it can tap into an aesthetic of bounty, when it accomplishes more than just work, and when it takes place in a network of specific, personalized relationships that recognize people's particularities.

Mutual aid must not be confused with egalitarianism. Often the call for cooperative labour of this kind only serves to widen the gap between the most prosperous and poorest households, because it was wealthier householders who were most often in a position to host such events, and they thus benefited disproportionately from mutual aid. There are no customary redistributive mechanisms in Don Khiaw based on the concept of mutual aid. Whenever I asked directly if better-off farmers were required to give to poorer ones during times of hardship, I consistently received a negative answer, even from poorer people. Instead, when gifts of this nature were made, they were phrased as examples of personal virtue and were mostly executed in secret. Part of my instruction in Lao etiquette on Don Khiaw was the explicit advice that gifting in large public donations to a generalized "village" was an inappropriate move in the personal relationships I was developing there. Instructing me against such generalized aid, Peng said, "Those to whom you want to give things, just give to those people." She added that, if I ever should feel compelled to give to her, I should do so in secret. Mother Nang, too, begged for help from me, saying "you help the school, why don't you help me?" She, too wanted any such gift to be secret. My closest friend, Suaay, valiantly attempted to help me in my effort to sponsor the school but advised me against it and noted at one point, wryly, "you help the school and I help you." What all of these unsolicited but well-meaning pieces of advice were aimed at was redirecting my sense of reciprocity away from any generalized sense of "the village" or "the community" towards specific relationships with individuals, marked if need be by secrecy as a sign of the intimacy of a dyad. These were redirections towards not only the most valued, but also the most successful forms of mutual aid actually existing in the south of Laos: ones existing in specific relationships, with always a person at the centre.

Mutual aid and state projects

The contrast between the success of such actually existing mutual aid—such as the *caeek*—and the failure of state-sponsored mutual aid events is striking. The policies of the Poverty Reduction Fund, irrigation and the collectivization drive each took the idea that Lao peasants do, or should, cooperate as a basic assumption and moved from there to build development and poverty reduction schemes that would exploit, in one way or another, this proclivity. This is a recurring theme, one might even say an obsession, of the Government of Laos policy towards the rural sector. Mutual aid is a Lao meta-narrative about the countryside. What is interesting about this meta-narrative is that it borrows from spontaneous events, such as the *caeek* described above, yet reconfigures these borrowings into forms that are apparently unpalatable to the very contexts they were appropriated from: the cooperation that seems so successful in events like the *caeek* becomes tense and difficult in events like the state requirement that villages cooperatively build and maintain their own schools. My argument is that by removing the person at the centre and replacing it with the soulless concept of state-loyal "solidarity", state-sponsored cooperation events cut out the heart of mutual aid.

In a school maintenance work day, for instance, local leaders confided in me their fear that their neighbours would come to hate them for asking them to do this communal work required of them by District policy. Leaders complained of the difficulties they faced in rallying the kind of mutual aid expected of them in the orders from the District. One man, the deputy Village Chief at the time, said of this work event:

> There were no leaders today, there was just me, but the people are not afraid of me. They don't listen to me and I can't tell them what to do. Today I was on the frame of the school building all day (putting on the roofing) following the instructions from the old men—when I looked around, all the others had left! They only came back at the end of the day for the summary in the meeting (so they would not be fined for non-attendance).

I asked him if he wanted to be a leader, and he replied:

> I do, but not in this way. I want to be a leader only if I am respected. Like if you are a teacher, and I am your student, I must be afraid of you. I will listen to you. But if I am not afraid of you—that is no good. If you are a leader, people must fear you. Not regular sort of fear, but orderly fear. Respect.

He spent all that night sleeping at Mother Fueang's house, whose shrunken mother was dying. It is customary when a person is deathly ill to sleep over at that person's house. He noted that he would be cold and uncomfortable there. The next day he would work on the roof of the school again, working and "afraid of falling and dying all day". He portrayed himself here as conforming to an ideal of the neighbour who diligently engages in mutual aid, but he expressed this in terms of a deeply felt frustration that this ideal was not more perfectly realized, and he gave way to fantasies that it was fear, not mutualism, that could attain real cooperation.

This example shows that the façade of mutual aid was fragile. It easily showed cracks of suspicion and blame. Nevertheless, the tussle over it ran deep. Mutual aid is co-opted into a variety of political and moral projects in Laos, both state-sponsored and private. It was both vaunted as part of the national, ethnic "we", and was also used for intimate critiques of "us". Even when mutual aid fails, when people grumble at the demands for labour days, or fail to attend or berate one another for not having this or that desired collectivist quality, the importance of mutual aid, and its presumed power and importance, is reaffirmed. That Lao people both engage in mutual aid, and that they do not, is in Laos "the ironic basis of intimacy and affection, a fellowship of the flawed, within the private spaces of the national culture" (Herzfeld 1997: 28).

Conclusion

Lao rural residents, as you will have gathered from the preceding chapters, are typically cynics when it comes to the state. Time and again I heard that development projects are motivated by greed and corruption, that taxation too is just another form of corruption, and that the state is an organ of violence and extraction. Cynicism about the state, as many observers have commented, is a way of participating in it, of recognizing the state as a central authority. I suggest that cynicism is also an important evaluation of the state that makes sense within the delirium of mutual aid.

The question concerns mutual aid as opposed to private gain. In the Lao political morality, a legitimate state is one that could and should *aid* its population. Rice and money, especially in times of crisis, are expected from the state. An illegitimate state, a corrupt one, is signalled in part by its failure to provide this kind of aid. Poverty was thus a sign of the illegitimacy of the current regime, although the possibility of a virtuous state is not precluded in this reading. Efforts to extract the people's "participation" during aid events, such as by distributing emergency food aid via work-for-food programmes, were thus interpreted as an infringement of these rights for pure aid, and as a failure of the state to provide the expected largesse.

This is why we need not be surprised when it is also observed that aspirations for the future in Don Khiaw included more, not less, incorporation with the state. Despite their cynicism, it was not autarky that they desired but roads, a bridge to the mainland one day, electricity, water supply—more, not less, education for their children leading ideally to an office job—perhaps working for one of those development projects they eyed so suspiciously, or for a state agency (not forgetting, here, that many petty bureaucrats earn their core income not from their wages, but from the "side benefits" of office, interpreted as corruption by the very people who aspire to move into these positions). The state is, despite the fear and revulsion with which it is perceived, still the object of desire. The delirium of mutual aid between state and society provides room for both virtue (where aid is enacted, and expectations are fulfilled) and disgrace (where aid is not extended, where expectations are not fulfilled).

Accusations of failing in mutual aid go both ways: the Lao state constantly exhorts Lao people to engage in more mutual aid, while rural residents accuse the Lao state of having failed in its duty to aid the populace. The delirium of mutual aid provides a rationality for both rightful rule and rightful resistance. Mutual aid is thus a site of multiple accusations. Rural residents accuse officials of corruption, and officials accuse farmers of insufficient mutual aid. In the super-abundant spectaculars of the *caeek khao*, the recriminations of a frustrated Village Chief berating a village meeting, and the explanations of what "we Lao" are like to a newly-arrived anthropologist, reference is made to the ideal of mutual aid. State narratives mirror this in policies that always require more of it. However, with no person at the centre, state-required mutual aid projects typically fail: the work is not done, or is done poorly, and inevitably poverty is not eased through it, and development is not delivered. Then come, predictably, the recriminations: not enough solidarity has been shown. I heard this at village meetings, but also from Provincial irrigation officers, and English foreign advisers, who likewise used the failure to cooperate on the part of the rural residents to suggest that these are not worthy poor after all. At perhaps its most obscene, it was phrased in these terms: if the rural poor cannot manage to work together, such as using irrigation pumps like catching a large bus together, then they should have their televisions seized.

The counter argument that wells up from the rural poor then is that it is in fact the state itself that has not filled its duty of aid. It is the state itself that has failed to fulfil its role and is thus corrupt and illegitimate. Vivid images of illegitimacy are offered: a state that lets its own people go hungry, that sells rice aid instead of giving it, that eats without return. There is an intimacy to this mirroring, this mutual posturing. Gestures are repeated and reciprocated in ways that make radical change in this scene more unlikely than ongoing, infuriating, but compelling exchanges of recognition and recrimination.

Consider this narrative from one of the Village Chiefs, comparing Laos to Thailand:

> Before, they (the Government of Laos), taught us to do everything together. But they lied. Their policy is: when I have enough I will let the people have some. They lie. Before, they didn't even let us listen to the radio—they were afraid we would hear about other countries. Lao people don't like to do things *suan huam* (together), they like to do things *suan tua* (individually). They are selfish. If something is being divided, they think only of themselves, *yaak day laay kwaa muu* (they want to get more than their friends). They don't think of the group. Like the money you gave to the school—you gave it for the group, but the Chief took it for *suan tua* (individual). We always leave someone in the house: we are afraid of thieves. The development workers speak of *suan huam* (together), but the *naew khit* (way of thinking) is *suan tua* (individual). The people will act together, but in their hearts they are *suan tua* (individual). We're all basically the same in Asia. We steal. We are poor so we steal. Rich people steal too. Look at the rules of Buddhism—they say not to steal. But people don't follow the precepts. People steal and kill and have sexual affairs.

This man indulges in a moment of self-orientalising, claiming that not only is the state immoral, but so too are local residents, indeed all Asians! The narrative ends with a claim that an amplified "we"—a grand "we all"—are so flawed that we cannot even stick to the five basic abstinences of lay Buddhism. This statement grows out of his narrative about a lack of mutual aid. It is a comment on the lack of *suan huam* (cooperation) that foregrounds this grandiose vision of failure and disgrace. This is a narrative that only makes any kind of sense from within the delirium of mutual aid. Of course on one level it is all untrue: Lao people do cooperate successfully, they are incredibly generous, and are not all thieves. This outburst was "nuts", to use Deleuze's phrase. However, given the delirium of mutual aid and the rationalities it generates, this statement also made some sense: it conveyed the speaker's sense of outrage directed not only at the state, but so intimately at "we" and indeed at himself.

In the Lao political field, the idea of mutual aid, rather than being a refuge of alternative culture, is co-opted and demanded by state policies. Meanwhile the language of state aid and largesse—the promise of development—is co-opted and demanded by rural residents in a rightful critique of the state. Rather than domination on one hand and resistance on the other, or state rationality versus local norms and ethics, the struggle over mutual aid in Laos has the intimacy (and extimacy) of a shared delirium. This is an intimate encounter formed where the other is encountered in the self, in mirrored gestures, echoed sentiments, inverted valuations and mutual recrimination.

9

Conclusion
Fieldnotes from the Postrevolution

The previous chapters were primarily based on fieldwork conducted in 2002–03. I kept a post-box in Pakse during that time, and once a month or so I would travel in to town to pick up the newspapers and mail that were delivered to it. Throughout 2003 a slow drip of violent incidents were reported in the papers: a bomb attack on the Pakse to Vientiane bus left one dead and 20 injured; a "group of unidentified gunmen shot at and threw a grenade into duty free shops on the Nam Ngeun Lao-Thai border checkpoint in Sayaboury province, on July 12" wounding a child (Vientiane Times 2003: July 15–17); The *Vientiane Times* dated 5–7 August reported a bomb attack "yesterday" at the morning market in Vientiane, with ten injured. There were six such incidents between February and August, with over 30 casualties (Thayer 2004: 111). It was difficult to know what to make of these: were they related? Were they political? The Lao government claimed that they were unrelated incidents undertaken by criminals. However, on 12 July, Lao Citizens Movement for Democracy (LCMD) announced that they had initiated a "revolution" to overthrow the "oppressive Communist government" (Thayer 2004: 111). In the same year, a sensational *Time Magazine* photo essay reported on Hmong resistance groups: a rag-tag army estimated at approximately 3,000, apparently living and fighting in desperate conditions.

However, most commentators at the time concluded that these attacks and resistance groups were not a serious threat to the LPRP regime. *The Economist* reported, for instance, that:

TO READ what little news emerges from secretive Laos, you would think one of the world's last communist regimes was on the verge of collapse.... Mysterious assailants have been launching attacks on highways all over the country. A long-forgotten insurgency is making headlines again. A bomb exploded last month in the centre of the capital, Vientiane. Laotian exiles in America have announced the beginning of a revolution. The contrast with recent years, when relative calm propelled foreign aid and tourism to record highs, is stark—and, it turns out, misleading (Economist 2003, capitalization in original).

Thayer (2004), in summing up 2003 in Laos, captured the mood in four words "Counterrevolution fails to ignite". It is true that from my position on Don Khiaw, the violence seemed distant and unlikely to spark a wider uprising. Indeed, my study of everyday politics in the south of Laos, conducted during this time of remarkable unrest, seemed at its conclusion to have been a study ultimately of political quietude.

This could be thought of as a post-rebellious moment for Don Khiaw, or as Baird and Le Billon (2012) have suggested, a "post-conflict" one. The basis for political and economic influence in Don Khiaw has been successively eroded: the decline of *mandala* polities and the rise of the nation state system has seen this region shift from being close to the centre of a political universe to being literally at its margins. The shift from riverine polities to national highway networks has made this once centrally-located and prosperous place obscure and poor. This region—historically westward leaning—found itself on the wrong side of the 1975 revolution. More recently, globalization has meant that poverty is now experienced in relative terms, and relative to a global system of steep inequality. In Chapter Three I described how the new nation's border sliced through the region and consolidated over time so that today, the border and the regime of citizenship that it enforces is one of the most profound causes of the poverty.

Early forms of resistance took the form of flight and fight, both of which depended on travels across that western border. However, the southern insurgency, which so many people had willingly joined, been caught up in or affected by, petered out in the 1990s. New technical aspects of the state such as taxation, land titling and citizenship papers were being progressively rolled out while I was there. Disgruntlement with the regime remained strong, but this was now expressed with a resignation and quietude maintained under sometimes extraordinary conditions. The lesson, as summed up by one returned insurgent and quoted in Chapter Three, was:

> These days it doesn't matter—we don't resist them now. We don't evade their policies. If we evade their policies, they'll arrest us for sure. But we go along with them now. It doesn't matter. It is nothing. We cooperate. We do whatever they tell us to do. We will build the school if they tell us to. Whatever they tell us: we can't not do it.

These were the attitudes conveyed by past rebels in post-rebellious Laos. In these and other cautionary tales, residents of Don Khiaw warned each other —and me—of the dangers and futility of resistance. In Chapter Five I used the example of collectivization of agriculture, together with other recollections of past state interventions shared in intimate settings to show how the state was reified in retrospective narratives. The image of the state that emerged was as a dangerous, violent and extractive entity. There were warnings about state violence and the impermissibility of dissent. Through stories about the past, an understanding of the current regime as entrenched and incontestable became part of the everyday political knowledge of rural Laos. The question of politics then was: how to manage this beast?

The state was perceived as beastly. However, this was a beast that was repeatedly turned to for help and assistance, was reproached and reprimanded for its beastly behaviour and yet could be seductive when it promised better futures. Some of the most passionate engagements that I observed in the south of Laos were engagements with the state, especially its promises of poverty reduction and development. For all that the state was demolished in these stories as a violent, rapacious, reified externality, it was nevertheless resurrected in daily lives, roles, hopes and endeavours. In Chapter Six I examined the attempted, but failed, resurrection of the irrigation project as an example of this desiring return to the state and its promises, despite disillusionment.

I have taken this return and resurrection as the topic and puzzle of this book: how is it that, when almost nobody believes anymore in the utopian development dreams, when almost everyone has been "de-mystified" about the nature of the state, almost everyone nevertheless continues to take part? Given the open secret of the flaws and failings of interventions that occur in the name of poverty reduction and development, why is not there more open opposition? How is it that the practice persists beyond belief, beyond ideology, perhaps beyond reason? The answer that I have offered is "desire".

I have approached desire not as a synonym for "hope" or "aspiration" but as a concept that points to the unconscious as social, structured and generative. Thinking of politics, the state, poverty and development interventions as fields of desire provokes a consideration not only of how they are structured in their public formulation (the official story, the known knowns, the public transcript), and not only in terms of those secret stories of state (revealed in intimate moments, the hidden transcript, the known unknowns, the things everyone in the know is meant to secretly know) but also in terms of the unknown knowns, the shared and structured rationalities underlying both these, linking them and providing the grounds for their mutual persistence. This is what Zizek called the "unconscious proper" and the appropriate field for intellectual enquiry. It is also what Herzfeld has called the "cultural intimacy" of the nation-state, that system of shared symbols that links public and private narratives. I have suggested here that we think of it also in terms of "extimacy". Extimacy describes an apparent paradox: although the state is reviled and feared, it is also approached with the most intimate demands. Some of these are for sheer bodily survival, and others are more extravagant, even utopian. But this is the key point: states, as Graeber has noted, always have this utopian aspect, even when they are at the same time forms of institutionalized raiding (2011: 1).

This formation is not unique to Laos and nor is it a universal condition (after all, states are not a human universal). Instead, the orientation towards political power that I have described for Laos is one variant of a more general formation. It is akin to what Sahlins has termed "the stranger-king" structure. Sahlins sums up this orientation with the phrase: "Power is a barbarian" (112: 1981). He draws the idea from myths and legends about polities founded by stranger-kings. In these instances, the king is described as originally foreign, either because the ruler was originally from somewhere else, or because he committed an act so extraordinarily barbaric that it was utterly foreign to the local people he came to rule. This original transgression—patricide, murder, incest, rape or something of that nature—is what Luc de Heusch (1982) called "the exploit". Often, both strategies of foreignness were evident at once, with an outsider arriving and transgressing local morality before being installed as king, often through the union with a local woman. Sahlins notes there are two kinds of power here—the external disruptive stranger-king power (*celeritas*) and the autochthonous nurturing female power (*gravitas*) that the stranger-king must unite with or subdue before taking power. The stranger-king's kind of power, then, is not understood as an innate property of social relations. Rather, "It is a usurpation, in the double sense of a forceful seizure of sovereignty and a sovereign denial of the prevailing moral order. Rather than a normal succession, *usurpation itself is the principle of legitimacy*" (1981: 113). This is the core of Sahlins' argument: that power in these formations is not understood as "everywhere," dispersed in capillary form, as so much Foucaultian-inspired writing has it. Rather, power is understood as an aberration, a permanent one in some cases, caused by an original transgression.

In an essay that traced this political formation further beyond his earlier interest in the Pacific, Sahlins (2008: 179) reports that stories of stranger-kings can be found throughout Africa, Eurasia and the Americas. Alexander the Great is a prominent example, especially given his violence and his practice of marrying local women. The story of Romulus and Remus and the rape of the Sabines is another. Sahlins reads these through the accounts of African kingships and headhunting practices of the Southeast Asian hinterlands to suggest that there is "a more general condition of human political order" (2008: 179) at play here in "the transformation of potent enemies into local benefactors" (2008: 185). He argues that this is not an understanding of power restricted just to those polities that actually have kings: "Even in so-called acephalous societies, the appropriation of outside potencies by hunters, shamans, warriors and traders bring them a certain differential standing in the community" (2008) he writes. What he is interested in is "the structural dynamic that makes foreign identity a condition of indigenous authority" (2012: 141).

It is evident that Sahlins has taken the idea of "stranger-king," first used to describe specific societies and legends, and asked it to work as a more general concept. Yet does it do the work he wants of it? The word "king" directs attention to a much narrower set of examples that involves male royals. For the Lao region I have dealt with in the previous chapters, the association of either *celeritas* or *gravitas* with a single gender, or with royal houses alone, is inappropriate. In Chapter Two I discussed the nurturing power that is such a common conception in Laos but also noted, following van Esterick (1999), that it is not limited to women. Nor is the kind of *celeritas* that Sahlins identifies, the auspicious power of foreign identities: Lao women may seek this too, and are capable of it. Reading charitably, perhaps what Sahlins really means is stranger-power, not stranger-kings.[1]

If thought of in terms of stranger-power, not stranger-kings, many examples can be found in the Lao mythic corpus to support Sahlins' argument. The first and perhaps most obvious example is Buddhism. It is not only known to have foreign origins: signs of its foreignness are conspicuously valued and preserved in story-telling and Buddhist practice today.[2] Likewise, the mythic-historical figure Fa Ngum, the founder of Lan Xang, is said to have acquired his power through a sojourn and union in a foreign land.[3] More locally, I recounted in Chapter Two the story of the rapacious dog father and his human wife. True to the stranger-king structure, this father-character was a very foreign element (a dog) and originally transgressed moral norms, in this case by eating his own off-spring. There are many more examples.[4]

However, stranger-power is not just the stuff of legends. It is also an important element in how politics play out today. Simon Creak, writing of how Laos' hosting of the 2010 Southeast Asian Games was funded and how plans to pay for the high-speed rail link to China unfolded, noted:

> …as a small polity surrounded in all directions by much larger ones, Laos and precolonial Lao kingdoms have always grown out of engagement with and even dependence on foreign powers. Lao leaders are comfortable with what may seem contradictory to some outsiders, proud of rather than embarrassed

by foreign assistance. As long as the party-state can project itself as conductor of foreign forces, as it did so effectively in the SEA Games, it (with the economy) will prosper with the help of the Chinese (Creak 2011: 122).

What I am arguing is that there is a political orientation, present but not inevitable in the Lao political mosaic, that does not shy from the efficacy of foreign power, and indeed seeks it out. This, of course, is one of the fundamental dynamics of the *mandala* form of politics, where smaller centres were not simply passively conquered, but where they often actively courted and sought out "in all directions" particularly successful, auspicious or efficacious leaders to pay tribute to (Wolters 1982: 17). One thinks, for instance, of the Kommadome *phuu mii bun* rebellion mentioned in Chapter Three, where the rebels requested in their demands the right from the French colonial administration to pay tribute to their former rulers in the Kingdom of Champassak. The request was phrased in these terms:

> If the *Résident Supérieur* wishes to extend his protection over we Khomes of the plain and the plateau and to make a *kong* of our region as part of the circumscription of Bassac, we would be grateful. The authorities of Bassac are in effect the former rulers of the Khome race (Gunn 1990: 166 cited in Baird 2013a).

Stranger-power can also be seen in the way foreign objects often hold a special power in Southeast Asia.[5] In the uplands, brass gongs and jars acquired through trade are often particularly important wealth items and may sometimes be thought to have healing powers. Scott (2009) has commented on how the uplands of Southeast Asia are scattered with objects that speak of their auspicious lowland origins, although often divorced from their original fields of meaning: he describes this as a "babble" of state imagery. Buddhist robes, pictures of Ho Chi Minh and temple paraphernalia are standard items that might be used by an uplands, non-Buddhist spirit medium. The classic example is provided by Leach (1954), in his account of the way the Kachin incorporated Shan titles and symbols in their claims to power. In the lowlands, likewise, Buddhist relics and royal palladia are often understood to have originated in distant places. They are considered all the more powerful for this, and are deployed to legitimate local authorities. Commenting on this widespread pattern, Sahlins encourages us to, "Note the retention of the marks of foreign origin" (2008: 187) as signs of stranger-power.

Echoes of this stranger-power in objects can be seen today in Don Khiaw in the special value given to the gifts and remittances that are sent home by migrants. In Chapter Four I described the shining toys held by Noy's relatives after her return from Thailand, the way she and her brother stood out on the island in their bright clothes, and the way Deng returned from Paksong proudly wearing an Adidas jacket, an ethnic minority *sihn*, and platform shoes. Deng seemed to want to let me know that she had been transformed by these experiences, too. She poured me a beer, showing me what she had learnt on her travels. I noted in that chapter that Deng's imaginary identification, even before her travels, was with being *otherwise*. On Don Khiaw, ambitions often lay elsewhere, and were pursued through links with other places, often by physically going to them. Travels themselves are often valued apart from any financial gain that they might entail: travels are themselves thought of as transformative and beneficial. Antecedents for this way of thinking can be found in the stories one hears of the power obtained by monks and laymen by virtue of long and arduous travels in the forest. Today, similar values can be found attached to the transformative potentials thought to be accessible through studying abroad, or at least in the city. These are elements of an imaginary investment in the "power of alterity" to which Sahlins points (2012: 131).

That this power of alterity is also an important element in the politics of the region today is evident in recent ethnographies. In the introduction I discussed what I called "the resistance to resistance studies," such as Walker's ethnography on politics in Thailand. I quoted his argument there that "Rural Thailand's new political society is energized by a fundamental *desire* to be productively connected to sources of power" (Walker 2012: 6 emphasis added). My question there, in the introduction, was about where the concept of desire stood in this emerging literature. What I note here is the link between desire and connection: what Walker seems to have put his finger on is the operation of a particular kind of political valuation of connection to alterity, one that I have described here as "stranger-power."

Sahlins, too, has noted "local desires of alterity" (2012: 151) in Southeast Asia and his point is that these desires are indigenous desires. Even when desires seem to be for things from afar, this does not mean that the desire itself *also* comes from afar. His is an argument against an interpretation of local desires in terms of domination, ideology or the brainwashing of globalization. He locates desires, instead, as part of a cosmological structure that operates in paired oppositions (*celeritas:gravitas; nurture:violence; local:foreign,* etc) and the generative dynamics between them (2008: 184). Sahlins is at pains to show how structuralism does not mean determinism. The structured pairs, he explains, are generative. The stranger-king dynamic allows for multiple outcomes, some of them diametrically opposed.[6] In short, he is interested in dualisms and their dynamisms.[7]

Sahlins observes this generative tendency of structures, but to my reading he does not adequately explain why structures are so generative. The psycho-analytically inspired use of the concept of desire that I have used can provide that explanation. Sahlins used the word "desire" to refer to what people want: the objects of desire that emerge from the structures he identified. By contrast, in the notion of desire developed by Lacan and anthropologically-inflected by Moore, it is desire that generates structures, not the other way around. Desire is understood as "arising from the incompleteness of representation" (Moore 2007: 21). No structure, no representation or symbolization, is ever finished or complete in itself: there are gaps, holes and inadequacies. Desire is itself these missing parts and the impossibility of ever fully compensating for them. The effort to do so by rearranging the symbolic pieces into a more complete form is a never-ending, impossible task. It is this effort that animates the structures we can observe into generative action. Moore writes persuasively: "We can say here, contra Freud, that culture does not repress desire, but rather is the product of its circulations and contradictions" (2007: 21). Without this understanding of desire as an impossibility, Sahlins can observe that cultural dualisms are generative without being deterministic, but he cannot explain where the spark that animates them comes from.

In the preceding chapters I have examined the politics of poverty in terms of desire and the dynamic dualisms it generates. In Chapter Two the dynamic I drew out was that which circulates around the ambivalence regarding food and eating. Common courtesies, sayings, religious observances and rice production suggest a dualistic reading of food and eating. Eating is basic to social solidarity, and the sharing of food is commonly associated with virtuous nurturing, cultivating and enhancing relationships. Yet to "eat with you" is also an expression of corruption and exploitation. I suggested that this ambivalence is indicative of a more general understanding of power as double-edged: power as a wild outsider is illegitimate and potentially destructive; power as a domestic and nurturing force is legitimate and virtuous. I suggested that this understanding of power helps us to understand the resurrection of the state that I mentioned in relation to the irrigation project in Chapter Six. Even when the irrigation project had been thoroughly critiqued and abandoned by the residents, and exposed as costly, unprofitable and even dangerous to engage with, still there is this capacity to "flip" into another mode of understanding, one which emphasized the potential for a nurturing, life-protecting capacity during a time of crisis. The stranger-power that Sahlins identified enables a more clear understanding of the "experimental ethic" that I identified there. I noted that there is an apparent willingness to experimentally engage with policies in Laos, even in the context of times of extreme fear and disillusionment. In Sahlins' formulation, one of the ways power attracts and seduces is through the very newness of the thing. The novelty of an item or idea itself has an intrinsic appeal. This, too, might help explain that constant regeneration of poverty reduction policies. Even though these so often seem to play out the same old themes, at the same time they are repackaged in novel ways and each time manage to recapture aspirations and hopes.

Mutual aid is another core instance of such repetitive but generative structures. I argued in Chapter Eight that a common theme running through collectivization, irrigation, the road to nowhere, and indeed a multitude of other state policies in rural Laos, was the idea that rural residents do, or should, engage in mutual aid. Rather than using models of domination and resistance, I argued that this was a shared delirium based on a capacity to flip between, or mirror, two structurally opposed but linked valences attached to mutual aid. Mutual aid is important in state-driven approaches to rural residents, but there is a substance to mutual aid as an ideal which exceeds the fabrications of policy. Mutual aid really does take place—at least some of the time, and particularly when there is a certain framework in place (a person at the centre, the dyadic relationships, a beauty of bounty). However, this ideal exists as much as a field of failure and recrimination as success, particularly when reproduced by the state, with no person at the centre. Mutual aid emerges neither as a fabrication of policy imposed through fear and intimidation nor as a genuinely autarkic element of a proud resisting peasantry. The reality is both more messy, and more compelling, than either of these suggestions. Mutual aid, like other features of the Lao political field, emerges from the structures of an unconscious, thoroughly social, thoroughly political, and deeply economic, field of desire. It provides political rationalities for actions and recriminations on all sides.

My aim in Chapter Seven was to show how these dynamic dualisms and their generated rationalities played out in action. People in Don Khiaw received the road to nowhere from the very beginning with suspicion, fear and distrust. They feared speaking their minds or asking questions. They were able to predict from the moment the project was announced that the road to nowhere would end in the non-provision of services. Yet, despite this fear and disillusionment, these people again and again participated in the project. They followed events with interest, attended meetings, and ultimately dug the soil of the "road" under a hot sun with the expectation that they would be paid wages. All of this was played in uncertain games. Interpretations were made and remade over time, drawing on different combinations of political rationalities—especially those of aid, mutual aid and exploitation—and these sustained the project to its limping and discordant end.

This book, then, has been a study of the politics of poverty as fields of desire. The conclusion of this study, which turned out to be a study of non-rebellion, need not indicate that no change is on the horizon for Laos. In one assemblage of desire are found the seeds of all others. The structures of desire are generative. The elements I have outlined here—fear and seduction, nurturance and devouring, aid and abandonment, virtue and corruption—do not offer a pre-set programme for political engagement. Rather, they are the building blocks with which people are able to cobble together their ongoing political engagements. I have described some of the engagements that were evident during my fieldwork, but these do not exhaust all the possibilities. I have no doubt that other potentialities were present there, too, many of them only in embryo form.

As I write this conclusion, some ten years after my first fieldwork, the newspapers carry very different news from the news they carried in 2002. The National Assembly is taking an increasingly vocal role in responding to concerns about land management, corruption and the rule of law. The controversy that broke out over the That Luang marsh showed that there *could* be political controversies in Laos (Stuart-Fox 2007). The disappearance of Sombath Somphone at the close of 2012, however, led to an international questioning of how effective recent moves towards opening a space for political debate have been. Given such limitations on political expression, people in Laos remain cautious, with good reason. However, they are also probing and testing new ways to find a political voice (High 2013b). The political context in which they find themselves is a field of desire, meaning that it is sedimented, but not certain.

Notes

Chapter One

1. This dance of mutual domestication is what Michael Pollan has, referring to quite a different context, playfully called the "botany of desire" (2002).

2. This approach was formulated by Scott in a number of monographs (1985, 1990 and 1998), a special issue of *Journal of Peasant Studies* 13, 2 (1986), in an edited collection (Scott and Kerkvliet 1986) and in a series of publications (1976, 1977a, 1977b, 1977c, 1977d, 1977e, 1979). For a more recent overview, see the special issue of *American Anthropologist*, 107, 3 (2005). This literature on rural politics in Southeast Asia has continued to inspire contemporary writers, such as Ong (1987, 1991), Mcelwee (2007) and Kerkvliet (1986, 1995).

3. But it is not quite fair to caricature contemporary economics by the terms laid out in an introductory textbook. The most influential economists today, such as Stieglitz, offer much more complex accounts which include the vagaries of politics, partial knowledge and power. The idea of rational action has come under particular critique from behavioural economics and neuro-economics. Opinions are so diverse in contemporary economics that a recent publication by *The Economist* concluded rather forlornly that economics can only really be defined as "what economists do, the best of them anyway" (*The Economist* 2011).

4. In the foreword to the second volume of his history of sexuality, he makes a more general comment about the ascendancy of desire in the theories and counter-theories of his day:

   > At the time the notion of desire, or of the desiring subject, constituted if not a theory, then at least a generally accepted theoretical theme. This very acceptance was odd: it was this same theme, in fact, or variations thereof, that was found not only at the very center of the traditional theory, but also in the conceptions that sought to detach themselves from it. It was this theme, too, that appeared to have been inherited, in the nineteenth and twentieth centuries, from a long Christian tradition. While the experience of sexuality, as a singular historical figure, is perhaps quite distinct from the Christian experience of the 'flesh,' both appear nonetheless to be dominated by the principle of 'desiring man.' (Vol 2: 5).

5. See for example Pfanner and Ingersoll 1962; Moerman 1966; Spiro 1966; Terweil 1976; Keyes 1983; Kirsch 1982; Little 1990; Rajavaramuni 1990; Sizemore and Swearer 1990.

6. The original passage is quite engaging and worth quoting in full:

    "Every society is at once rational and irrational. They are necessarily rational in their
    mechanisms, their gears and wheels, their systems of connection, and even by virtue
    of the place they assign to the irrational. All this presupposes, however, codes or
    axioms which do not result by chance, but which do not have an intrinsic rationality
    either. It's just like theology: everything about it is quite rational if you accept sin, the
    immaculate conception, and the incarnation. Reason is always a region carved out of
    the irrational—not sheltered from the irrational at all, but traversed by it and only
    defined by a particular kind of relationship among irrational factors. Underneath all
    reason lies delirium, and drift. Everything about capitalism is rational, except capital
    or capitalism. A stock-market is a perfectly rational mechanism, you can understand
    it, learn how it works; capitalists know how to use it; and yet what a delirium, it's
    nuts. This is what we mean when we say that the rational is always the rationality
    of an irrational ... it is demented and it works. So then what is rational in a society?
    Once interests have been defined within the confines of a society, the rational is the
    way in which people pursue those interests and attempt to realise them. But under-
    neath that, you find desires, investments of desire that are not to be confused with
    investments of interest, and on which interests depend for their determination and
    very distribution: an enormous flow, all kinds of libidinal-unconscious flows that con-
    stitute the delirium of this society. In reality, history is the history of desire. Today's
    capitalist or technocrat does not desire in the same way a slave trader or a bureaucrat
    from the old Chinese empire would have. When people in a society desire repression,
    for others and for themselves; when there are people who like to harass others, and
    who have the opportunity to do so, the 'right' to do so, this exhibits the problem
    of a deep connection between libidinal desire and the social field. There exists a
    'disinterested' love for the oppressive machine" (Deleuze 2004: 262–263).

7. Stuart-Fox (1997) has argued that in the pre-colonial era, the region did not feature
    "states" but rather "*mandala*" where power was concentrated at the centre but fainter
    on the peripheries, much like the light cast by a candle (Tambiah 1977). An exem-
    plary central figure, a "man or woman of prowess", relied on an exceptional store of
    "soul stuff" (in the case of Laos, Buddhist merit) to attract a retinue of supporters
    and extend political control. Thus, *mandala* were spiritual as well as political centres.

8. Evrard and Goudineau (2004: 942) suggest that roughly half of the population re-
    located as a result of the hostilities.

9. In fact, since the 1975 revolution the LPRP have been oscillating between centraliza-
    tion and decentralization. The motivations seem to stem in part from an ambition to
    curb the authority of Provincial Chiefs who in some cases hold considerable auto-
    nomy. Some decentralization efforts are aimed at circumventing the Provincial level
    altogether and "empowering" the District and Village level authorities below them.

10. The foremost government document on poverty at the time of this research was
    the National Poverty Eradication Program (*NPEP*). This document used an absolute
    poverty line based on a minimum requirement of 2100 calories per person per day
    in combination with an assessment of government services in order to define and
    enumerate poverty. The government services considered in poverty assessments are:
    schools, medical facilities, water supply and access to roads. Thus, the *NPEP* explains,
    a household is considered poor if income falls below the poverty line, and a village
    as a whole is considered poor if it lacks most of these government services and most

houses are below the poverty line. The assessment of Districts is made on the basis of the poverty rating of its villages in terms of the poverty line and access to services. It is on the basis of these criteria that 72 Districts were identified as poor, and subsequently targeted for poverty eradication. This had two important effects: first, with four out of five poverty indicators being government services, poverty was considered largely a lack of government services. Secondly, with the primary units of poverty measurement villages and Districts, poverty was delineated spatially, generalized by administrative area, rather than as a feature of individuals or particular families. The primary means of reducing poverty thus emerged as providing government services to these administrative units, either villages or Districts. In the *NPEP*, Champassak Province was listed as having 160 poor villages, or about 50% of the Province in total. Don Khiaw was one of those officially poor villages (LPDR 2003: 31).

Chapter Two

1. White notes that the P'an Hu complex of myths in and around China attribute ethnogenesis of certain "barbarian" groups, including the Yao, to the union between a dog and a Princess (White 1991: 14, 140–60). He suggests these were commentaries about inter-ethnic relations: the dog myths may have had indigenous Yao origins, but in relations with the Chinese empire these were converted into an ideological vehicle expressing the hierarchical incorporation of the Yao into imperial Chinese politics, society and culture. The myth served as a vehicle for explaining both their subhuman status and their occasional exemption from tax (an interpretation that was then "re-exported" to the Yao).

   The Katu, an upland group proximate to Don Khiaw, tell of an original ancestral couple (a woman and a dog) who were the only survivors of a great flood (Institute of Research on Lao Culture and Society and Costello 1993). The ancestral couple lived in a house (not a cave) and conducted swidden agriculture (not hunting). The father lived in the swidden field, far from the house where the mother nurtured their son. One day, the mother asked her son to take some food to the father in the swidden field. On arriving in the field, the son saw no person who could be his father—there was only a dog. The dog greeted the boy with a warm embrace. The boy, mistaking this for the crazed behaviour of a strange dog, beat the father off and killed him. He returned to his mother to report what had happened. The mother was horrified and ordered her son to leave the house immediately. She told him that, one day, after wandering far and wide, he would meet a woman and that he should take this woman to be his wife. This eventually happens, and it is their children who go on to form the populations we see today. The narrator of this myth notes, in two places, that "no one knows" if this woman was in fact the mother herself, or another woman. True to the patterning that White observes, the myth goes on to recount the varying fates of the off-spring of this original couple: the Katu stayed in the highlands, while Vietnamese, more clever, found their ways to the fertile lowlands.

   In comparison to the Katuic version of the myth, the Don Khiaw version is abbreviated, simplified and generalized. It occurs in an entirely imagined realm of forest and caves (rather than the oddly familiar and domestic scenery of the Katuic version) and makes no commentary on interethnic relations. I interpret this tale in terms of the contemporary concerns of residents in Don Khiaw, rather than an enduring myth.

2. The landless were particularly mobile, they were also particularly difficult to account for through survey forms. In my initial survey I found that nine households reported owning no land at all. However, in subsequent conversations I concluded that the figure was much higher. For instance, when new fields were opened for a resettlement project (High 2008), ten families moved (of 66 households in Don Khiaw at the time), claiming to have had no land in Don Khiaw. Not all of these were reported in my original survey because some of these were splinters from other households that remained, such as young couples or sibling pairs, and other landless families had moved elsewhere in the interim.

3. Elsewhere I have written about how, because I shared so many meals with one particular family, I was adopted into that family (High 2010 and 2011a).

4. I have written elsewhere of this rite (High 2010). See also Tambiah 1968; Evans 1998: 77–82, Van Esterik 1999, Keyes 1970: 224–8.

5. Kaufman, writing in 1961, notes eerily similar complaints about the burden of state extraction to those that I recorded in 2002–03. He notes laxity in tax collection (1961: 25), complaints from canton (*tasseng*) leaders about the lack of remuneration for their work and about the difficulties of raising taxes and corvée from the populace, "They feel that official duties require too much of their time, interfere with their personal interests, and are detrimental to their economic pursuits" (1961: 25). He added, "Several headmen stated that they had seriously considered joining the priesthood as a means of escaping their frustrating duties" (1961: 27).

6. One reviewer asked if it was fair to think of the requirements to build and maintain a school as a state requirement: are not schools, in fact, something for the village, not the state? My view is that schools in Laos are state institutions. This is not to say that they do not have local benefits, nor even that they are not locally desired: they clearly are. But schools are a key part of the broader project of the modernist state. In Don Khiaw the school was one of the benefits the state had promised to deliver, but was perceived to have delivered poorly or not at all.

7. It seems that the boat-racing festivals were originally held to honour the 15 nagas of the river on behalf of the king (Sachchidanand 2005: 22). In a useful contribution to the literature, Platenkamp (2008) builds on a 1966 essay by Archaimbault to track the changes that have affected this emblematic Lao event in Luang Prabang. His argument is that there, at least, the events continue to be ritualized renditions of the spiritual efficacy of the king and his consorts, now in the form of mythical nagas, although the LPRP state and Buddhist authorities have attempted to appropriate these popular events to shore up their own claims to power. In the south there have likewise been moves to define the festivals as explicitly secular events. They were held by administrative centres and used to entertain exceptionally high-ranking state employees and other secular power brokers from the local area and from further afield. What is most notable at these expressively hierarchical events is the sectioning off of space: there is always a cordoned area for dignitaries where a meal is served. The District Chief presides inside this zone, with tables of invited guests. Young women and pubescent girls were allowed in to pour drinks for them. Monks and

religion were notable by their absence. The Chief may leave the cordoned off area to present prizes and lead the ordinary people and low ranking officials milling outside in dance.

8. I have provided an extended account of the gap between planned and actual policy outcomes elsewhere (High 2013a), where I understand these in terms of an experimental orientation.

9. While all of the homes on Don Khiaw spoke Lao as the first language, some neighbouring areas spoke Khmer as the first language, although school instruction is in Lao. For more on language and state education, see Cincotta 2009.

Chapter Three

1. Literally, "people who send"; perhaps the best translation is "migration agents." I thank one of the reviewers for suggesting that the phrase can also refer to spirit mediums.

2. Literally, "there is no one in the house."

3. While I was not able to obtain exact figures for local migration rates, one illustration of the frequency and importance of migration is the prominence that these have gained in ritual in Laos. The village temple, for instance, is now crammed with structures built from the 1990s onwards with money remitted from abroad, particularly from those who had moved to the USA. Likewise, one of the territory cult shrines in the village was rebuilt with money remitted from locals who had moved to Australia. In the twice yearly "feeding of the *puutaa* (territory spirit)", the *puutaa* is informed (by means of a series of snaps on a bamboo skewer) of each of the residents of each household so that he will extend care and protection to them. When I tracked these bamboo skewers, and asked people who each snap represented, I found that households often included these relatives abroad as members of the household and thus as children of the village indicating that many of these relationships are ongoing (High 2006a, 2009).

4. The New York Times 28/11/2005. "The War on Third-World Remittances." Accessed at www.nytimes.com (10 June 2009).

5. This was featured on their website: http://www.ifad.org/remittances/maps/asia.htm that was accessed on 5 April 2011.

6. Baird (2013a: 8) reports that Champassak's influence extended as far north as Khammouane Province in Laos.

7. Formally "Siam", the nation adopted the current moniker of "The Kingdom of Thailand" on 23 June 1939.

8. The enthusiasm of the Thai to absorb the area is indicated by this ecstatic commentary at the time:

> The fall of Champassakdi City was an occasion for nation-wide rejoicing and Bangkok welcomed the announcement with great popular enthusiasm. The Ruler of Champassakdi had always remained a friend of Thailand. He was a Thai himself by racial connections and social inclination and the Ruler's son who was bought up under French tutelage and deliberately prevented from getting friendly with the Thais, proved himself to be a real Thai when he visited Bangkok sometime after the incorporation of Champassakdi into the Thai Kingdom and broadcast over the radio in excellent Thai. The occupation of Champassakdi was no annexation of territory; it

> was merely a reunion of people of the same flesh and blood, same language, same
> culture and same religion, who were forcibly separated by circumstances beyond their
> control at the time (Sivaram 1941: 97–99).

9. I am referring here specifically to experiences in the south of Laos: the bombings in
    the north of Laos began earlier, in 1962.

10. An illuminating comparison can be drawn with the border between East and West
    Germany. Residents of a borderland area there remembered the period when the
    border was intensified (1952–61) and normalized (1969–81), as a time when people
    "ceased" moving back and forth across the border altogether (Berdahl 1999: 146).
    This contrasts with the memories related to me of the southern border between
    Thailand and Laos between 1975–88. People associated this period with regulation
    of the border but also with significant movements across it, especially as refugees and
    insurgents, as I will discuss below.

11. One of the best summaries is given by Stuart-Fox (2004: 383–4). Gunn wrote an
    early account (1983). Evans and Rowley briefly discuss a movement they call the
    "White Lao" in the south of Laos (1990: 225). Baird also refers to the "White Lao"
    in his recent addition to the literature (2012) which discusses the role of Buddhist
    monks in the insurgency. Baird and Le Billon, commenting on how outsiders operating
    in Laos are typically ill-informed about the post-1975 conflict, suggest instead that
    Laos be recognized as in a "'post-conflict' situation" (2012: 294). A summary also
    appears in Baird's account of the special relationship that developed between a group
    of Thai monks and Hmong (2013b: 132). See also Ivarsson et al. (1995: 20).

12. They were referred to by the Lao government, by contrast, as *phattikan* (counter-
    revolutionaries) (Baird 2012, personal communication).

13. Most of the ethnic Lao asylum seekers were housed in Ban Napho, reaching a popu-
    lation of 23,000 in 1986 (Van Esterik 1992: 13). The camp was aimed at "humane
    deterrent", with the Spartan living conditions purportedly discouraging additional
    asylum seekers. After 1985, new screening procedures were introduced intended at
    separating out political from economic refugees. Those deemed as economic refugees
    and thus rejected were confined in detention camps for eventual return to Laos: Si
    may have been confined in one of these camps.

14. This came across clearly in a news report on smuggling across the Mekong:

    > "Goods smuggling spread widely throughout the 1980s and '90s, and was mainly
    > caused by limitations on imports and exports of everyday consumer goods. Laos, like
    > Thailand, has made continuous efforts to eradicate the practice. Thanks to the good
    > relationship between the two countries, and the agreement to broaden import and
    > export laws, smuggling has declined since 2000" (Phinith 2006).

15. As recently as July 2011, Amnesty (2011: 6) was continuing to condemn the treat-
    ment of these asylum seekers. However, Baird reports that the 158 Hmong were
    eventually able to be resettled as refugees abroad, although this was not reported
    in the media, and that, of the 4,500, many have subsequently returned to Thailand
    (personal communication 2012).

16. Mr Suang Sengsouliya, Mr Vixay Xayachak, Mr Bounloth Khensouvan, Mr Lom
    Salyhom, Mr Thongdy Homnuan, Mr Souliya Samart, Mr Teum Phomthevy and
    Mr Seng Saybounya received sentences of 12 years. Mr Kham Sayavong, Mr Napha

Phothibandith, Mr Phailin Saybounya, Mr Phaysan Linthang, Mr Kaen Singkhoum-khong and Mr Keobuathong Vongphachan received sentences of seven years. Mr Seng Champa and Mr Som Sayavong received sentences of two years and six months (VT 2004, 22 October).

17. See for instance IRIN news website "Laos: Domestic Trafficking goes undetected" which reports a UNICEF spokesperson saying, "We encounter women on a regular basis [who] don't know they were trafficked, but who want to escape exploitation". Brennan (2005) writing of trafficking workers in the US likewise was told "None of the women tell me 'I'm a victim of trafficking', rather they say 'I need help to not get deported'". Nadra Qadeer, Director of the Anti-Trafficking Program at Safe Horizon in New York City, echoed this observation: "People do not talk about trafficking ever. They talk about abuse, things like 'my boyfriend beat me." (2005: 41).

18. This was never more clear than in the arrest in 2007 of US citizen and former CIA ally, Vang Pao, in the US on charges of planning an attack on the government of Laos.

19. I also thank Ian Baird (personal communication) for reporting in addition that smuggling is continuing across the Vang Tai/Chong Mek border as some Lao traders pay export tax on only part of what they carry across the border. This resonates with the findings Walker (1999) made about the way even tightly controlled borders create zones for profit. Baird also suggests that forest paths that avoid the Vang Tai/Chong Mek border crossing are also still used today.

Chapter Four

1. He wrote, "In every social system, you will always find lines of escape, as well as sticking points to cut off these escapes, or else (which is not the same thing) embryonic apparatuses to recuperate them, to reroute and stop them, in a new system waiting to strike." (Deleuze 2004: 269–70).

2. This echoes what Gell calls "conventional western attitudes" about the meaning of skin (1993: 24). There is a tendency, he suggests, to reason that "the skin is on the outside of the body (and) what is outside is always less important/true/real than what is inside (and) hence the skin cannot tell us about the real person" (1993: 24, symbols removed, parentheses added). I have written on this elsewhere (see High 2004).

3. There is also evidence that race matters in Laos, too. Baird has recently written about the apparently race-related restrictions on Hmong settlement in the south of Laos (2010).

4. Turner noted some time ago that skins are always significant, if only because they mediate between "the self and the other, the individual and society" (1980: 139). Thus, the skin is a particularly powerful "symbolic stage" where both self making and socialization are dramatized. Turner suggested that, "the surface of the body seems everywhere to be treated, not only as the boundary of the individual as a biological and psychological entity but as the frontier of the social self as well" (1980: 112). In Japan, Ashikari (2005) suggests that white skin is understood as an innate feature of the Japanese race, so that skin whitening cosmetics are not understood as making skin white, but as bringing out an underlying core of Japanese whiteness. Ashikari suggests that in this context, skin colour and cosmetics are firmly entrenched in a

racial discourse. In contrast, O'Hanlon notes that among the Wahgi of Papua New Guinea's Western Highlands Province, it is the "axis of gloss/glow:matt/dull, not that of colour, which is crucial in assessing appearance" (1989: 118). For the Wahgi, skin is of an abiding interest: it is decorated, oiled, discussed and cultivated. But it is not blackness and whiteness that are the main concern of these interventions. Instead, aesthetics favour the glow, luminousity, lustre and gloss of skin. Skin that is burnished, glittering and iridescent is valued. Skin that is dry, dull, matt, flaky, and ashen is devalued. O'Hanlon links this preference for sheen and glow to the importance of pig fat, which is a symbol of growth, fertility and well-being. Pig fat and glowing skin alike are symbols of people's productive and harmonious social relationships. Dull skin can indicate pollution, sorcery or betrayal by one's kin. While these transgressions may be verbally denied, they are evident in skins, because appearances are "felt to disclose the true state of moral relations, otherwise obscured by doubt and rival verbal accounts" (1989: 111).

5. This interweaving of skin colour with other valued traits, as well as its achievability, is evident in some of the literary traditions of the region. Sachchidanand writes:

> The discrimination on the basis of colour is a dominant theme in the classical literature of Laos and other countries of Indo-China. The heroes and the gifted persons are presented as persons with light colour, while the people with dark colour are defined Kha, uncivilised and incapable. The Kha are made themselves responsible for their present state. One of the texts says: Men and women descended from the mountain to drink the purifying water of the pond at the foot of the hill. Those who washed themselves well and drank its water, obtained a brilliant, beautiful, light-colour physique as well as conscience, intelligence and ability to govern the country. Afraid of the cold the Kha Che came out of the pond first, without washing themselves properly and without drinking its water. So they remained dark in colour and in (sic) deplorable state. (2005: 30–1).

6. Green has noted a similar emphasis on building a personal house in Tanzania. She links the desire for a house to a notion of "personal development" based on a "recognition of the potentiality of individual agency in bringing about social transformation" (2000: 2). Green points out that such a personal, agency-focused view of development stands at odds with state development policies and the "participatory" community development interventions of foreign NGOs and donors, which draw on assumptions about "'traditional' collectivist values of rural African communities" (2000: 15). The disparity, as Green has noted, is between the intensely personal and the resolutely generalising.

7. In Laos, the *kip* has been notoriously unstable, prone to hyperinflation.

8. Gold was not always the supreme standard. He argues that in the past this mantle was shared with silver and cowrie shells (1997: 250). Gregory, drawing on Rist, interprets the ongoing attachment to gold and resistance to state-backed currencies as an aspect of a larger struggle between individuals and the state for power over the future (1997: 252).

9. Deleuze and Guattari wrote: "But our 'object choice' itself refers to a conjunction of flows of life and of society that this body and this person intercept, receive, and transmit, always within a biological, social, and historical field where we are equally immersed or with which we communicate." The people we love "intervene only as

points of connection, of disjunction of flows whose libidinal tenor of a properly unconscious investment they translate" (1983: 293).

10. Turner, for instance, suggested that concerns with appearances may be one of the human universals that is able to reveal so much about cultural difference: "(T)he adornment and public presentation of the body, however inconsequential or even frivolous a business it may appear to individuals, is for cultures a serious matter" (1980: 112). Miller has noted that consumption, especially of items deemed non-essential, is devalued in much analysis through an association with the "surface" and thus superficiality, while true "meaning" is to be found in "deeper" topics (1994). On a related point, Friedman comments that through the commonly drawn distinction between needs and luxuries, it seems "all non-productive consumption is simply unnecessary and therefore somehow a product of error, false consciousness, compensatory behaviour, ostentation; all in all, a misconstrual of reality" (1994: 2). This is especially true in the discourse of poverty in the international development bureaucracy, where recent trends have emphasized "basic needs", and communal goods, rather than the consumptions described above: cosmetics, gold, houses and household goods, and clothing.

11. Lai had arrived at this expectation by speaking to returned migrants and the *khon song*. I collected similar estimations from the numerous other would-be or return migrants that I spoke to, many reporting even higher figures. It is possible that some inflation of the wages expected has been caused by return migrants exaggerating their successes, or migrant agents overstating the benefits of working in Thailand. According to 2006 minimum wage rates, if a person worked in a Bangkok factory six days a week for a month at minimum wage, they could expect to earn 4,316 baht, so these figures may not be as inflated as they appear at first glance. On the other hand, labour activists estimate that only a fraction of labourers in Thailand are paid the minimum wage.

12. Walker (2009) reports that in his fieldsite in rural northern Thailand, the daily wage was 120 baht during his fieldwork in the mid-nineties.

13. Noy's envelope contained about 7,000 *baht*, Win's about 9,520 *baht*, and Daaw's about 4,000 *baht*. About 50 *baht* was paid to the *maee khaa*, for the cost of the telephone calls.

14. In economics, the debate on how best to measure poverty has centred often on the choice between "relative" and "absolute" poverty lines. Proponents of the absolute measure of poverty argue that its merits lie in its wide applicability and its conformity to the populist notion of poverty as "absolute", in a more general sense of extreme and dire. By applying an absolute measure of poverty to post-war Britain, it was found that poverty in the working classes had dropped from 31 percent to just 3 percent, prompting the Labour Party to claim that poverty had been "banished" (Sen 1983: 154). Commentators such as Townsend rejected such victory claims, arguing that poverty is relative both to time and to place (1979: 17). They proposed a "relative" poverty line that is variable both over time and in different global contexts. The relative poverty line is one that measures poverty in relation to the rest of society. The relative poverty measure has gained recent support in industrialized countries, because it highlights not just basic needs, but inequalities. The relative poverty line

has become "the accepted" measure of poverty in affluent economies (Sen 1983: 153). There are several weaknesses in the relative poverty line approach, particularly around the question of "relative to whom?" Invariably relative poverty lines are set relative to "a society". In practice, the basic unit of this "society" is the nation-state. This means that the definition of what it is to be poor in one nation-state is different from the definition in another. This raises two problems: first, it overlooks the fact that, although poverty is experienced as a social relation, these relations are not severed by the borders of nation-states. In migrations to Thailand, international news and relatives abroad, the rural poor of Don Khiaw experience their poverty relatively, yes, but relative to a trans-national context. By contrast, people in Don Khiaw rarely compared themselves at all to their highlander compatriots, who, it has been suggested, are arguably more impoverished (Goudineau 2003). Second, the significant divergences in poverty lines between nation-states engendered by the relative poverty line amounts to an institutionalized variation in standards, whereby what a person can reasonably expect for a basic living depends on his or her nationality and citizenship. The relative poverty line asks us to find acceptable for some what would be unacceptable for others.

Chapter Five

1. A number of high-profile cases had made this clear. Three high-ranking government officials were arrested in October 1990 for writing letters demanding political and economic change in Laos. They went on trial in November 1992, where they faced charges such as "making preparations for rebellion", "propaganda against the Lao People's democratic republic" and "libel and slander" (AI 2004). Two were released to France on 16 December 2004, the third died in prison. In October 1999, the "Lao Students Movement for Democracy" reportedly attempted to raise banners of protest. Five were arrested. One died in prison, another was released in 2002, and three remain behind bars. Amnesty International considers them as prisoners of conscience. When the Asia-Europe Meetings were held in Laos in 2012, Amnesty International attempted to use the occasion to draw attention to the men's political imprisonment, but with little discernable impact. Foreign nationals also have strong disincentives to express open dissent: in June 2003, Belgian reporter Thierry Falise, French photographer Vincent Reynaud, and their American interpreter Naw Karl Moua were arrested along with their Lao guides while attempting to access a Hmong group. After diplomatic talks, the foreign nationals were expelled, Falise commenting on the regime "I would call it an injustice system, there was no justice, no fair trial" (AI 2004). That said, this context has shifted during the ten years plus or so of my research. Recently, there have been moves to enhance and increase spaces for public dissent, although the outcome of these efforts and experiments remains uncertain (see High 2013b).

2. Taussig suggests that fear has a "silencing" effect, but this silence only confirms terror, as it drives stories of the state into the realms of myth and nightmare. Taussig warns that silencing is not to be confused with forgetting. He writes: "The point about silencing and the fear behind silencing is not to erase memory. Far from it. The point is to drive memory deep within the fastness of the individual so as to create more

fear and uncertainty in which dream and reality commingle" (1992: 27). "What distinguishes cultures of terror," Taussig writes, "is that the…problem of reality-and-illusion, certainty-and-doubt, becomes infinitely more than a 'merely' philosophical problem. It becomes a high-powered tool for domination and a principal medium of political practice" (1984: 492).

3. It continues to elaborate:

> "The National Assembly is a state organ representing the rights and interests of the Lao multi-ethnic people. The National Assembly is the supreme organ of state powers and also the legislative branch with the powers to make decisions on fundamental issues of the country, to oversight the activities of the executive organs, the people's courts and the offices of the people's prosecutors. The election of the National Assembly members is carried out on the basis of the principles of universality, equality, direct suffrage and secret ballot" (19 June 2012), http://www.mofa.gov.la/index.php/en/about-lao-pdr/64-about-lao-p-d-r/112-lao-political-structure.

4. The full quotation makes Zizek's point clear:

> In March 2003, Donald Rumsfeld engaged in a brief bout of amateur philosophizing about the relationship between the known and the unknown: 'There are known knowns. These are things we know that we know. There are known unknowns. That is to say, there are things that we know we don't know. But there are also unknown unknowns. There are things we don't know we don't know.' What he forgot to add was the crucial fourth term: 'the unknown knowns', things we don't know that we know—which is precisely the Freudian unconscious, the 'knowledge that doesn't know itself', as Lacan used to say, the core of which is fantasy. If Rumsfeld thinks that the main dangers in the confrontation with Iraq are the 'unknown unknowns', the threats from Saddam or his successors about which we do not even suspect what they may be, what we should say in reply is that the main dangers are, on the contrary, the 'unknown knowns',…which nonetheless determine our acts and feelings." (Zizek 2006a: 52).

5. References in this format refer to "Summary of World Broadcasts" (SWB), the Far East section (FE).

6. A comprehensive account and analysis of collectivization in Laos is provided by Evans (1988; 1990) and Stuart-Fox also describes the scheme (1996).

7. Toro (2012) provides an overview of the collectivization efforts in the Bolaven. He reports that these took place from 1981–84.

8. This entails a mode of state-society relations that I have elsewhere described as an "experimental consensus" (High 2013a).

9. Singh (2009), for instance, has provided a detailed ethnography of low-ranking officials in the Nakai Plateau attempting to gain secure government jobs by "volunteering" in District offices. For income, they relied on the per diems dispensed by aid projects. Such work was allocated by higher ranking officials who expect a portion of the per diem to be returned to them in thanks. Baird (2010c) describes corruption in logging in Champassak and Attapeu. Officials reported collecting "fees" even from householders who held all the correct permission papers as their most lucrative form of income.

10. Two politburo members were dismissed in 1991 under allegations of corruption. Sisavat Keobounphan, one of the dismissed, was reinstated in 1996 and served briefly

as Vice-President. Laos signed the United Nations Conventions against Corruption in 2003 and now celebrates the infectious "Anti-corruption day" each year. On that occasion one year, Mr Asang Laoly, Deputy Prime Minister, stated: "Corruption is a serious bug that eats into a nation, and it will finally topple the nation" (2005).

Chapter Six

1. The metaphor of such interpretations as "catching" people is an idiom drawn from the way people discussed witchcraft in the Bocage that Favret-Saada studied: to be bewitched was to be "caught".

2. Baird was present in the area when the project was first launched, and he remarks that there was considerable enthusiasm at first, with people eagerly demanding pumps (personal communication 2012).

3. He goes on, "Ruination is not just death, loss, and absence; it is vitality, survival, and insistent presence against all expectations. Ruins…surprise because they manifest a positivity where there should be nothing but negativity, a presence where all there should be (is) absence" (Beasley-Murray 2011: 160).

4. For instance, in an influential essay, Timothy Mitchell argued that the boundary between state and society "appears elusive, porous, and mobile" (1991: 77). He did not specify to whom the boundary appears this way—presumably this was a free-floating perception, perhaps among his readers, or perhaps within the "modern state" where he locates so much of his analysis. Yet, at the same time and in a contradictory vein, his essay is perhaps best remembered for his argument that a perception of a distinction between state and society *is* produced by the modern state, powerfully so, and that in fact the production of this distinction is defining of the modern state. He writes: "The ability to have an internal distinction appear as though it were the external boundary between separate objects is the distinctive technique of the modern political order" (1991: 78). Mitchell is thus credited with unveiling the state not as an entity, but as an "effect".

5. Ireson-Doolittle and Moreno-Black (2004) describe a much more intensive role for the Women's Union elsewhere in Laos.

6. Sahlins' formulation is worth considering at length:

   > "If people really were in control of their own existence they would not die. Or fall ill. Nor do they govern the natural reproductive processes of their food supplies or themselves. They cannot control the weather on which their prosperity depends. And most notably in the present connection, neither do they control other peoples of their ken: peoples whose cultural existence may be enviable or scandalous to them, but in any case, by their very differences from themselves, strangers who thus offer proof of a transcendent capacity for life. As symptoms of life powers, even the dangers of outside presences may factor into desires for them…marriage is the archetypal form of life-from-without, the actual experiential synthesis of intimacy and alterity that prospers the consanguineous group through the incorporation of external reproductive powers. In this regard, marriage or stranger-kinship epitomises stranger kingship, as conversely the dynasty of the stranger-king is typically founded by an alliance of cosmic dimensions with a princess of the autochthonous people" (2010: 379–80).

7. It was further developed by Miller (1994).

Chapter Seven

1. Li (2007) has provided an anthropological reading of the original Kecamatan Development Project on which this project was based.

Chapter Nine

1. Sahlins himself draws on many examples that involve no kings, such as ideas of potency among headhunters. He argues that, nevertheless, "as modes of political authority, they are structurally commensurable" (2008: 188), that is, there is a general structure of the stranger-king that underlies all these different examples, even when royalty or men are not the key factor, and this is that "All achieve their authority by their instantiation or command of external sources of vitality and mortality." (2008: 188).

2. The Urangadhatu, a Chronicle kept at the That Phanom on the bank of the Mekong in Nakom Phanom, Thailand, describes the Buddha's airborne journeys along the Mekong in the company of his disciple, Ananda. They encounter nagas that dwell in the river, spirits of the place and local leaders. In some places he is honoured and asked to leave a footprint, in others he is attacked by nagas but they cannot prevail. They surrender instead and become his followers. In various ways, a series of indigenous powers, human and non-human, either yield to him or are overcome, and he then imprints his traces on the land (Sachchidanand 2005: 24).

3. This is a key variation of stranger-kingship, where the king is in fact a native son who for one reason or another is separated from his native land before returning to conquer and rule it. Fa Ngum is revered even by the current LPRP-endorsed literature as the foundational leader of the Lao nation: he has been installed as first of a sequence of "great kings" in a single line of "patriotic ancestors" (Grabowsky and Tappe 2011: 1). The chronicles explain that Fa Ngum was born in Xieng Dong Xieng Thong (now Luang Prabang) but was forced to spend his childhood in the Cambodian court. There he married the daughter of the Khmer king and returned with her father's army to retake Xieng Dong Xieng Thong and force the surrounding areas to accept his leadership (Stuart-Fox 1997: 9). His subsequent violent exploits united the various *muang* into the Kingdom of Lan Xang, thought of as the predecessor of contemporary Laos.

4. An excellent one is the *Phra Lak Phra Lam*, a version of the Ramayana epic rewritten to be set along the length of the Mekong River. The text was copied to its present form in 1850 but internal evidence suggests that it goes back at least to the 17th century. Until the 1970s, it is reported that these legends were recited by Buddhist monks from palm-leaf manuscripts during the rains retreat, and listened to by laypeople (Sachchidanand 2005: 61). In this version of the myth, Rama's father is the founder of Vientiane and Ravana is his younger brother, in Phonom Phen. Rama's sister Chantha is abducted by Ravana. Lak and Lum are born to rescue their sister. They do so, and along the way have many adventures that often culminate in marrying local women, typically the daughters of local chiefs (including the daughter of one "Kha" chief). They also marry a series of nagas, thevadas and water spirits. Rama himself marries the sister of the naga-king.

The subsequent brideprices entail the brothers building important roads between power centres and also further adventures which see the brothers' retainers meet and fall in love with local women: they escape and found new cities. The city of Bassak, for instance, the old capital of the Kingdom of Champassak, is said in this legend to be founded when a young retainer, Thao Pan Dam, fled with Lady Sakta, the name of the city they founded being composed of one element from each of their names (Sachchidanand 2005).

5. This is noted by Sahlins in his 2008 paper.

6. The key example is the contrast between the fate of Captain Cook, who Sahlins argues was ultimately killed because of his recognition as a stranger-king by the Hawaiians, and James Brooke who was the first "white rajah of Sarawak" on the same principle. Sahlins explains, "the big argument I am making is that Cook was a god-figure who died as a function of the same kind of structural relations that allowed Brooke to be the man who became king" (2012: 148).

7. He explains that, "Abstractly, the life of society is generated through the combination of opposed yet complementary qualities, each incomplete without the other" (1981: 121).

Bibliography

Agamben, G. (1999). "Absolute Immanence," in *Potentialities: Collected Essays in Philosophy*. Stanford: Stanford University Press.

Amnesty International (2001). "Thailand: Time to end human rights violations," in *Amnesty International Submission to the UN universal periodic review*, October.

————— (9 May 2006). "Urgent Action, Laos: Further information on forcible return/arbitrary detention/torture/ill-treatment," <http://web.amnesty.org/library/Index/ENGASA260032006?open&of=ENG-LAO> [accessed 14 May 2006, page no longer available].

————— (8 July 2004). "Fear of torture/fear for safety/unfair trial," <http://web.amnesty.org/library/Index/ENGASA260032004?open&of=ENG-LAO> [accessed 8 January 2004, page no longer available].

Archaimbault, C. (1961). "L'Historie de Campassak," *Journal Asiatique* 249, 4.

Ashikari, M. (2005). "Cultivating Japanese Whiteness: The 'Whitening' Cosmetics Boom and the Japanese Identity," *Journal of Material Culture* 10, 1: 73–91.

Aymonier, E. (2000). *Isan Travels: Northeast Thailand's Economy in 1883–1884*, tr. Walter E.J. Tips. Bangkok: White Lotus Press.

Baird, I.G. (2007). "Contested History, Ethnicity, and Remembering the Past: The Case of the Ay Sa Rebellion in Southern Laos," *Crossroads* 18, 2: 119–59.

————— (2010a). "Land, Rubber and People: Rapid Agrarian Changes and Responses in Southern Laos," *The Journal of Lao Studies* 1, 1: 1–47.

————— (2010b). "The Hmong Come to Southern Laos: Local Responses and the Creation of Racialized Boundaries," *Hmong Studies Journal* 11: 1–38.

————— (2010c). "Quotas, Powers, Patronage and Illegal Rent-Seeking: The political Economy of Logging and the Timber Trade in Southern Laos," in *Forest Governance, Markets and Trade: Implications for sustainability and livelihoods* <http://www.forest-trends.org>.

————— (2012). "Lao Buddhist Monks' Involvement in Political and Military Resistance to the Lao People's Democratic Republic Government since 1975," *The Journal of Asian Studies* 71: 655–77.

————— (2013a). "Millenarian movements in Southern Laos and North Eastern Siam (Thailand) at the turn of the twentieth century: Reconsidering the involvement of the Champassak Royal House," *Southeast Asia Research* 21, 2: 257–79.

———— (2013b). "The Monks and the Hmong: The Special Relationship between the Chao Fa and the Tham Krabok Buddhist Temple in Saraburi Province, Thailand," in *Buddhism and Violence: Militarism and Buddhism in Modern Asia*, ed. V. Tikhonov and T. Brekke. New York and London: Routledge.

Baird, I.G. and K. Barney, et al. (2009). "Internal Resettlement in Laos," *Critical Asian Studies* 41, 4: 605–20.

Baird, I.G. and P. Le Billon (2012). "Landscapes of political memories: War legacies and land negotiations in Laos," *Political Geography* 31: 290–300.

Beasley-Murray, J. (2001). Comments to "Ships Stranded in a Forest: Debris of Progress on a Phantom River" by Gastón Gordillo, *Current Anthropology* 52, 2: 160.

Berdahl, D. (1999). *Where the World Ended: Re-Unification and Identity in the German Borderland*. Berkeley, Los Angeles and London: University of California Press.

Bray, F. (1986). *The Rice Economies: Technology and Development in Asian Societies*. Oxford: Basil Blackwell.

Brennan, D. (2005). "Methodological Challenges in Research with Trafficked Persons: Tales from the Field," *International Migration* 43, 1–2: 35–54.

Brown, M.F. (2008). "Cultural Relativism 2.0," *Current Anthropology* 49, 3: 363–83.

Caldwell, I. and D. Henley (2008). "Introduction: The Stranger who would be King. Magic, logic, polemic," *Indonesia and the Malay World* 36, 105: 163–75.

Carsten, J. (1995). "The Substance of Kinship and the Heat of the Hearth: Feeding, Personhood, and Relatedness among Malays in Pulau Langkawi," *American Ethnologist* 22, 2: 223–41.

Col, G. da and D. Graeber (2011). "Foreword: The return of ethnographic theory," *HAU: Journal of Ethnographic Theory* 1, 1: vi–xxxvii.

Condominas, G. (1990). *From Lawa to Mon, from Saa' to Thai: Historical and Anthropological Aspects of Southeast Asian Social Spaces*, ed. G. Wijeyewardene and tr. S. Anderson, M. Magannon, and G. Wijeyewardene. An occasional paper of the Department of Anthropology in association with the Thai-Yunnan Project, Research School of Pacific Studies, The Australian National University, Canberra.

Costello, Nancy A. (1993). *Katu Folktales and Society*. Ministry of Information and Culture, Vientiane: Institute of Research on Lao Culture and Society.

Cowlishaw, G. (2004). *Blackfellas, Whitefellas, and the Hidden Injuries of Race*. Cornwall: Blackwell Publishing.

Creak, S. (2011). "Laos: Celebrations and Development Debates," *Southeast Asian Affairs 2011*, ed. Daljit Singh. Singapore: Institute of Southeast Asian Studies, pp. 107–28.

Deleuze, G. (2004). *Desert Islands and Other Texts, 1953–1974*. Los Angeles: Semiotext(e).

Deleuze, G. and F. Guattari (1983). *Anti-Oedipus: Capitalism and Schizophrenia*. Minneapolis: University of Minnesota Press.

Devereux, G. (1980). *Basic Problems in Ethnopsychiatry*. Chicago and London: The University of Chicago Press.

Dumézil, G. (1988). *Mitra-Varuna: An Essay on Two Indo-European Representations of Sovereignty*. New York: Zone Books.

Evans, G. (1998). *The Politics of Ritual and Remembrance: Laos since 1975.* Honolulu: University of Hawaii Press.

———— (1990). *Lao Peasants under Socialism.* New Haven and London: Yale University Press.

Evans, G. and K. Rowley (1984). *Red Brotherhood at War: Indochina since the Fall of Saigon.* London: Verso.

Evrard, O. and Y. Goudineau (2004). "Planned Resettlement, Unexpected Migrations and Cultural Trauma in Laos," *Development and Change* 35, 5: 937–62.

Favret-Saada, J. (1980). *Deadly Words: Witchcraft in the Bocage.* Cambridge: Cambridge University Press.

Foucault, M. (1984). *The Use of Pleasure. The History of Sexuality, Vol. 2.* London: Penguin Books.

———— (1976). *An Introduction. The History of Sexuality, Vol. 1.* Harmondsworth: Penguin.

Frazer, J.G. (1966). "Preface," in *Argonauts of the Western Pacific: An Account of Native Enterprise and Adventure in the Archipelagoes of Melanesian New Guinea,* B. Malinowski. London: Routledge and Kegan Paul Ltd.

Ferguson, J. (1994). *The Anti-Politics Machine: "Development," Depoliticization, and Bureaucratic Power in Lesotho.* Minneapolis and London: University of Minnesota Press.

Friedman, J. (1994). "Introduction," in *Consumption and Identity,* ed. J. Friedman. Chur, Switzerland: Harwood Academic Publishers, pp. 1–23.

Garnier, F. (1996). *Travels in Cambodia and Part of Laos: The Mekong Exploration Commission Report (1866–1868)—Volume 1.* Bangkok: White Lotus Press.

Gay, B. (2002). "Millenarian movements in Laos, 1895–1936: Depictions by Modern Lao Historians," in *Breaking New Ground in Lao History: Essays on Seventh to Twentieth Centuries,* ed. M. Ngaosrivathana and K. Brezeale. Chiangmai: Silkworm Books.

Geertz, C. (1963). *Agricultural Involution: The Processes of Ecological Change in Indonesia.* Berkeley, Los Angeles and London: University of California Press.

Gell, A. (1993). *Wrapping in Images: Tattooing in Polynesia.* Oxford: Clarendon Press.

Gesick, L.M. (May 1976). "Kingship and Political Integration in Traditional Siam, 1767–1824," unpublished thesis, Faculty of the Graduate School of Cornell University.

Gordillo, G. (2011). "Ships Stranded in the Forest: Debris of Progress on a Phantom River," *Current Anthropology* 52, 2: 141–67.

Goudineau, Y., ed. (2003). *Laos and Ethnic Minority Cultures: Promoting Heritage.* Paris: UNESCO Publishing.

Grabowsky, V. (1995). "The Isan Up to Its Integration into the Siamese State," in *Regions and National Integration in Thailand 1892–1992,* ed. V. Grabosky. Harrassowitz Verlag: Wiesbaden.

Grabowsky, V. and O. Tappe (2011). ""Important King of Laos": Translation and Analysis of a Lao Cartoon Pamphlet," *Journal of Lao Studies* 2, 1: 1–44.

Graeber, D. (2011). "The divine kingship of the Shilluk: On violence, utopia, and the human condition, or, elements for an archeology of sovereignty," *HAU: Journal of Ethnographic Theory* 1, 1: 1–62.

Green, M. (2000). "Participatory Development and the Appropriation of Agency in Southern Tanzania," *Critique of Anthropology* 20, 1: 67–89.

Gregory, C.A. (1997). *Savage Money: The Anthropology and Politics of Commodity Exchange*. Amsterdam: Harwood Academic Publishers.

Guéguen, P.-G. (2006). "The Intimate, the Extimate, and Psychoanalytic Discourse," in *Jacques Lacan and The Other Side of Psychoanalysis*, ed. J. Clemens and R. Grigg. Durham and London: Duke University Press, pp. 263–73.

Gunn, G.C. (1983). "Resistance Coalitions in Laos," *Asian Survey* 23, 3: 316–40.

Hanks, J.R. (1960). "Reflections on the Ontology of Rice," in *Primitive Views of the World*, ed. S. Diamond. New York and London: Columbia University Press, pp. 151–4.

Harmand F.J. (1997). *Laos and the Hilltribes of Indochina: Journeys to the Boloven Plateau, from Bassac to Hué through Laos, and to the Origins of the Thai*, first published in French as articles in Le Tour du Monde 1878–9. Bangkok: White Lotus Press.

Hertzfeld, M. (1997). *Cultural Intimacy: Social Poetics in the Nation-State*. New York and London: Routledge.

Heusch, L. de (1982). *The drunken king, or, The origin of the state*. Bloomington: Indiana University Press.

High, H. (2013a). "Experimental Consensus: Negotiating with the Irrigating State in the South of Laos," available online to subscribers of *Asian Studies Review*.

———— (2013b). "Laos in 2012: In the Name of Democracy," in *Southeast Asian Affairs 2013*, ed. Daljit Singh. Singapore: Institute of Southeast Asian Studies, pp. 135–50.

———— (2011a). "Melancholia and Anthropology," *American Ethnologist* 38, 2: 217–33.

———— (2011b). "Poverty and Merit: Mobile Persons in Laos," in *Everyday Life in Southeast Asia*, ed. K.M. Adams and K.A. Gillogly. Bloomington: Indiana University Press.

———— (2010). "Ethnographic exposures: Motivations for donations in the south of Laos (and beyond)," *American Ethnologist* 37, 2: 308–22.

———— (2009). "The Spirit of Community: Puta Belief and Communal Sentiments in Southern Laos," in *Tai Lands and Thailand: Community and State in Southeast Asia*, ed. A. Walker. Copenhagen: NIAS Press, pp. 84–95.

———— (2008). "The Implications of Aspirations: Reconsidering Resettlement in Laos," *Critical Asian Studies* 40, 4: 531–50.

———— (2006a). "Ritualising Residency: Territory Cults and a Sense of Place in Southern Lao PDR," *The Asia Pacific Journal of Anthropology* 7, 3: 251–64.

———— (2006b). "Join Together, Work Together, for the Common Good—Solidarity: Village Formation Processes in the Rural South of Laos," *SOJOURN: Journal of Social Issues in Southeast Asia* 21, 1: 22–45.

———— (2004). ""Black" skin "white" skin: Riches and beauty in Lao women's bodies," *Thai-Yunnan Project Bulletin* 6: 7–9.

INTERPOL (24 November 2005). "People Smuggling." <http://www.interpol.int/contentinterpol/search?SearchText=PEOPLE+SMUGGLING&x=0&y=0> [accessed 15 May 2006].

Ireson, R.W. (1995). "Village Irrigation in Laos: Traditional Patterns of Common Property Resource Management," *Society and Natural Resources: An International Journal* 8, 6: 541–58.

Ireson-Doolittle, C. and G. Moreno-Black (2004). *The Lao: Gender, Power and Livelihood*. Boulder, Colorado: Westview Press.

Ivarsson, S. (2008). *Creating Laos: The Making of a Lao Space between Indochina and Siam, 1860–1945*. Copenhagen: NIAS Press.

Ivarsson, S., T. Svensson, and S. Tonnesson (1995). *The Quest for Balance in a Changing Laos: A Political Analysis*. Copenhagen: NIAS Press.

Kaufman, H.K. (1961). *Village Life in Vientiane Province (1956–1957)*. Waltham, Massachusetts: Department of Anthropology, Brandeis University.

Kerkvliet, B.J.T. (1995). "Village-State Relations in Vietnam: The Effects of Everyday Politics on Decollectivisation," *The Journal of Asian Studies* 54, 2: 396–418.

——— (1986). "Everyday Resistance to Injustice in a Philippine Village," in *Everyday Forms of Peasant Resistance in South-East Asia*, ed. J.C. Scott and B.J.T. Kerkvliet. London: Frank Cass, pp. 107–23.

Kerr, A.D. (1972). *Lao-English Dictionary*. Washington D.C.: Catholic University of America Press.

Keyes, C.F. (1983). "Economic Action and Buddhist Morality in a Thai Village," *Journal of Asian Studies* 42, 4: 851–68.

——— (1983). "Merit-Transference in the Kammic Theory of Popular Theravāda Buddhism," in *Karma: An Anthropological Inquiry*, ed. C.F. Keyes and E.V. Daniel. Berkeley, Los Angeles and London: University of California Press, pp. 261–86.

——— (1977). "Millennialism, Theravāda Buddhism, and Thai Society," *The Journal of Asian Studies* 36, 2: 283–302.

Kipnis, A. (2004). "Anthropology and the Theorisation of Citizenship," *The Asia Pacific Journal of Anthropology* 5, 3: 257–78.

Kirsch, A.T. (1982). "Buddhism, Sex Roles, and the Thai Economy," in *Women of Southeast Asia*, ed. P. Van Esterik. De Kalb, Illinois: Northern Illinois University, pp. 13–32.

Laoly, A. (2005). "Speech of His Excellency Mr. Asang Laoly, Deputy Prime Minister of Lao PDR, on the meeting to celebrate the International Day Against Corruption, 9 December 2005," *Vientiane Times* 241, 5, 12 December.

Lea, T. (2008). *Bureaucrats and Bleeding Hearts: Indigenous Health in Northern Australia*. Sydney: UNSW Press.

Leach, E. (1954). *Political Systems of Highland Burma: A Study of Kachin Social Structure*. Cambridge, Massachusetts: Harvard University Press.

Lee, G.Y. (2007). "The Hmong Rebellion in Laos: Victims or Terrorists? in *A Handbook of Terrorism in Southeast Asia*, ed. A.T.H. Tan. Cheltenham, UK and Northampton, MA, USA: Edward Elgar, pp. 352–73.

Li, T.M. (2007). *The Will to Improve: Governmentality, Development, and the Practice of Politics*. Durham and London: Duke University Press.

_______ (2014). *Land's End: Capitalist Relations on an Indigenous Frontier*. Durham: Duke University Press.

Lichbach, M.I. (1994). "What makes Rational Peasants Revolutionary? Dilemma, Paradox, and Irony in Peasant Collective Action," *World Politics* 46, 3: 383–418.

Little, D. (1990). "Ethical Analysis and Wealth in Theravāda Buddhism," in *Ethics, Wealth, and Salvation: A Study in Buddhist Social Ethics*, ed. R.F. Sizemore and D.K. Swearer. Columbia: University of South Carolina Press.

LPDR (2003). "*The Lao PDR's National Poverty Eradication Programme (NPEP): A Comprehensive Approach to Growth with Equity*," draft. Vientiane: Central Planning Committee.

Lyttleton, C. (1999). "Any Port in a Storm: Coming to Terms with HIV in Lao PDR." *Culture, Health and Sexuality: An International Journal for Research, Intervention and Care* 1, 2: 115–30.

Malinowski, B. (1966). *Argonauts of the Western Pacific: An Account of Native Enterprise and Adventure in the Archipelagoes of Melanesian New Guinea*. London: Routledge and Kegan Paul Ltd.

Marx, K. (1987). "Peasantry as a Class," in *Peasants and Peasant Societies: Selected Readings*, ed. T. Shanin. Oxford, New York: Basil Blackwell, pp. 331–7.

_______ (1976). *Capital. Volume 1: A Critique of Political Economy*, tr. B. Fowkes. Middlesex, New York, Ringwood, Ontario and Auckland: Penguin Books in association with Left Review.

Marx, K. and F. Engels (Originally published in 1888). *The Manifesto of the Communist Party*. Adelaide, The University of Adelaide Library: ebooks@Adelaide. <http://ebooks.adelaide.edu.au/m/marx/karl/m39c/>

Mcelwee, P. (2007). "From the Moral Economy to the World Economy: Revisiting Vietnamese Peasants in a Globalizing Era." *Journal of Vietnamese Studies* 2, 2: 57–107.

Miller, D. (1994). "Style and Ontology," in *Consumption and Identity*, ed. J. Friedman. Chur, Switzerland: Harwood Academic Publishers.

Miller, J.-A. (1994). "Extimité," in *Lacanian Theory of Discourse: Subject, Structure and Society*, ed. M. Bracher, M.W.J. Alcorn, R.J. Corthell and F. Massardier-Kenney. New York and London: New York University Press.

Ministry of Labour, Thailand (2006). "Announced Minimum Wage Rate increased for 2006." <http://eng.mol.go.th/statistic_01.html> [accessed 14 May 2006, page no longer available].

Moerman, M. (1966). "Ban Ping's Temple: The Center of a 'Loosely Structured' Society," in *Anthropological Studies in Theravada Buddhism*, ed. M. Nash. New Haven: Yale University Southeast Asia Studies.

Molland, S. (2011). "'I am helping them': 'Traffickers', 'anti-traffickers' and economies of bad faith." *The Australian Journal of Anthropology* 22, 2: 236–54.

Moore, H. (2011). *Still Life: Hopes, Desires and Satisfactions*. Cambridge: Polity Press.

_______ (2007). *The Subject of Anthropology: Gender, Symbolism and Psychoanalysis*. Cambridge: Polity Press.

Mosse, D. (2005). *Cultivating Development: An Ethnography of Aid Policy and Practice.* London and Ann Arbor, Michigan: Pluto Press.

Ngaosyvathn, M and P. Ngaosyvathn (1994). *Kith and Kin Politics: The Relationship between Laos and Thailand.* Manila, Philippines and Wollongong, Australia: Journal of Contemporary Asia Publishers.

Nevins, J. and N. Peluso (2008). *Taking Southeast Asia to Market: Commodities, Nature, and People in the Neoliberal Age.* Ithaca: Cornell University Press.

O'Hanlon, M. (1989). *Reading the Skin: Adornment, Display and Society among the Wahgi.* London: British Museum Publications.

Ong, A. (1991). "The Gender and Labor Politics of Postmodernity." *Annual Review of Anthropology* 20: 279–309.

——— (1987). *Spirits of Resistance and Capitalist Discipline: Factory Women in Malaysia.* New York: SUNY Press.

Ortner, S.B. (1995). "Resistance and the Problem of Ethnographic Refusal." *Comparative Studies in Society and History* 37, 1: 173–93.

Pavie, A. (1999). *The Pavie Mission Indochina Papers: 1879–1895, Volume 1.* Bangkok: White Lotus Press.

Pfanner, D.E. and J. Ingersoll (1962). "Theravada Buddhism and Village Economic Behaviour: A Burmese and Thai Comparison." *The Journal of Asian Studies* 21, 3: 341–61.

Phinith, L. (2006). "Laos-Thailand: Open Borders Ease Smuggling." <http://www.newsmekong.org/laos-thailand_open_borders_ease_smuggling> [accessed 17 May 2006, page no longer available].

Pholsena, V. (2006). *Post-war Laos: The Politics of Culture, History, and Identity.* Ithaca, New York: Cornell University Press.

Phomvihan, K. (1979). "Address on 24 April Opening Ceremony of First National Congress of Agricultural Cooperatives in Vientiane." Summary of World Broadcasts (SWB).

Platenkamp, J. (2008). "The Canoe Racing Ritual of Luang Prabang." *Social Analysis* 52, 3: 1–32.

Polanyi, K. (1957, reprinted in 1960). *The Great Transformation: The Political and Economic Origins of Our Time.* Beacon Hill, Boston: Beacon Press.

Pollan, M. (2002). *The Botany of Desire: A Plant's-Eye View of the World.* London: Bloomsbury.

Rajavaramuni (1990). "Foundations of Buddhist Social Ethics," in *Ethics, Wealth, and Salvation: A Study in Buddhist Social Ethics,* ed. R.F. Sizemore and D.K. Swearer. Columbia: University of South Carolina Press.

Randolph, R.S. (1986). *The United States and Thailand: Alliance Dynamics, 1950–1985.* Research Papers and Policy Studies No. 12. Berkeley: Institute of East Asian Studies, University of California.

Rehbein, B. (2005). "The Lao Economic Field." *Sojourn* 20, 1: 23–38.

Reynolds, C.J. (2005). "Power," in *Critical Terms for the Study of Buddhism,* ed. D.S. Lopez, Jr. Chicago and London: The University of Chicago Press.

Rigg, J.D. (2006). "Forests, marketization, livelihoods and the poor in the Lao PDR." *Land Degradation and Development* 17, 2: 123–33.

Sachchidanand, S. (2005). *The Mekong River: Space and Social Theory.* Delhi: B.R. Publishing Corporation.

Sahlins, M. (2012). "Alterity and authochthony: Austronesian cosmographies of the marvelous. The 2008 Raymond Firth Lecture." *HAU: Journal of Ethnographic Theory* 2, 1: 131–60.

———— (2010). "Infrastructuralism." *Critical Inquiry* 36, 3: 371–85.

———— (2008). "The Stranger-King or, Elementary Forms of the Politics of Life." *Indonesia and the Malay World* 36, 105: 177–99.

———— (1996). "The Sadness of the Sweetness: The Native Anthropology of Western Cosmology. Sidney Mintz Lecture for 1994." *Current Anthropology* 37, 3: 395–428.

———— (1981). "The Stranger-King or Dumézil among the Fijians." *The Journal of Pacific History* 16, 3: 107–32.

Salemink, O. (2012). "The art of upland governmentality and the desire for improvement in the Southeast Asian highlands." European Association of Social Anthropologist (EASA) Conference, Nanterre, 2012, unpublished manuscript.

———— (2011). "A View from the Mountains: A Critical History of Lowlander-Highlander Relations in Vietnam," in *Upland Transformations in Vietnam*, ed. T. Sikor, N.P. Tuyen, J. Sowerwine and J. Romm. Singapore: NUS Press, pp. 27–50.

———— (2003). "Social Science Intervention: Moral versus Political Economy and the Vietnam War," in *A Moral Critique of Development: In Search of Global Responsibilities*, ed. P. Quarles van Ufford and A.K. Giri. London: Routledge, pp. 159–78.

Sarasin, V. (1985). "Reflections on Thai-Lao Relations." *Asian Survey* 25, 12: 1260–76.

Schiller, J.M., M.B. Chanphengxay, et al., ed. (2007). *Rice in Laos.* Australian Centre for International Agricultural Research (ACIAR).

Schneider, D.M. (1972). *American Kinship: A Cultural Account.* Englewood Cliffs, New Jersey: Prentice-Hall.

Scott, J.C. (2009). *The Art of Not Being Governed: An Anarchist History of Upland Southeast Asia.* New Haven and London: Yale University Press.

———— (1998). *Seeing Like a State: How Certain Schemes to Improve the Human Condition have Failed.* New Haven and London: Yale University Press.

———— (1990). *Domination and the Arts of Resistance: Hidden Transcripts.* New Haven and London: Yale University Press.

———— (1986). "Everyday forms of peasant resistance." *Journal of Peasant Studies* 13, 2: 5–35.

———— (1985). *Weapons of the Weak: Everyday Forms of Peasant Resistance.* New Haven and London: Yale University Press.

———— (1979). "Revolution in the Revolution: Peasants and commissars." *Theory and Society* 7, 1/2, Special Double Issue on State and Revolution: 97–134.

———— (1977a). "Peasant Revolution: A Dismal Science." *Comparative Politics* 9, 2: 231–48.

———— (1977b). "Patronage or Exploitation," in *Patrons and Clients in Mediterranean Societies*, ed. E. Gellner and J. Waterbury. London: Duckworth, pp. 21–40.

———— (1977c). "Protest and Profanation: Agrarian Revolt and the Little Tradition, Part I." *Theory and Society* 4, 1: 1–38.

———— (1977d). "Protest and Profanation: Agrarian Revolt and the Little Tradition, Part II." *Theory and Society* 4, 2: 211–46.

———— (1977e). "Hegemony and the Peasantry." *Politics & Society* 7, 3: 267–96.

———— (1976). *The Moral Economy of the Peasant: Rebellion and Subsistence in Southeast Asia*. New Haven and London: Yale University Press.

Scott, J.C. and B.J.T. Kerkvliet, ed. (1986). *Everyday Forms of Peasant Resistance in Southeast Asia*. London and Totowa: Frank Cass.

Sen, A. (1983). "Poor, Relatively Speaking." *Oxford Economic Papers* 35: 153–68.

Simms, P and S. Simms. (1999). *The Kingdoms of Laos: Six Hundred Years of History*. Surrey: Curzon.

Singh, S. (2012). *Natural Potency and Political Power: Forests and State Authority in Contemporary Laos*. Southeast Asia Series: Politics, Meaning and Memory. Honolulu: University of Hawai'i Press.

———— (2009). "Living within the State: A Dormitory Community in Central Laos," in *Tai Lands and Thailand: Community and State in Southeast Asia*, ed. A. Walker. Singapore: NUS Press, pp. 141–65.

Sivaram, M. (1941). *Mekong Clash and Far East Crisis: A Survey of the Thailand-Indochina Conflict and the Japanese Mediation and Their General Repercussions on the Far Eastern Situation*. Bangkok: Thai Commercial Press.

Sizemore, R.F. and D.K. Swearer (1990). "Introduction," in *Ethics, Wealth, and Salvation: A Study in Buddhist Social Ethics*, ed. R.F. Sizemore and D.K. Swearer. Columbia: University of South Carolina Press.

Spiro, M.E. (1966). "Buddhism and Economic Action in Burma." *American Anthropologist* 68, 5: 1163–73.

Stuart-Fox, M. (2007). "LAOS: Politics in a Single-party State." *Southeast Asian Affairs 2007*, ed. Daljit Singh. Singapore: Institute of Southeast Asian Studies, pp. 159–80.

———— (2006). "The Political Culture of Corruption in the Lao PDR." *Asian Studies Review* 30: 59–75.

———— (2004). "Laos," in *Revolutionary and Dissident Movements of the World*, ed. B. Szajkowski. London: John Harper Publishing.

———— (1997). *A History of Laos*. Cambridge, New York and Melbourne: Cambridge University Press.

———— (1996). *Buddhist Kingdom Marxist State: The Making of Modern Laos*. Bangkok: White Lotus Press.

———— (n.d.). *Political Culture and Power in the Lao People's Democratic Republic*.

Tambiah, S.J. (1977). "The Galactic Polity: The Structure of Traditional Kingdoms in Southeast Asia." *The Annals of the New York Academy of Sciences* 293: 69–97.

———— (1968). "The Ideology of Merit and Social Correlates of Buddhism in a Thai Village" in *Dialectic in Practical Religion*, ed. E. Leach. Cambridge: Cambridge University Press.

Tan, A.T.H. (2007). "Old Terrorism in Southeast Asia: A Survey," in *A Handbook of Terrorism and Insurgency in Southeast Asia*, ed. A.T.H. Tan. Cheltenham, UK and Northampton, Massachusetts, USA: Edward Elgar.

Taussig, M. (1992). *The Nervous System*. New York and London: Routledge.

———— (1984). "Culture of Terror—Space of Death. Roger Casement's Putumayo Report and the Explanation of Torture." *Comparative Studies in Society and History* 26, 3: 467–97.

Terweil B.J. (1976). "A Model for the Study of Thai Buddhism." *Journal of Asian Studies* 35, 3: 391–403.

Thalemann, A. (1997). "Laos: Between Battlefield and Marketplace." *Journal of Contemporary Asia* 27, 1: 85–105.

Thayer, C.A. (2004). "Laos in 2003: Counterrevolution Fails to Ignite." *Asian Survey* 44, 1: 110–4.

The Economist (September 2003). "Laos: The Phantom Menace. Myth and Reality in Indochina." <http://www.economist.com/node/2076531?story_id=E1_NDSGVPT> [accessed 13 April 2011].

Thongchai W. (1994). *Siam Mapped: A History of the Geo-Body of a Nation*. Honolulu: University of Hawai'i Press.

Time Asia (2004). "Welcome to the Jungle," photo essay.

Toro, M. (2012). "Coffee Markets, Smallholder Credit, and Landscape Change in the Bolaven Plateau Region, Laos," University of Miami, unpublished MA thesis.

Toye, H. (1968). *Laos: Buffer State or Battleground*. London, New York, etc.: Oxford University Press.

Tucker, I.B. (2011). *Economics for Today's World*. Canada: South-Western Cengage Learning.

Turner, T.S. (1980). "The Social Skin," in *Not Work Alone: A Cross-Cultural View of Activities Superfluous to Survival*, ed. J. Cherfas and R. Lewin. London: Temple Smith.

Van Esterik, P. (1999). "Ritual and the Performance of Buddhist Identity among Lao Buddhists," in *American Buddhism: Methods and Findings in Recent Scholarship*, ed. D.R. Williams and C.S. Queen. Surrey: Curzon Press.

———— (1992). *Taking Refuge: Lao Buddhists in North America*. Program for Southeast Asian Studies: Arizona State University.

Walker, A. (2012). *Thailand's Political Peasants: Power in the Modern Rural Economy*. Madison, MI: University of Wisconsin Press.

———— (2009). "'Now the Companies have Come': Local Values and Contract Farming in Northern Thailand," in *Agrarian Angst: Resistance in Contemporary Southeast Asia*, ed. D. Caouette and S. Turner. London and New York: Routledge, pp. 61–81.

———— (2001a). "Introduction: Simplification and the ambivalence of community." *The Asia Pacific Journal of Anthropology* 2, 2: 1–20.

———— (2001b). "The 'Karen Consensus,' Ethnic Politics and Resource-Use Legitimacy in Northern Thailand." *Asian Ethnicity* 2, 2: 145–62.

———— (1999). *The Legend of the Golden Boat: Regulation, Trade and Traders in the Borderlands of Laos, Thailand, China and Burma.* Honolulu: University of Hawai'i Press.

White, D.G. (1991). *Myths of the Dog-Man.* Chicago and London: University of Chicago Press.

White, C.P. (1974). "The Vietnamese Revolutionary Alliance: Intellectuals, Workers, and Peasants," in *Peasant Rebellion and Communist Revolution in Asia,* ed. J.W. Lewis. Stanford, California: Stanford University Press, pp. 77–95.

Wolters, O.W. (1982). *History, Culture and Region in Southeast Asian Perspective.* Singapore: Institute of Southeast Asian Studies.

Wyatt, D.K. (1997). "History and Directionality in the Early Nineteenth-Century Tai World," in *The Last Stand of Asian Autonomies: Responses to Modernity in the Diverse States of Southeast Asia and Korea, 1750–1900,* ed. A. Reid. London: Macmillan Press.

Zizek, S. (2006a). *How to Read Lacan.* London: Granta Books.

———— (2006b). "Philosophy, the "unknown knowns," and the public use of reason." *Topoi* 25, 1–2: 137–42.

———— (1989). *The Sublime Object of Ideology.* London and New York: Verso.

———— (1996). ""I Hear You With My Eyes"; or, the Invisible Master," in *Gaze and Voice as Love Objects,* ed. R. Salecl and S. Zizek. Durham and London: Duke University Press.